Generating Texts
*The Progeny of
Seventeenth-Century Prose*

Generating Texts
The Progeny of Seventeenth-Century Prose

Sharon Cadman Seelig

University Press of Virginia
Charlottesville and London

The University Press of Virginia
© 1996 by the Rector and Visitors of the University of Virginia

First published 1996

∞ The paper used in this publication meets the minimum requirements of the American National Standard for Information Sciences — Permanence of Paper for Printed Library Materials, ANSI Z39.48-1984.

Library of Congress Cataloging-in-Publication Data

Seelig, Sharon Cadman.
   Generating texts : the progeny of seventeenth-century prose / Sharon Cadman Seelig.
     p. cm.
   Includes bibliographical references and index.
   ISBN 0-8139-1676-3 (cloth : alk. paper)
   1. English prose literature — Early modern, 1500–1700 — History and criticism. 2. Donne, John, 1572–1631. Devotions upon emergent occasions. 3. Browne, Thomas, Sir, 1605–1682. — Religio medici. 4. Burton, Robert, 1577–1640. Anatomy of melancholy. 5. Eliot, T. S. (Thomas Stearns), 1888–1965. Four quartets. 6. Thoreau, Henry David, 1817–1862. Walden. 7. Sterne, Laurence, 1713–1768. Life and opinions of Tristram Shandy, gentleman. 8. American literature — English influences. 9. Influence (Literary, artistic, etc.)
10. Intertextuality. I. Title.
PR769.S44 1996
828'.40809 — dc20   96-18964
                                                                            CIP

Printed in the United States of America

*For my family, past and present —
strong shapers and nurturers all*

CONTENTS

Acknowledgments *ix*

I
Questions of Genre *1*

II
Donne: *Devotions upon Emergent Occasions*
as Meditative Form *13*

III
Eliot: *Four Quartets*: The Pattern in Revision *36*

IV
Browne: *Religio Medici* as Normative Autobiography *62*

V
Thoreau: *Walden*: The Rhetoric of Time Illumined by Eternity *83*

VI
Burton: *The Anatomy of Melancholy*: "I Have
Overshot My Selfe" *105*

VII
Sterne: *Tristram Shandy*: The Deconstructive Text *128*

VIII
Questions of History *155*

Appendix *163*

Notes *167*

Select Bibliography *189*

Index *199*

ACKNOWLEDGMENTS

A BOOK LIKE THIS, so long in the process of generation, has deep roots and many debts. My teachers at Carleton College and Columbia University taught me to read with pleasure a number of the texts considered here—especially Owen Jenkins, who introduced me to *Tristram Shandy* and Aristotle; Philip Sheridan, who opened the door to the seventeenth century; Scott Elledge, who sent me off to England with *The Poetry of Meditation* under one arm and Sir Thomas Browne under the other; Wayne Carver, who never forgot that literature was part of life. At Columbia Edward Tayler, ironist, patient observer, and teacher par excellence, dared his students to encounter alien minds and assumptions; Joseph Mazzeo shared his enthusiasm for Dante and the seventeenth century and continued to teach me even as I rediscovered his critical essays. Early in my teaching life Marjorie Kaufman and Richard Johnson helped me read and think about *Walden*. Andrea Sununu, friend and colleague who never seemed to doubt that this project was a good idea, generously supplied references early and late. I wish that I could thank Joan Webber and Rosalie Colie, whose critical insights and standards have been a model and inspiration for many years. But I can thank those students who—even if they couldn't altogether share my enthusiasm—listened as I illustrated Shakespeare and Milton with passages from *The Anatomy of Melancholy* and *Religio Medici*. Perhaps they too breathe a sigh of relief at the completion of this book.

My colleagues at Smith have cheered me on and offered helpful criticism: Bill Oram, with characteristic generosity, read the entire manuscript and made many excellent suggestions; Betsey Harries, an unfailing source of good sense and clarity, helped me think about genre, organization, and Sterne; Douglas Patey, just when I thought I was finished, made extremely useful suggestions for further thinking and reading; Ronald Macdonald helped me find my way through some of my own sentences. A Picker Fellowship at Smith College lightened my teaching load so that I could finish the manuscript, and the Office of the Dean of the Faculty provided additional support.

Early versions of several portions of this book were presented at the John Donne Conference in Gulfport, Mississippi (1989), the Purdue Conference on Renaissance Prose (1987 and 1992), the Five College Re-

Acknowledgments

naissance Seminar (1992), and the Hofstra Conference on Autobiography (1994). I'm grateful to Clayton Lein, John Shawcross, and Thomas Hester for comments that forced me to re-examine assumptions and assertions. As chapters came closer to completion, Jonathan F. S. Post, Louis Martz, and Anna Nardo offered further suggestions and challenges.

Earlier versions of two sections of this book have appeared elsewhere: parts of chapter 2 as "In Sickness and in Health: Donne's *Devotions upon Emergent Occasions*" in *The John Donne Journal* 8 (1989): 103–13; and of chapter 6 as "Sir Thomas Browne and Stanley Fish: A Case of Malpractice," in *Prose Studies* 11 (1988): 72–84. My thanks for permission to reprint this material. I also acknowledge the permission of Harcourt, Brace & Company and of Faber and Faber Ltd. to quote passages from *Four Quartets*, copyright 1943 by T. S. Eliot and renewed 1971 by Esme Valerie Eliot. I am grateful for permission to use an illustration from the copy of *Tristram Shandy*, vol. 6, published 1760, in the Amherst College Rare Book Room, and for the courtesy of its curator, John Lancaster.

Special thanks go to Cathie Brettschneider, editor at the University Press of Virginia, whose willing suspension of disbelief and subsequent enthusiasm and good cheer did so much to further this project, and to Gerald Trett, who exercised remarkable care, good judgment and good humor, generosity and tact in the editing of the manuscript. Two anonymous readers for the University Press of Virginia buoyed me with their enthusiasm, and offered specific and helpful suggestions for clarification.

If this book is not all that these friendly critics might wish, it is immeasurably better for their critical acumen and counsel.

My longest and deepest debt is to my family: especially to my father and mother, whose unfailing integrity and belief in learning enabled me to do things they ought to have had the opportunity to do; to my uncle Tore Olsen, who taught me to read only by patiently reading and perhaps by drifting off at crucial moments; to my brother Norman to whom I am indebted for information about the Shandy syndrome in medicine and a great deal else; to my husband Harry and our children Catherine and David, who took on an extra measure of dishwashing, cooking, and visits to the orthodontist while I sat at the computer or in the library, and who are the best reminders that life exists beyond the printed page. This book is for all of them.

Generating Texts
*The Progeny of
Seventeenth-Century Prose*

For books are not absolutely dead things, but do contain a potency of life in them to be as active as that soul was whose progeny they are; nay, they do preserve as in a vial the purest efficacy and extraction of that living intellect that bred them.

— John Milton, *Areopagitica*

I

QUESTIONS OF GENRE

THIS STUDY OF GENRE and the generation of texts began a number of years ago with my noticing similarities between Eliot's radical dissolution of time and space in the *Four Quartets* and Donne's in the *Devotions upon Emergent Occasions;* in finding sentences in Thoreau's *Walden* that could have been written by Sir Thomas Browne; in seeing, despite the clear and significant differences between them, some kinship between the methods of Burton's *Anatomy of Melancholy* and *Tristram Shandy,* some similarities in their subversion of forms and their subversive personae.

But the similarities I found are not simply to be understood as literary influence. Not that it did not exist. Eliot, whose essays contributed so much to the renewed interest in metaphysical poetry in the twentieth century and who found in Donne the very embodiment of the nature of poetry, was profoundly influenced by the earlier poet. Thoreau, whose enthusiasm for sixteenth- and seventeenth-century poetry and prose began during his undergraduate days at Harvard, has often been heard by critics to echo his English predecessors.[1] And in the multitudinous bits and pieces that went into the making of *Tristram Shandy,* others before me have seen traces, indeed slices, of Robert Burton.

But in describing the relationships among these texts, I do not simply find literary influence, nor do I mean to trace the history of ideas. Each of the later writers with whom I am concerned was at the least aware of, interested in, and, arguably, affected to some degree by the earlier. The evidence exists in the form of quotation, comment, expressed admiration, and apparent similarity. But the connections I want to ponder have to do with the nature and structure of each work and, finally, with generic and generative connections between them. While one may begin with echoes of one writer in another, far more intriguing and more central to my approach are the ways in which the later writer adopted a similar method, a similar set of assumptions, or indeed, in which the assumptions seem to generate the method. Beyond the Renaissance notion that style is a garment for thought is the more basic proposition that

I

one's way of looking at the universe may be the determinant of one's syntax—that is, that the relationship between idea and expression is not merely large and general but rather elemental and radical and that a view of the world or a definition of one's task *generates* a particular literary form, rhetorical stance, or stylistic mode. Such a notion is related to Northrop Frye's suggestion, derived from Aristotle, that logic grows out of grammar, or Ralph Cohen's assertion that different literary types imply different conceptions of experience, or the Renaissance notion that external features proceed from subject matter or from a set of attitudes.[2] According to this view, genre is not merely taxonomic, not merely a matter of formal qualities, but in the deepest sense the expression of "a larger epistemological system, a way of seeing and interpreting the world."[3] Genre, in this view, is neither static nor merely formal but functional.

In exploring this notion I shall consider three pairs of works, the first in each case of the seventeenth century, the second from a later century: Donne's *Devotions upon Emergent Occasions* and Eliot's *Four Quartets,* Browne's *Religio Medici* and Thoreau's *Walden,* Burton's *Anatomy of Melancholy* and Sterne's *Tristram Shandy.* At first the differences between these paired works will be more striking than the similarities. Donne writes in prose, Eliot, in verse; Browne sets out to define that acknowledged oxymoron, the religion of a physician, Thoreau, to give an account of his months at Walden Pond; Sterne writes a novel, or "private history," Burton, a medical treatise. What connections can there be that are not arbitrary or accidental?

If one conceives of genre in conventional terms and particularly in terms of external characteristics, such a study may be thought to have debilitating practical and theoretical difficulties; indeed, it may seem perverse to deal in one book with a group of poems, a novel, a meditation on sickness and health, two quasi-autobiographical works, and a large medical treatise. Moreover, if one thinks of literary criticism as historically grounded, the mingling of texts from four centuries and the introduction of at least one work of American literature into the mix may seem at best odd.

But despite what may appear decisive differences in genre, there are significant relationships among these texts. Most striking perhaps are the thematic ones: of the six writers, four—Donne, Eliot, Browne, and Thoreau—are concerned with time and eternity, with eternity's intersection with or interruption of time. These writers also share a strong concern with the nature of the self, its relation to the past, to the world or the universe, to larger social, theological, or philosophical systems. And particularly if one defines the self in secular as well as religious terms, this interest is shared also by Burton and Sterne. All six texts are deeply concerned with process, the process of discovery and presentation, particularly self-discovery and self-presentation; they deal with the relationship between a single moment and its larger implications, with the discovery of infinite regress, or progress. And finally, each of these superbly conscious writers gives explicit attention to occasion and genre.

As these last points suggest, the similarities among these texts are not only those of subject matter but of approach; they are rhetorical as well as conceptual. Donne and Eliot, though the one concentrates almost obsessively upon the health of his body and his soul and the other, on the relationship between events and literary structure, meditate alike upon the nature of reality, upon the position of man in the universe. Both, as James Olney has said of Eliot, "weave together personal allusions . . . to create generalized significance."[4] As for Browne and Thoreau, although one writes to place himself within the Church of England and the other to place himself beyond the bounds of organized religion, each in so doing defines himself and, by implication, the nature of mankind. Each articulates a relationship between the mundane and the cosmic; each sees through the reality we know to a world beyond, and, most significant, each creates rhetorical forms that force us to make the leap he does, that enable us to see what he sees. Burton and Sterne, despite a good deal of explicit attention to formal structure—in the first case in an elaborate system of divisions and subdivisions, in the second, the attempt to get through an autobiographical account in reasonable space and comprehensible form—are both engaged in a radical undermining of form. They use quotation, apparently to support the substance of the text, but in fact to alter, even call into question, the pattern and direction of the whole, to create, in short, a subversive subtext.

The differences among these texts are evident: yet in undertaking this study I intend to test the notion of genre as a more flexible and, I believe, thereby more useful category than it has often been taken to be. The most illuminating kinds of comparisons, I suggest, may be not those based on considerations of external form but rather on a view of the world and of the self, seen in relation to rhetorical approach, indeed, as a determiner of that approach. In bringing these diverse texts together I shall consider the extent to which they share authorial impulses or strategies, attitudes toward their tasks, or shaping conceptions and the extent to which a similar conceptual approach leads to a similarity in structure, large or small, to a particular rhetorical or syntactical approach. I shall approach these six works, not simply from the point of view of external form, but in terms of what each *does,* of its undertaking; the second, related task will be to consider each work in relation to another but later work of the same kind or mode. This process will illuminate shifts of attitude or approach from one period to another; it will also show that the seventeenth-century texts with which I begin are not sui generis but profoundly generative.

The first pair of works, Donne's *Devotions upon Emergent Occasions* (1624) and Eliot's *Four Quartets* (1936–42), are both examples of meditative form, texts in which ideas are put forth, incrementally elaborated, modified and adjusted, the one in highly rhythmic prose, the other in rhythmic verse, both moving associatively to show the interconnections, the structure of reality, as these are progressively realized by the writer. Donne's *Devotions,* growing out of his own serious illness, gives rise to passionate meditations on the state of mankind and on the sickness of sin for which physical illness is a vivid image. Eliot, using particular locations as the starting point for his meditation, probes the meaning of those places and the conceptions or experiences they suggest, endlessly seeking orientation, not so much in specific doctrines as in the accumulation of perceptions or traditions, in the aggregate meaning of a place or a phrase. In exploring these works as meditations I shall consider first how the very elaboration of the idea generates the form and, second, what differences in idea and tone this meditative approach produces. The juxtaposition of these two works shows, on the one hand, the connections between their metaphors and themes; on the other, the differences of voice, of intensity, and of tone that distinguish the two authors and the centuries in which they wrote.

Like Donne and Eliot, Browne and Thoreau strain the limits of the possible, exploring the boundary between time and eternity, pointing out their intersection in often quite startling ways. Browne in *Religio Medici* (1643) and Thoreau in *Walden* (1854) are both concerned with, in Thoreau's phrase (and orthography), "*extra- vagant* expression." Browne revels in the paradoxes of faith and the possibilities of language; he uses language to point to that which it cannot adequately express; he delights in attempting the precise articulation of those truths that escape our verbal and logical powers. "Who can speake of eternitie without a solœcism, or thinke thereof without an exstasie," Browne asks, pointing to the inadequacy of verb tenses to present timelessness, of the human mind to comprehend the infinite, at the same time that he gives us linguistic tools with which to attempt these things.[5] The effect of Browne's prose is to strain our minds, to point, in its deliberate confusion of tenses and images, to the mind of God that conceived and contains all and to force the reader to experience the inadequacy of his own intellect to deal with the irreconcilables of faith.

Although *Walden* is much more firmly grounded in the physical world than *Religio Medici*, Thoreau's minute account of particulars, his description of objects or experiences, like Browne's, opens up a vision of the universal. This aspect of Thoreau's work is not simply a matter of philosophy but of rhetoric: a sentence or a paragraph seems to be moving in one direction, seems to make perfect sense on one level, only to shift, thereby revealing a dimension always potentially present yet not before suspected by the reader. As Thoreau writes toward the end of *Walden*, "If you are chosen town-clerk, forsooth, you cannot go to Tierra del Fuego this summer: but you may go to the land of infernal fire nevertheless. The universe is wider than our views of it."[6] Both Browne and Thoreau, then, share a delight in the power of prose that, paradoxically, reflects their capacity to handle the awesome and shows their prowess as stylists. My emphasis will be on the way rhetoric creates a dual apprehension of reality, on the way single sentences reflect and create the worldview of the whole, on the extent to which similarities of conception are modified in articulation between the seventeenth and the nineteenth centuries.

The earliest pair of works chronologically and the last to be considered are Burton's *Anatomy of Melancholy* (1621–39)[7] and Sterne's *Tristram Shandy* (1759–61), the one a compilation of knowledge and received authority regarding a common physical and psychological complaint, the other a personal history, a fictionalized autobiography that apparently gets out of hand and never accomplishes its declared purpose. Both are characterized by excess; each puts forward a form only to undermine it, to tease our expectations, or to manipulate our responses. Burton's three-volume treatise on melancholy, which gives in painstaking detail the causes, symptoms, and cures of this disorder, appears to be a scholarly attempt to order and comprehend a complex subject. But in fact it is a highly personal, idiosyncratic work, one in which the writer's voice, ceaselessly interrupting, modifying, offering another phrase or translation, thrusts itself to the forefront, belying and defeating its formal organization. Burton's massive citation of instance and authority, ostensibly offered to reinforce the point and the validity of his work, tends rather to undermine authority itself, to create chaotic diversity.

Sterne's delight in disorder is more open and explicit than Burton's and his attitude to the reader more obviously teasing, as he moves backward and forward in time, inserting hints, black pages, and Latin maledictions. But his rhapsodic, freely associative style, with its parodies and distortions of narrative convention and temporal sequence, owes a great deal to Burton. Both writers subvert the form they have chosen, using it as a measure of their excess, of their violation of order and control. The chief fact is not that one of these works is a novel and the other a quasi-scientific treatise but that each author has created a persona or a form that is not what it seems but is used to play games with the reader, treating him both as partner and as object. A juxtaposition of these two works, commonly considered in the context of their own genre or period, will illustrate the more clearly their virtuoso handling of form and digression, their creation of a persona, and their manipulation of the reader.

Although I have described the genesis of this study in my noticing a series of interrelationships between texts, such an undertaking of course raises difficult theoretical questions. If, as I have suggested, genre is not only a matter of external form but also has something to do with occasion, with the generating impulse variously conceived, the question of genre persists, leading us to ask, On what terms does one consider a literary work? What are its own terms? What is its kind, its genre?

Anyone concerned with the matter must first face the question of whether, as has sometimes been claimed, genre is dead, or whether it still exists as a viable category of analysis. Some twenty years ago Rosalie Colie began her study of genre theory in the Renaissance by declaring: "In a period like our own, in which forms seem generally restrictions — . . . self-made prisons in which we acquiesce — the protracted discussion of literary form and forms, in a period long past, may seem at best antiquarian and at worst irresponsible. Indeed, even in literary circles, the idea of 'kind,' of genre, is hardly popular nowadays."[8] Fredric Jameson went further, to declare that genre criticism has been "thoroughly discredited by modern literary theory and practice."[9] But at about the same time, Alastair Fowler asserted, in *Kinds of Literature:* "Much of our best criticism is taken up with matters of genre."[10] And in 1986 Barbara Lewalski was able to state: "Genre-based studies of old and new kinds are now flourishing, as Crocean antagonism to the idea of genre has given way to a very general recognition of its importance."[11] Fowler's revised appraisal of the central importance of genre theory derives in part from the work of Colie herself and relates to the significant treatments of Renaissance genre theory by Lewalski, Dubrow, and Imbrie. But Colie's opening statement may also be seen as an instance of a minor genre, the modesty topos: in addition to the early work of Northrop Frye (especially *Anatomy of Criticism*), the importance and the variety of genre theory is amply attested to by the work of Paul Hernadi, whose book *Beyond Genre* (1972) sketches some sixty examples of genre theory, and Claudio Guillén, whose massive *Literature as System* (1971) moves toward newer and more flexible approaches to the question of genre, treating it less as literary category than as a strategy for communication with the reader.

Not only has literary genre received a good deal of recent critical attention, but there is also ample assertion that, like it or not, we cannot do without it. As Heather Dubrow reminds us, how we read a text depends on what genre we take it to be.[12] And in the words of E. D. Hirsch, "All understanding of verbal meanings is necessarily genre-bound," and "in fact, every disagreement about meaning is usually a disagreement about genre."[13] Both critics argue persuasively for the dependence of interpretive decisions on genre and our conception of genre: what we think of a work depends to a significant extent on what kind of work we think it is; our understanding and our judgment of quality depend on our sense of conventions handled or responded to. To mistake the genre is to mistake tone, context, meaning. Nor is genre simply a matter of nomenclature, as Dubrow observes: "The way a critic chooses to describe and define genres — whether in terms of, say, their linguistic patterns or their underlying assumptions about time or their effects on the reader — reveals his presuppositions about the very nature of art" (46).

But if we agree that genre is important, even crucial, to our interpretation of literary and other texts, it still remains to clarify what genre is, how it is to be determined, how it functions in literary discussion. For centuries it has been common to approach the question of genre in terms of the three major categories, lyric, drama, and epic; but as often as these have been invoked, so have they been found wanting, rejected as too general to be of much practical use. Claudio Guillén argues that "even within the bounds of Western literature, the tripartite division into narrative, drama, and lyric has been insufficient for several centuries now. The rise of the essay as a genuine — certainly, since Montaigne, not spurious or marginal — literary genre has made the point quite clear." D. W. Robertson concurs, asserting that these categories are artificially perpetuated as the bases of undergraduate courses in literature, and are, even in that context, misleading.[14]

For my purposes, moreover, these three large divisions are particularly inadequate, because, as Guillén's reference to Montaigne suggests, Renaissance nonfiction prose does not fit neatly — or at all — into any one of them.[15] The large grouping of nonfiction prose tells us more about what such works are not than about what they are: only the time period is specified, and that rather broadly. Northrop Frye addresses the problem by making prose a separate category within which he includes some nonfiction forms, most notably the anatomy and the confession, but he groups these under the category of fiction, thus blurring rather than clarifying the issue (332). Earl Miner counters by describing prose and verse as alternate approaches or separate rhythms (verse being the "marked form") rather than separate genres.[16] But for some, nonfiction prose is simply considered less artful than poetry or fiction.[17]

Given the traditional exclusion of prose from the major generic categories and the difficulty of finding a category appropriate to nonfiction prose in particular, one may question whether such systems are useful, whether there are rules or even paradigms by which nonfiction prose may be judged or understood. One strategy might be to consider individual works in relation to very specific subgenres according to the use for which they were intended: hence, we would consider Renaissance prose under such categories as sermon, allegory, meditation, political theory, essay, character, scientific treatise, biography, autobiography, utopia, travelogue, or satire. A good deal of fine criticism has gone on under those headings, and the categories themselves may prove historically interesting. Yet although they will help us understand the nature of a text, they will not sufficiently illuminate the interconnectedness — if such there be — of these texts, since each of the major examples seems to inhabit its own category. Moreover, the categories don't really help us understand how the texts in question escaped over the menagerie fence into the realm of literature. Graham Hough's suggestion, that texts once intended to be useful but which no longer are may become literature, helps us determine what we will consider literature, not how we will talk about it.[18]

Fowler, in what purports to be an introduction but is in fact an extensive and helpful survey of recent and historical considerations of genre, offers a list of the many aspects of a work that have been used to determine genre, including representational strategies (narrative, dramatic, or discursive), external structure, metrical structure, size, scale, subject, value, emotional coloration or mood, occasion, attitude, character, action, and style. In this discussion not only is genre not restricted to a few categories, but even the basis of that determination, seen in historical context, is remarkably diverse. Rather than understanding genre in terms of definitive and exclusionary categories, Fowler asks that we look to these determinative aspects as ways of differentiating texts from one another and associating them into groups, suggesting that "genres appear to be much more like families than classes."[19] In other words, Fowler argues, works of literature are related in various ways, without necessarily having any single feature shared by all.[20] As David Radcliffe puts it, "The notion of family resemblance" enables us to regard literary kinds "not as essential types but as mutable sets of relations among relatives."[21]

The point is extremely helpful because it shows how we may see connections among works, indeed link them meaningfully together, without insisting that they conform in every respect to a preconceived generic category. Yet Fowler is finally so generous about making way for another genre or subgenre, admitting that the particular qualities of a work may necessitate another special grouping if we are to understand it properly, that his system, though certainly not so rigid as some, may nevertheless offer us so many small generic packages that it provides too little framework for the comparison within a genre or between genres.[22] There are ultimately so many categories that each work is in danger of becoming sui generis, thus destroying the function of genre, which is not only to help understand individual works but also to see them in relation to other works of the same kind. The result is a world made up of families of texts rather than of tribes or nations. This approach undermines Fowler's own understanding, shared by Hirsch and Guillén, that the real function of genre is not classification but interpretation, that it serves as a guide to understanding rather than mere categorization.

But Fowler's critique of Northrop Frye, which finds Frye's treatment of genre excessively synchronic, taking too little account of the historical transformation and development of genres, does point to something I want to stress in this study: that genre is not fixed outside of time, that works do indeed respond to other works, and that our conception of genre is influenced by every work considered part of that genre. As Earl Miner observes, a generic term, once used to describe an existing group of works, will subsequently be applied to other, necessarily somewhat different works. For Ralph Cohen, "since each genre is composed of texts that accrue, the grouping is a process, not a determinate category."[23]

Thus genre, though rooted in time, is not altogether bound by the fixed forms of the past. Rather, genre develops within time; notions of individual works, of genres, and of the nature of genre itself are all subject to change. I turn briefly to Renaissance attitudes toward genre, both because these conceptions contribute to an understanding of the nature of genre and because they are particularly suited to the texts in which my study originates.

That the Renaissance was a time of considerable interest in genre is recalled by Rosalie Colie's question: "Why should there have been such bitter critical battles in sixteenth-century Italy over Dante's *Commedia* . . . , Ariosto's and Tasso's epics, Guarini's tragicomical play? . . . Why weren't critics and readers able to take them gratefully for whatever they were, instead of making them objects of critical inquiry and even disapproval?" (2). Colie finds part of the answer in the well-known Renaissance enthusiasm for the recovery and transmission of classical texts, seen as models to be imitated by the aspiring poet or scholar and to be discovered *by kind*.[24] The interest in genre was also manifested in the great variety of literary forms: J. C. Scaliger describes more than one hundred different genres and subgenres; Fowler, in noting the point, suggests that the proliferation of genres in the Renaissance may be a consequence of its significant body of genre theory.[25] The notion of *genera mista* (mixed genres), though subject to criticism by Sidney and parodied in *Hamlet,* testifies to the desire to adapt the formal structures of the past to new occasions and purposes, to combine previously distinct approaches for particular rhetorical occasions. Imbrie points out how in the great encyclopedic works of the Renaissance (for example, Burton's *Anatomy*) "generic indeterminacy is a function of its comprehensive accumulation of generic forms and attitudes, some of them conflicting with each other" (68). In such cases the conflict may not be simply incidental or accidental but in fact a vehicle of meaning. Indeed, as Jonathan Culler notes, writing against a genre is as significant as writing within it.[26]

While generic questions were the subject of spirited debate, generic criteria were unusually varied: in the *artes poeticae* of the late sixteenth and early seventeenth centuries, as Colie notes, we often find a list of possible forms with their distinctions drawn in terms of topic or content; and both Scaliger and Sidney based their notions of genre on a variety of criteria, sometimes external features or formal properties, sometimes subject matter, and sometimes values and attitudes that are expressed, codified, and preserved.[27] Renaissance nonfiction prose forms, as Imbrie puts it, extend from "prose genres that have rigorously organized structures and highly codified external features to those whose forms are almost exclusively a function of attitude" (61).

These studies demonstrate the historical basis for a broader understanding of the nature and purpose of genre and the particular appropriateness in applying such criteria to Renaissance texts. The realization that texts may be grouped by subject matter or by attitude toward the material as well as by formal qualities provides a basis for a more careful and accurate reading of texts. The awareness that our reasons for grouping texts may vary in particular instances can facilitate comparison, for example, of texts in verse and prose.[28] As Heather Dubrow argues, "Genres that seem far apart from each other in other ways should in fact be seen as allied if they 'put into play the same faculties of the authors, the same tastes of the public.'" She continues, "This observation has . . . the broadest of implications for studying generic evolution; in particular, it encourages us to note subterranean parallels between literary forms that may be totally different in their subject matter and their prosodic patterns."[29] Such notions of genre, then, are not only more appropriate to the Renaissance nonfiction texts with which I begin but also offer fruitful ways of exploring and joining the later texts that are, in my view, their progeny.

The notion of generic determination as fluid, a matter of familial resemblances rather than particular characteristics that remain set over time, is basic to the present inquiry, which deals with a number of works that have on the one hand highly codified features—the elaborate formal structure of Burton's *Anatomy of Melancholy*, for example, or the tripartite structure of Donne's *Devotions upon Emergent Occasions*, even the less pronounced divisions of Browne's *Religio Medici*—and yet whose essence is certainly not explained by such formal structure, whose essential features, I shall argue, are "almost exclusively a function of attitude," or, perhaps more precisely, within which attitude has a significant determinative and formative function. I shall explore ways in which Donne's

Devotions, Browne's *Religio Medici,* and Burton's *Anatomy* may be understood, generically and structurally, as a function of attitude, ways in which genre is related to occasion, defined in both internal and external terms; then by looking at other works in which similar kinds of attitudes and occasions obtain—*Four Quartets, Walden,* and *Tristram Shandy*—I shall explore the generic and rhetorical relationships between them. The obvious variety of the works considered reflects the richness of seventeenth-century nonfiction prose; it also enables us to test the idea of generic interconnectedness in a wide range of works, texts that practice a variety of forms of communication, that are meditative, autobiographical, celebratory, and deconstructive.

Although I shall be arguing for interconnectedness by affirming the generic relationships of diverse texts, I shall also take note of divergence, using one text as a marker for the other, to consider how writers are distinguished in voice, tone, intensity, and frame of reference, not only as individuals, but as products of different centuries. The generic links will make evident how similar impulses or conceptions are modified in altered philosophical, religious, or cultural climates, from one century to another. There are not timeless moments, but there are intersections of literary forms that let us examine the relationship between the conception and the articulation, between the smaller and the larger structures of a work, that will allow us to see the generation of texts in time.

II

DONNE
Devotions upon Emergent Occasions
as Meditative Form

T‍HE PAIRED TEXTS in this study, however various, have important similarities of theme, subject matter, and approach, links, I have been suggesting, that are at least as important as the external features by which genre is frequently defined. But I am less interested in the thematic unity of these works than in the variety of ways in which the generic qualities I have outlined may operate, in the manifestation of what Cohen describes as "concepts of experience" or Imbrie as a "function of attitude." Hence, I consider a trio of pairs, representing by turn meditative, autobiographical and celebratory, and deconstructive or transgressive approaches.

Donne's *Devotions upon Emergent Occasions* and Eliot's *Four Quartets* are both meditations, not only in the general sense of the word as commonly used, but also in the more specific sense elaborated by Louis Martz in *The Poetry of Meditation*. Rejecting the notion that metaphysical poetry derives simply from Donne, Martz outlines a meditative tradition, a widespread practice with important consequences for seventeenth-century literature, and speaks of the poetry of meditation as a genre that may be composed in different styles. Citing St. François de Sales, Martz describes meditation as "thinking deliberately directed toward the development of certain specific emotions" and, according to St. François, as "an attentive thought iterated, or voluntarily intertained in the mynd, to excitate the will to holy affections and resolutions."[1]

Meditation so defined has both structural and functional aspects: the primary basis of Martz's discussion is the *Spiritual Exercises* of St. Ignatius Loyola, characterized by a threefold structure of meditation: a composition of place, drawing on the power of memory in a vivid imagination of the scene or subject of the meditation; an analysis of the scene, depending on the power of the intellect or understanding; and a final colloquy, involving a movement of the will. Such a meditative method has implications both for the structure and movement of poem or meditation and for the involvement of the writer's or devotee's psyche, his memory, understanding, and will. Martz acknowledges a good deal of variation in the practice of these meditative patterns, allowing for differences of emphasis as well as the adaptation of meditative exercises to the needs of the individual (46). He also suggests a wider applicability of the notion of meditation, asserting, for example, its relevance for more modern poetry and arguing "that the art of meditation represents yet another aspect of the deep affinity between the seventeenth and the twentieth centuries."[2]

The account of the meditative tradition offered by Martz has been both challenged and supplemented by Barbara Lewalski, who in *Protestant Poetics and the Seventeenth-Century Religious Lyric* takes issue with Martz's reliance upon continental Catholic sources and stresses instead the relation of meditation to the great Protestant drama of salvation, with its emphasis upon experience as well as upon biblical texts. According to Lewalski, these sources of typology and of images, stories, and paradigms are far more central to the practice of meditation in Protestant England than are the continental sources cited by Martz. My purpose here is not to choose between these two analyses, each of which enriches our understanding of seventeenth-century devotional practice, but rather to draw on both for a broad sense of the nature and scope of the meditative tradition.[3] The formal, paradigmatic practice of meditation clearly operates in Donne's *Devotions,* but the work is also a drama of salvation of a most fervent kind; it fuses the formal and the intensely personal. The patterns and traditions of meditation outlined by Martz and Lewalski, taken together, illuminate the relationship between Donne and Eliot, both of whom use a carefully developed meditative structure, first to focus on questions that emerge from their own experience, and second, to extend the implications of these questions to the human condition itself.

Meditation, as we see it in Donne and Eliot, and as it grows out of the meditative tradition, is intellectual and emotional: in the words of Donne's contemporary Joseph Hall, "It begins in the braine, descends to the heart, begins on earth, ascends to heaven."[4] Meditation deliberately cultivates the powers of the mind and the affections; it also responds to experience. In that it constitutes a spiritual journey of the mind, it is essentially exploratory, but it also takes place in relation to a larger religious or social structure. As Lewalski notes, meditation either interprets individual experience in relation to religious texts or typology or puts the meditator into the world of the spiritual text, event, or experience.[5] Meditation, as Martz describes it, is the action of an inward search, but the search is undertaken deliberately, with the guidance of tradition, whether in the form of a method, a text, or a pattern. "A meditative poem," says Martz, "is a work that creates an interior drama of the mind; this dramatic action is usually (though not always) created by some form of self-address, in which the mind grasps firmly a problem or situation deliberately evoked by the memory, brings it forward toward the full light of consciousness, and concludes with a moment of illumination, where the speaker's self has, for a time, found an answer to its conflicts."[6]

Such marked meditative characteristics are found in both Donne's *Devotions upon Emergent Occasions* and Eliot's *Four Quartets*. One must of course acknowledge some obvious differences: Donne uses the complex and muscular Senecan prose of his day, Eliot, the verse, sometimes free, sometimes rhymed and complex, of the mid-twentieth century; Donne's text is insistently theological, Eliot's only tentatively, progressively so; Donne's prose is energetic, in the view of some, almost obsessively personal; Eliot's verse, although dealing with matters of equal concern to him, is less intense, even (paradoxically) more prosaic than Donne's prose. The formal structure of Donne's *Devotions* is clear and explicit; the structure of Eliot's poems is less obvious and its significance more open to interpretation; the *Devotions* was written within a month; *Four Quartets* took the better part of seven years. Yet in each case meditative practice and pattern are decisive.

Both Donne and Eliot are deliberate, persistent, insistent; both explore, question, associate, seek to understand the parts in relation to the whole, probe the implications and consequences of an acknowledged or hypothesized truth. Both use a particular place or event as the focus of a search for truth, a process of discovery; both move from an individual experience or question to a larger religious or philosophical framework. In both, the process of exploration is incremental, with the elements of discovery expressed rhythmically and syntactically. Both use formulation and reformulation, statement and restatement, to drive ever further into the heart of truth. With Donne, it may be a matter of categories ruthlessly explored, analyzed into oblivion; with Eliot, of a groping toward clarity through the nearly endless modification of insight and articulation. But in Donne's sometimes ferociously energetic prose and Eliot's sometimes laconic and diffident verse, the method of exploration and of presentation is strikingly analogous: it is meditative. Seeing Donne and Eliot in relation to the meditative mode will help us place the elements of the personal and impersonal in their work.

Donne's *Devotions upon Emergent Occasions* originated in 1623, in the course of a potentially life-threatening illness. The work recreates the progress of the illness, its symptoms and treatment, in some detail; it recounts the consultation of the physicians and Donne's eventual recovery. But throughout this account, Donne's attention is focused as much on his mental as his physical state, not only because of his long-standing and absorbing interest in his own psyche, but because he sees the sickness of the body as an image of the sickness of the soul, and indeed as the result of it, sickness having come into the world only through the sin of Adam and Eve.[7] Donne's *Devotions* has sometimes been considered an embarrassingly private work, an instance of his obsessive self-absorption. But however intense Donne's interest in the health of his body and his soul, the *Devotions upon Emergent Occasions* always extends to the life of the human race, and, particularly in the expostulations, moves to place Donne's own experience within the context of biblical precepts and language.

Although the meditative structure of Donne's *Devotions upon Emergent Occasions* is evident and important, too little attention has been given to the complex duality of that structure, which interweaves the obvious formal organization of twenty-three meditations, expostulations, and prayers with the larger narrative of Donne's descent into physical illness and his return to health.[8] The formal structure is cyclical, a series of small circles made up of a meditation upon the patient's state and a response to it; the narrative structure is progressive and linear, leading through sickness to recovery. The larger narrative structure depicts an extended encounter with death that concludes with an ambiguously figured rescue; each of the intense local cycles draws full meaning from a particular circumstance or event that is connected to more universal concerns. I shall deal with both these structures, the formal, or cyclical, and the extended narrative structure. I begin with the formal structure, by which Donne is joined to the earlier meditative tradition described by Martz and Lewalski, as well as to the later work of T. S. Eliot.

For each of the twenty-three days of Donne's illness as recorded in the *Devotions,* we have a meditation, expostulation, and prayer; each of these elements has its own characteristic mode and function. The meditation typically opens with a principle of human nature or a statement of the speaker's condition that then becomes the subject of that particular section: "Variable, and therfore miserable condition of Man; this minute I was well, and am ill, this minute" (Med. 1); or "There is *more feare*, therefore *more cause*. If the *Phisician* desire help, the burden grows great" (Med. 7). Often, as in this second instance, the opening is both transitional and intensifying. The meditations are the most personal part of the work, focusing on Donne's analysis of the nature of his own illness in relation to a universal principle, his symptoms and their emblematic meaning. Perhaps owing to this personal quality, the meditations have received particular attention from readers, even though to detach them from the other parts of the *Devotions* is to destroy the very structure I'm describing.

In the expostulations Donne characteristically undertakes to speak to God, often rising up out of his misery to protest against his condition and insisting on his rights to dialogue with the Almighty: "If I were but meere *dust* & *ashes*, I might speak unto the *Lord*, for the *Lordes* hand made me of this *dust*, and the *Lords* hand shall recollect these *ashes*" (Exp. 1). Donne finds justification for his stance in scriptural precedent: "I have not the *righteousnesse* of *Job*, but I have the desire of *Job*, *I would speake to the Almighty, and I would reason with God*" (Exp. 4).[9] He cites the examples of Martha (Exp. 5), Jeremiah (Exp. 3), David and Saul (Exp. 2), Augustine (Exp. 7), the Preacher (Exp. 8), James (Exp. 12), Gregory of Nazianzen (Exp. 10), and others who have questioned God with what Donne calls a "pious impudencie." The expostulations are always full of questions, some of them rhetorical, others more genuinely troubled; sometimes the tone is almost querulous, consistent with the *OED* definitions of expostulate: "to complain, set forth one's grievances" (1561); "to complain of grievances, to plead or remonstrate with a person about his conduct" (1586); "to reason earnestly and kindly with a person" (1574). They are genuine expostulations ("uttered remonstrance, protest or reproof" [1597]): "But *Lord*, thou art *Lord of Hosts*, & lovest *Action*; Why callest thou me from my calling?" (Exp. 3).

But although the expostulation is characteristically the section in which Donne expresses his discomfort and struggles to fathom God's dealings with him, it is also the section in which he tries to align himself with the holy patterns that he cites, setting himself and his actions in the context of biblical history: "*Thy Samuel* spake unto all the house of thy *Israel*, and sayd, *If you returne to the Lord with all your hearts, prepare your hearts unto the Lord.* If my heart bee *prepared,* it is a *returning* heart; And if thou see it upon the *way,* thou wilt carrie it *home"* (Exp. 11).[10] It is here too that Donne ponders biblical sayings, figuring and refiguring their meanings, taking God at his word, registering question or complaint. In Expostulation 15, for example, he begins "My *God,* my *God,* I know, (for thou hast said it) *That he that keepeth Israel, shall neither slumber, nor sleepe:* But shall not that *Israel,* over whom thou watchest, sleepe?" Donne then meditates further on the meaning of sleep, its association with sloth on the one hand and with death on the other. By the end of the expostulation, he has recast his sleeplessness, initially a state of torment, into a condition of positive watchfulness: "for since I finde thy whole hand light, shall any *finger* of that hand seeme heavy? since the whole sicknesse is thy *Physicke,* shall any accident in it, bee my poison, by my murmuring? The name of *Watchmen* belongs to our *profession;* Thy *Prophets* are not onely *seers* indued with a *power* of seeing, able to see, but *Watchmen,* evermore in the *Act* of seeing" (Exp. 15).

In the third of these meditative units, the prayer, Donne characteristically reconciles the problem constituted by his own stance as articulated in the meditation with the biblical perspective first glimpsed in the expostulation. The tone is generally much calmer and more conciliatory than either the meditation or the expostulation, with the speaker at rest in a newly achieved vision of things. The action of refiguring that takes place in these sections may be compared to that of a magnet on iron filings, or perhaps a Rorschach test differently seen: the material is the same, but the shape, direction, or significance is altogether altered. This triple sequence, then, comprises the intense statement or exploration of a problem; the attempt to place it, though not without questioning, in a biblical context; and finally, the speaker's reconciliation to his situation.

These individual tripartite sections are not only formally but also organically unified. Each section focuses on a single theme, sometimes on a principle articulated at the opening of the meditation, or simply on a word, frequently a word given in the Latin or English headings. For example, section 1 treats the "Variable, and therfore miserable condition of Man," that is, the radical insecurity of all we know and are; sections 2 and 3 treat the frustrating instability of man, who lives neither in heaven nor on earth, who is neither truly upright nor prone; section 5 treats the anxiety of solitude; section 6, fear, in its dual meaning; section 7, sickness, in its dual meaning. The middle sections are even more strictly focused: section 11 on the heart of man; section 12 on vapor; section 13 on the spots of illness; section 14 on the critical days; section 15 on sleep; sections 16–18 on bells; section 19 on the seasons of illness.

The later sections of the *Devotions* are generally more complex in their focus than the earlier ones: section 19 represents the physicians as "*patients,* patiently attending" on the disease. Such word play is related to the point Donne makes in Expostulation 19 about the texture of God's word, that different readers will find in it varying and often antithetical virtues — simplicity, majesty, or power of argument. Section 20 treats purgation but also the relation between decision and action; section 21 is on rising and falling but also on the relation between physical and spiritual movement; sections 22 and 23 emphasize the sinful nature of humanity and the effect of divine intervention on that condition.

Whether single or complex in emphasis, each of these tripartite sections comes full circle in its treatment of the topic, in stating, struggling with, and resolving a problem; these are the most basic and intense structural elements of the *Devotions.* Yet each small unit is also part of the larger structure of the work, which not only traces a much greater arc but within which further cyclical motions follow. Thus, while an issue is resolved in the prayer that concludes the section, it, or a related question, is raised again in the following meditation and expostulation, thereby reinforcing the cyclical nature of these meditations even within their progression. The resolution comes quickly, within the unit of meditation, expostulation, and prayer, but it is only temporary and partial, a sign that in this world, although divine comfort is never long in coming, its presence too is partial, awaiting a final resolution.

This evident, formal structure, embodied in the small repeating cycles of meditation, expostulation, and prayer, is counterbalanced by the narrative structure; that narrative is primarily progressive in that it treats the day-by-day development of the speaker's condition, but it also suggests a cycle in that it depicts a movement from health to the loss of health to the return to health. Donne begins his work with "*The first alteration, The first grudging of the sicknesse,*" with a moment so close to the inception of illness that we are chiefly aware of health receding from us: "Variable, and therfore miserable condition of Man; this minute I was well, and am ill, this minute" (Med. 1). He proceeds through the stages of his illness: the loss of strength; taking to his bed; sending for the physician, who, fearful, consults with others; the prescription of remedies; the appearance of spots signifying infection and malignity; the reaching of a critical stage; the lack of sleep; the nearness to death; purgation; recovery; the arising from the bed; and the final warning of the dangers of relapse. In these complex and complementary qualities—the cyclical mode, the progression through repetition, the deeper understanding that emerges by revisiting a mental or physical place—Donne's meditative practice is analogous to Eliot's.

In this narrative of physical illness, Donne also depicts the progress of his soul. He does so directly, representing the misery of uncertainty, his solitude, his fear, his anxious observation (especially in Meditation 6, where his acute awareness of process is coupled with the knowledge that such keen insight may well be the very reverse of helpful). Moreover, throughout the *Devotions* but especially marked in the later part, physical symptoms either give way to spiritual aspects or are taken as emblematic of a spiritual state. The spots of fever (Med. 13) not only aid the physicians in their diagnosis but are also images of the spots of sin; the patient's inability to sleep (Med. 15) leads to a disquisition on the relation between sleep and death. The applying of pigeons to draw out the vapors (Med. 12) and the purging (Med. 19 & 20) are clearly emblems for the expiation of Christ and the purging of sin from the soul; the later sections of the *Devotions* represent the purgation of infection, both bodily and spiritual, necessary to recovery. The three sections devoted to the bells (Med. 16–18) constitute a memento mori in several senses: the patient, keenly aware of his state, lies close to death, while reminders of death—of individuals and of the human race—resonate around him. The rising from the bed allowed by his recovery in the final sections has obvious analogues with Christ's resurrection.

In its narrative movement from loss of health through sickness to recovery, the *Devotions* has a kind of structural symmetry that has generally been overlooked: the work rises to its climax at its midpoint in Meditation 12, an ars moriendi with its roots in the biblical Epistle of James, and in Meditation 13, in which the illness makes itself known through spots. Thereafter one has the feeling of having crossed a decisive border, of having endured a medical and spiritual crisis. Although death seems closer in the later part of the *Devotions,* health returns, and the mood becomes more tranquil, at least until one arrives at the highly conditional, highly suspended concluding section.

Thus the relation in the *Devotions* between the formal structure made up of small units and the larger narrative line is more complex than at first appears. For while each of the twenty-three individual sections comes full circle, stating a problem and resolving it, so too does the work as a whole, descending into illness and returning from it, but also moving from its opening articulation of the variable condition of man to its concluding, even more resounding, affirmation of that point. Thus these bipolar structures — the individual and the general, the local and the universal, the cyclical and the linear — both complement and strain against each other; for while Donne records his progress toward health, that linear movement is also a return to his previous state. Moreover, the significance of such movement is dual and complex: the final meditative sequence at once celebrates health and expresses fears of a relapse, for it suggests that although bodily sickness may be an emblem of spiritual sickness, bodily health may also lead to a falling away from God.

In addition to the complementarity between the linear, narrative structure and the cyclical, formal structure of the *Devotions,* there are also tensions within these structures, two instances of which I want to consider in some detail. The large movement of the *Devotions* contains two curious points, the moment of tranquility just past the midpoint of the *Devotions,* when "the bell rings out, and tells me in him, that I am dead" (Med. 18), and the moment of agitation at the end, in the apparent recovery of health. At first sight problematic in showing a divergence between the speaker's external circumstances and his emotional response, these instances fully exemplify the particular vision of reality of Donne's meditations and the method by which it is achieved. These points reflect the conflict between spiritual and physical reality, which form an inverse pattern, carefully and systematically recorded: Donne describes this opposition, in which a loss in one sphere is by definition a gain in the other, in Prayer 2, where he addresses that God who "cald me up, by casting me further downe, and clothd me with thy selfe, by stripping me of my selfe, and by dulling my bodily senses, to the meats, and eases of this world, hast whet, and sharpned my spirituall senses, to the apprehension of thee. . . . My tast is not gone away, but gone up to sit at *Davids* table, *To tast, & see, that the Lord is good:* My stomach is not gone, but gone up, so far upwards toward the *Supper of the Lamb,* with thy *Saints* in *heaven.*"

Donne's perspective here is by definition divided, for he draws our attention simultaneously to the heavenly and the earthly aspects of an issue. As his earthly fortunes decline, his heavenly ones rise. The notion is a theological one, but the persuasiveness of this point depends on Donne's dramatic use of spatial metaphor and on his firm placing of like clauses expressing opposite motions within a single syntactic framework.

He speaks of the relationship between heaven and earth in terms of a shifting, vertically organized balance: as he leaves earth, he approaches heaven; as we diminish here, we prosper there. Thus every human experience is capable of two opposing interpretations, depending upon whether the interpreter's point of reference is the heavenly or the earthly realm.

In taking this approach, Donne of course partakes of a central precept of medieval and Renaissance Christianity—that the things of this world are valueless when weighed against the things of heaven. But his use of the notion is particularly dramatic, for he insists on the conflation of the positive and negative moment, the simultaneity of time and eternity, of point and infinity. As he writes in the concluding words of Prayer 13: "Onely be thou ever present to me, O *my God*, and this *bed-chamber*, & thy bed-chamber shal be all one roome, and the closing of these bodily *Eyes* here, and the opening of the *Eyes* of my *Soule*, there, all one *Act*." What is seen by other writers as an opposition, a tension, is represented by Donne both as an absolute antithesis and a simultaneous occurrence.

The variable readings of the text that is reality derive from the God who is at the heart of that reality, as we may see in Donne's supplication of a rather geometrical deity: "O eternall, and most gracious *God*, who considered in thy selfe, art a *Circle*, first and last, and altogether; but considered in thy working upon us, art a *direct line*, and leadest us from our *beginning*, through all our wayes, to our *end*, enable me by thy *grace*, to looke forward to mine end; and to looke backward to, to the considerations of thy mercies afforded mee from the beginning" (Prayer 1). The duality and complexity of the Deity here, his circularity and linearity, produce an imitative complexity in the speaker, who moves backward and forward in his articulation of the nature of the divine being and his action upon human life. The speaker understands God as part of two realms, time and eternity; as immanent and transcendent; as complete unto himself and as acting directly on our lives. For Donne, both visions of reality are true, and although one cannot focus on both at once, Donne's articulation of both within the same sentence forces upon his reader a realization of a nature beyond human logic or notions of consistency.

Such tranquillity as the *Devotions* offers, then, derives not from peaceful external circumstances but from the refiguring of death, from the acceptance, expressed in Prayer 18, that death is not so much a future as a present state: "Thou toldst me in the other *voice*, that I was *mortall*, and approaching to *death*; In this I may heare thee say, that I am *dead*, in an *irremediable*, in an *irrecoverable* state for bodily health. . . . *I am dead*,

I was *borne dead,* and from the first laying of these *mud-walls* in my *conception,* they have *moldred* away, and the whole course of *life* is but an *active death.* Whether this *voice instruct* mee, that I am a *dead man now,* or *remember* me, that I have been a *dead man* all this while, I humbly thanke thee for speaking in this *voice* to my *soule.*" In figuring death as "the *cure* of my *disease,* not as the *exaltation* of it," Donne treats death less as a future threat than a present reality, not to be feared but accepted, seen in a new perspective. The mood of resignation and reconciliation here is remarkably like that in act 5 of *Hamlet:* "If it be now, 'tis not to come; if it be not to come, it will be now; if it be not now, yet it will come — the readiness is all" (5.2.220–22), and the rhetoric depends similarly on powerful yet understated repetition.

In contrast to the hopeful acceptance of death in Prayer 18, the final section of the *Devotions* contains remarkably little joy or relief at the return of health. After the tranquillity of sections 19–21, section 23 is remarkably agitated, expressing fears — though immediately repressed — that someone once pardoned and again relapsing is in a state so dire as to tempt God to show no mercy. And even in claiming *"as thy Majestie, so is thy Mercie,* both *infinite"* (Exp. 23), Donne is fearful lest he presume: "I speak not this, O my *God,* as preparing a way to my *Relapse* out of *presumption,* but to *preclude* all accesses of *desperation,* though out of *infirmity,* I should *Relapse"* (Exp. 23). Donne, having fallen ill and recovered, having fallen into sin and been forgiven, is if anything more fearful of falling than before, or to put it another way, as his faith and his experience have increased, so has his fear.

There are practical as well as psychological reasons for such an ending: the relapsing fever was epidemic in London in 1623, and though Donne himself did not relapse, there was ample cause for medical concern.[11] And there is Donne's native anxiety, expressed so often in his work, as, for example, in the "Hymne to God the Father":

> When thou hast done, thou hast not done,
>   For, I have more.
>
> I have a sinne of feare, that when I have spunne
>   My last thred, I shall perish on the shore.[12]

But what we have at the end of the *Devotions* is not simply medical prudence, native anxiety, or theological caution; it is a new ambivalence about health itself — a knowledge that if death come not now, yet it will come, that one lives under a sentence of death, and only by means of that death within sight of life. The real danger in this refigured conclusion is not of dying, for although immediate death has been averted, death is also an absolute certainty. The real danger is of relapsing into sin. And as with *Hamlet,* when recovery comes, it does so precisely when it has lost some of the meaning earlier attributed to it, for it is when the patient ceases to hope desperately for health that health returns.

In the context of the *Devotions* as a whole, it is clear that the conclusion of the work is not, as has sometimes been suggested, a sudden failure of nerve, an inability to accept good fortune, or a perverse turning of it into ill;[13] rather, the conclusion grows directly out of the last five sections; it is a principle of faith discovered, made real, in the process of meditation, expressed in syntactical forms that highlight its paradoxes. Once death has been accepted in the passing bell and the death knell, health returns, in the first instance spiritual health, owing to man's proper understanding of his true state, but also, by divine mercy, bodily health. The precarious balance Donne strikes, not just by temperament, but by theology, is articulated in the opening of Prayer 22, which describes a radical duality in the nature of God that leads to a radical duality in the human condition: "O eternall and most gracious *God,* the *God* of *securitie,* and the *enemie* of *securitie* too, who wouldest have us alwaies *sure* of thy *love,* and yet wouldest have us alwaies *doing something* for it, let mee alwaies so apprehend *thee,* as *present* with me, and yet to *follow* after thee, as though I had not apprehended thee."[14]

The way in which we understand experience is not, according to Donne, a function of fixed material reality, nor of human interpretation, but of divine intention and divine power to shape events and meanings. Donne makes the point in Prayer 3: "As thou hast made these *feathers, thornes,* in the sharpnes of this sicknes, so, *Lord,* make these *thornes, feathers,* againe, *feathers* of thy *Dove,* in the peace of Conscience, and in a holy recourse to thine *Arke,* to the Instruments of true comfort, in thy Institutions, and in the Ordinances of thy *Church.*" The event itself is less crucial than the divine motive in creating it, an impulse that can transform opposites into one another.

The mingling of the cyclical and the progressive that I've been describing in Donne's *Devotions* emerges from a duality of vision, a kind of radical ambivalence toward life. This fact of radical indeterminacy is not the result merely of personal fear, arbitrariness, or whim; it is the product of Donne's approach to reality as a text to be read figuratively, a text whose literal details are full of meaning and whose interpretation may vary as absolutely as a photographic negative and its print. Donne's expression of these attitudes, which he shared with many of his contemporaries, is so emphatic that he has seemed to modern critics more idiosyncratic than he is. But although Donne is a particularly brilliant articulator of this vision, his attitudes and his methods reflect central Christian tenets; they derive from a homiletic and theological training that prepared him to examine every text, every circumstance, to probe it for all possible meaning. Donne characteristically sees opposed meanings in objects or events, which he quite clearly takes to be not simply objects or truths but figures, and figures capable of, even inviting, conflicting interpretations.[15]

As we may see from Donne's account of death as giving life, of God as line and circle, one of the chief accomplishments of the *Devotions* is a figuring, or refiguring, of reality, achieved through meditation. The elements of Donne's experience—illness, sleeplessness, solitude—are givens, but the interpretations he places upon them are radically diverse, ranging from absolutely negative to wholly positive. Experience is a given, but its meaning is not inherent, is rather conditional on the will of God and on human understanding of that will; thus a single object, fact, or event may have diverse and opposed significance.

A particularly dramatic instance of such refiguring is found in the treatment of fear in section 6. In the meditation Donne vividly represents fear, making us feel his panic in the repetition of a quick succession of active verbs and of the word itself so that fear, his fear, is at the center: "I observe the *Phisician*, with the same diligence, as hee the *disease;* I see hee *feares,* and I feare with him: I overtake him, I overrun him in his feare, and I go the faster, because he makes his pace slow; I feare the more, because he disguises his fear, and I see it with the more sharpnesse, because hee would not have me see it" (Med. 6). Donne is here watching himself, watching others watching him; he is aware of the potentially negative effects of such intense scrutiny, but all of his self-conscious intelligence cannot free him from his own self-conscious intelligence. Donne creates the effect of a hall of mirrors with a series of clauses of the same length and structure (isocolon and parison) within which he uses emphatic patterns of repetition: he begins a sequence of clauses with *I* (anaphora) and ends them with *him* (epistrophe); he laces the passage through and through with the central word *feare.* The increased rhythmic energy of these short repetitive phrases is further heightened by forces in a state of dynamic tension, the one attempting to balance and forestall the other, but in fact being overbalanced by it: "I feare the more, because he disguises his fear, and I see it with the more sharpnesse, because hee would not have me see it." Even the subject-verb complexes that begin the clauses give us in small format the essence of Donne's anxiously watchful position: "I observe," "I see," "I feare," "I overtake," "I overrun," "I go [the faster]," "I feare," "I see." With its nearly perfect symmetry of "I observe," "I see," surrounding "I feare," and in the center the panic activity of "I overtake," "I overrun," "I go the faster," this passage vividly recreates Donne's frantic, self-perpetuating state, one in which fear is intensely active.

Than this nothing could be more dramatic, but in the expostulation the meaning of the emotion and of the situation is altered as Donne places the event and the word in a new context. Donne shifts his emphasis from fear, seen as destructive, to the fear of God, that fear which is the beginning of wisdom, so that he can pray at last: "So give me, *O Lord,* a *feare,* of which I may not be *afraid*" (Prayer 6). The word remains constant throughout the meditation, expostulation, and prayer, but under the powerful influence of the Divine Word its significance is absolutely reversed. These diverging perspectives emerge from the process of meditation: they are contained within the whole, within cyclical units, within paragraphs and sentences. Donne's *Devotions* is a text that goes nowhere in that it is made up of twenty-three little circles of meditation, expostulation, and prayer or in that it begins in the loss of health and returns to health; but it may also be seen as a text that goes the distance from sickness (spiritual) to health (spiritual and physical).

This complex and complementary structure, cyclical as well as progressive, I have argued, grows out of Donne's vision of reality as taking place simultaneously in time and in eternity. Thus any given act or circumstance may have dual and contrasting, even contradictory, meanings. The meditative patterns of the *Devotions* show how the mind in meditation, by focusing on a physical or spiritual circumstance, can transform that circumstance, can make us understand it in a new light. That probing of experience, that setting of it in a new context, though handled more aggressively, more schematically, and in a more explicitly theological way by Donne, is the meditative practice that links his text to Eliot's. Such significant form, apparent in the familiar structural units of meditation, expostulation, and prayer, may be seen, I want to argue now, in the even smaller but no less mimetic structure of sentences.

Like all writers of his time, Donne learned early to use the devices of classical rhetoric to emphasize meaning.[16] But Donne is particularly remarkable for the extent to which he combines a rhetorical structure that implies and seems appropriate to logical argument with an unusual intensity of emotion. Joan Webber comments briefly on this aspect of Donne's work when she says that Donne "has a good time with logic when he is not forced to depend on it."[17] But whereas Webber sees a kind of disjuncture, I find Donne's use of logic fully functional, if unusual. Webber's further remark, "In the poetry, logic is made into a kind of affective superstructure," might equally apply to Donne's prose, which creates the impression of rational structure through balanced syntactical form. But that rational structure is used in the service of emotional intensity, of passionate conviction. On the one hand Donne exhausts the possibilities of logic; on the other hand, the structure of his work is not logical but associative, and he uses logic to win emotional assent.[18] Donne characteristically pushes a point as far as it can go, indeed, one might say, much farther than it can go, and certainly much farther than one would have imagined possible, at the same time that he insists on its converse. He does so by parallel syntactic form used to express two divergent ideas, ideas that grow more divergent all the time: the result is repetitiously incremental yet brilliantly contrastive and revelatory.

An example is the opening passage of Meditation 2: "The *Heavens* are not the lesse constant, because they move continually, because they move continually one and the same way. The *Earth* is not the more constant, because it lyes stil continually, because continually it changes, and melts in al the parts thereof." The parallel form here expresses not unity but opposition as Donne takes on a problem that appears insoluble— the coexistence of constancy and constant change. To make his point, Donne juxtaposes constancy and motion, but in asserting, apparently illogically (though in fact in harmony with prevailing attitudes), the constancy of the heavens, he also creates a moment of stasis at the midpoint of the first sentence by repeating the image of motion: "because they move continually, because they move continually one and the same way." Essential to the rhetorical force of the argument is Donne's use of anadiplosis, the repetition not only of a word but of a whole clause to create a moment of stasis, and commutatio, the reversal of the order, not only of words but of clauses, to create a mirror effect. The changeablity of the earth, by contrast, is communicated subtly by a shift in that same pattern: "because it lyes stil continually, because continually it changes"; until the sentence ends in dissolution: "and melts in al the parts thereof."

Donne further intensifies this opposition within a confining structure in the passage that follows, giving us a sense on the one hand of a rational, intellectually sound perception of the situation, and on the other hand a terribly intense, deeply persuasive vision. The elements of the sentence quoted below are perfectly parallel, as Donne uses parison and isocolon to emphasize the synchronized but divergent motion of his body and soul:

> *Earth* is the *center* of my *body,*
> *Heaven* is the *center* of my *Soule;*
>   these two are the naturall place of those two;
>   but those goe not to these two, in an equall pace:
> My *body* falls downe without pushing,
> my *Soule* does not go up without pulling:
>   *Ascension* is my *Soules* pace & measure,
>   but *precipitation* my *bodies.*

Even the points of divergence within this parallel scheme are emphatic and purposeful: "My *body* falls downe without pushing, / my *Soule* does not go up without pulling." That the one action is natural and effortless, and the other difficult, is evident in the structure of the prose itself, as the ease and naturalness of "falls downe" is contrasted with the difficulty — felt in a series of heavily accented monosyllables — and awkward wordiness of "does not go up," which comes at a shift from iambic to trochaic rhythm.[19] Similarly, the deliberate moderation of the doublet in "*Ascension* is my *Soules* pace & measure," contrasts with the quick and elliptical economy of "*precipitation* my *bodies.*"

Donne completes the sequence with a series of parallel clauses that make the same point repeatedly, balancing the supposed relative slowness of the heavenly bodies (here, the sun and stars in the Ptolemaic system), conveyed in long initial clauses, with the speed of his falling, expressed by the shorter elliptical one that concludes the sentence:

> The *Sunne*   who goes so many miles in a minut,
> The *Starres* of the *Firmament,* which go so very many more,

Donne: *Devotions upon Emergent Occasions*

>>goe not so fast,
>>as my *body* to the *earth*.

Once again rhythm reinforces meaning, as Donne uses triple rhythms to convey speed ("in a minut," "of the *Firmament*," "as my *body*," "to the *earth*"). In the following passage Donne not only uses parallelism for emphasis (parison and isocolon, reinforced by anaphora, alliteration, and rhythmic repetition); he also combines such emphatic balance with an intensity of forward motion to stress the rapidity of human decline.

>In the same instant that I feele the first attempt of the
>>disease,
>>>>I feele the victory:
>In the twinckling of an eye, I can scarce see;
>instantly the tast is insipid, and fatuous;
>instantly the appetite is dull and desirelesse:
>instantly the knees are sinking and strengthlesse;
>and in an instant, sleepe,
>>which is the picture,
>>the copy of death,
>>>>is taken away,
>that the *Originall*,
>>*Death* it selfe
>>>>may succeed,
>and that so I might have death to the life.

The series concludes with the longer, more complex units that dwell on the paradoxical patterns by which sleep gives way to death, and death, to life.

    In this passage one sees Donne engaged in meditation, not only in the large structure of his work, or even within the individual units of meditation, expostulation, and prayer, but also in the radical structure of sentences. Donne, considering a point, considers it always to the uttermost, bringing us not to logical comprehension but to emotional assent, indeed surrender. Such an instance of the use of logic to overwhelm the reader is found in the stunning annihilation of the possibility of human happiness in Meditation 14. Like the second meditation, this section begins with syntactically balanced statements that give the impression of rationality and moderation at the same time that they emphasize the contrast between God's infinite praiseworthiness and man's unspeakable degradation:

> I would not make *Man* worse then hee is,
> Nor his Condition more miserable then it is.
> But could I though I would?
> As a Man cannot *flatter God,* nor over prayse him,
> so a Man cannot *injure* Man, nor undervalue him.

The passage itself is symmetrical, placing Donne's expressed wish ("I would not") and the reality ("Man cannot *flatter God*") on either side of the short rhetorical question ("But could I though I would?"), so that the emphatic contrast is underscored by parison and alliteration in the first pair, by absolute parallelism in the second.

The appearance of logic continues as Donne begins to examine the elements of human happiness, their dependence on time and space, each of which he considers in its turn. But as he examines them, they turn to nothing in his hands, so that intensity of analysis brings the immediate dissolution of human hopes before the reader's very eyes.

> What poore *Elements* are our *happinesses* made off, if *Tyme, Tyme* which wee can scarce consider to be *any thing,* be an essential part of our happines? All things are done in some *place;* but if we consider *place* to be no more, but the next hollow *Superficies* of the *Ayre, Alas,* how thinne, & fluid a thing is *Ayre,* and how thinne a *filme* is a *Superficies,* and a *Superficies* of *Ayre?* All things are done in *time* too; but if we consider *Tyme* to be but the *Measure of Motion,* and howsoever it may seeme to have three *stations, past, present,* and *future,* yet the *first* and *last* of these *are* not (one is not, now, & the other is not yet) And that which you call *present,* is not *now* the same that it was, when you began to call it so in this *Line,* (before you sound that word *present,* or that *Monosyllable, now,* the present, & the *Now* is past,) if this *Imaginary halfe-nothing, Tyme,* be of the Essence of our *Happinesses,* how can they be thought *durable? Tyme* is not so; How can they bee thought to be? Tyme is not so; not so, considered in any of the *parts* thereof. (Med. 14)

Donne's prose here has an apparently clear logical structure: he considers first place and then time, these being the two elements of happiness. Within this topical organization there is also forceful syntactic organization; the heavy use of parallelism, of parison and isocolon, is underscored by repetition of words and phrases to create climax: "how thinne, & fluid a thing is *Ayre,* and how thinne a *filme* is a *Superficies,* and a *Superficies* of *Ayre?*" In this instance Donne uses a series of clauses and phrases to intensify his meaning, to give it incremental weight. But

Donne doesn't in fact abide by his initial scheme; for, having considered time and then place, he returns once again to time, treating it with an intensity that seems to derive from his foregoing annihilation of place. The section becomes even more powerful and alarming as he dips inside his categories, disrupting the parallelism of past, present, and future to discover that none of them exists. The parallelism holds at first to articulate a contrast: "one is not, now, & the other is not yet"; but finally the very time in which the reader lives and reads vanishes in a radical attack upon reality as we know it, not merely in an abstract philosophical sense but in the most basic and existential way: "And that which you call *present*, is not *now* the same that it was, when you began to call it so in this *Line*"; even as we stop to examine this possibility the text unravels before us and the words disappear in our mouths: ("before you sound that word *present*, or that *Monosyllable, now*, the present, & the *Now* is past."[20] Reading becomes the most dangerous of activities; existence itself is threatened; and the categories that we use to mean no longer exist, destroyed by an incremental process of close examination.

Sometimes the element of balance in such structures is dominant; at other times the intensity of the forward motion predominates, but there is usually in Donne's prose the sense of a balance that can be, or has been, tipped. And this contributes to our dual perception: first, that there is a logic to what Donne does, that his argument deserves our rational assent; and second, that logic has gone wrong, that the categories that ought to pertain do not, that order itself is lost, and that we too join in this overarching ruin. There is a conceptual echo of the *First Anniversarie*, the notion that all is lost, that contributes to the powerful emotional impact of Donne's work.[21] The repeated theme of the *Devotions*, a principle expressed with the syntactic, logical, and persuasive force of parallelism, is that articulated in Meditation 10, the belief that the common center is decay: "This is *Natures nest of Boxes*; The *Heavens* contain the *Earth*, the *Earth, Cities, Cities, Men*. And all these are *Concentrique;* the common *center* to them all, is *decay, ruine*." Even in the statement of the contrary, of the exception that proves the rule in the passage that follows, Donne uses anaphoric repetition of "only that," "even," and "they" to stress decay, rather than angelic permanence:

> Only that is *Eccentrique*, which was never made; only that place, or garment rather, which we can *imagine*, but not *demonstrate*, That light, which is the very emanation of the light of *God*, in which the

Saints shall dwell, with which the *Saints* shall be appareld, only that bends not to this *Center,* to *Ruine;* that which was not made of *Nothing,* is not threatned with this annihilation. All other things are; even *Angels,* even our *soules;* they move upon the same poles, they bend to the same *Center;* and if they were not made immortall by *preservation,* their *Nature* could not keepe them from sinking to this *center, Annihilation.* (Med. 10)

Ruin, annihilation, and decay are the center of the universe, as Donne's repetitions and circling phrases emphasize in Meditation 10. But Donne makes us feel that point the more keenly by placing human limitation in the context of human aspiration, as he does in the brilliant fourth meditation. With the use of epistrophe, Donne first builds himself up to a position of great power and comprehension: "My thoughts reach all, comprehend all." Next, a moment of balance expresses the paradox of Donne's position: "Inexplicable mistery; I their *Creator* am in a close prison, in a sicke bed, any where, and any one of my *Creatures,* my *thoughts,* is with the *Sunne,* and beyond the *Sunne,* overtakes the *Sunne,* and overgoes the *Sunne* in one pace, one steppe, every where" (Med. 4). Then, as counterpart to the multiplicity and extent of Donne's thoughts, comes the expansive elaboration of the multitudinous and malignant creatures of disease — before the conclusion in which, again with epistrophe and ploce, Donne puts the genie back into the bottle, circling back to the center that is ruin and decay: "Call back therefore thy Meditations again, and bring it downe; whats become of mans great extent & proportion, when himselfe shrinkes himselfe, and consumes himselfe to a handfull of dust; whats become of his soaring thoughts, his compassing thoughts, when himselfe brings himselfe to the ignorance, to the thoughtlesnesse of the *Grave?*" These two sections of Meditation 4 stand in brilliant contrast to each other, the one celebrating the power of man ("It is too little to call *Man* a *little World*"); the other elaborating his puniness. Taken together with Meditation 10, in which ruin is seen as central, these passages span the inevitable contradictions of human nature in theological and rhetorical form.

We have been observing the duality of Donne's prose as it relates to the duality of the human condition: man is both a little lower than the angels and the quintessence of dust, infinitely imaginative and ultimately earthbound. Donne expresses these visions in prose that uses balance and symmetry yet tips into passionate, asymmetrical climax, giving us a sense of stasis and equilibrium accompanied by a dramatic and climactic movement forward. These mixed techniques are exemplified in the very opening of the *Devotions,* where the apparent balance and symmetry of the opening—"Variable, and therfore miserable condition of Man; this minute I was well, and am ill, this minute"—in fact presents a state of radical uncertainty, for the apparent security of health is balanced by the surprising reality of sickness. The second clause of the opening sentence ends as it begins—"this minute I was well, and am ill, this minute"—giving not a sense of stasis, but a sense of how quickly the balance can shift from well to ill.

Thus, as I have suggested, while each of the twenty-three individual sections of the *Devotions* comes full circle, stating a problem and resolving it, so too does the work as a whole, descending into illness and returning from it, but also moving from its opening articulation of the variable condition of man to its concluding, even more resounding, affirmation of that point. In seeking to purge the body of illness, the physicians have looked even more closely at the nature of that body, leading to Donne's exclamation in the opening of Meditation 22, "How *ruinous* a *farme* hath *man* taken, in taking *himselfe?*" Although Donne rises from his bed, like Lazarus from his tomb, it is the more apparent that what rises can also fall: "I am readier to fall to the *Earth* now I am up, than I was when I *lay* in the bed" (Med. 21). And human nature is seen to be ruinous at its center. At the end we are once again where we began, with the "Variable, and therfore miserable condition of Man." This cyclical aspect of the *Devotions* brings us again to the work's conclusion, which not only represents the outcome of the illness but also creates the point of symmetry with the opening. And one may argue that the *Devotions* as a whole constitutes one grand instance of such symmetry, beginning with a rhetorical example of the figure of epanalepsis (mirroring repetition) in the opening sentence, and concluding with a similarly symmetrical fear of illness and sin. Donne too is back where he began, in a state of health, but given the "Variable, and therfore miserable" human condition, such health may well be the forerunner of illness.

Earlier I mentioned the oddly anxious concluding sentences of the *Devotions,* which have been seen as evidence of Donne's idiosyncratic and obsessive fear. But I have argued for the *Devotions* as a work cyclical as well as progressive, a structure within which a return to the opening may be differently valued. I want now to set those sentences within the context of Prayer 23 and within the larger structure of the work. Throughout the final prayer, as before, Donne asserts paradoxes by means of sentences that are both balanced and asymmetrical. He sets the contradictory notions of infinity and incrementality against one another in constructions that look as if they will be of equal weight but that rapidly shift toward asymmetry through the addition of further phrases and clauses: "O eternall and most gracious *God,* who though thou beest *ever infinite,* yet *enlargest* thy selfe, by the *Number* of our prayers, and takest our *often petitions* to thee, to be an *addition* to thy *glory,* and thy *greatnesse,* as *ever* upon all occasions, so now, O my *God,* I come to thy *Majestie* with *two Prayers, two Supplications."* Throughout the final prayer Donne sets before his readers divine faithfulness and human weakness, repeatedly placing himself within the divine care and asserting its sufficiency, yet in the next breath asserting his own tendency to waver. Faced with the theologically and emotionally powerful notions of divine infinitude and mercy, which typically are stated in the first unit of each sentence or pair of sentences, Donne is nevertheless drawn in the second unit or sentence to add further petitions—just in case that divine sufficiency should not anticipate all the dangerous possibilities that occur to Donne himself. Prayer 23 contains not one but two petitions—that God preserve the writer from relapsing and that, if he relapse, he may be pardoned. The division of attitude is expressed in a divided syntax: Donne is willing to trust God if God will act: "I durst deliver my selfe over to thee this *Minute,* If this *Minute* thou wouldst accept my *dissolution."* But if God will not act, then Donne remains in the world in which the necessity of human actions brings uncertainty, along with the hope of divine rescue: "Thy holy *Apostle, Saint Paul,* was shipwrackd *thrice;* & yet *stil saved."*

The prose of Prayer 23 is fraught with concern, even anxiety. Yet the sentence quoted above, "I durst deliver my selfe over to thee this *Minute,* If this *Minute* thou wouldst accept my *dissolution,"* with its use of mirroring in mid-sentence, also recalls the very opening lines of the *Devotions*— "Variable, and therfore miserable condition of Man; this minute I was well, and am ill, this minute.[22] Thus the powerfully articulated uncertainty of the ending of the *Devotions* is not a matter of individual fear but of return to the radical insecurity of the human condition itself. At the last Donne has returned to the first, to an awareness of the cyclical quality of human life, its rising and falling, its participation in the whole, and in the divine disposing of that whole, as he says: "Since therefore thy *Correction* hath brought mee to such a *participation of thy selfe* . . . to such an *intire possession* of thee, as that I durst deliver my selfe over to thee."

Donne: *Devotions upon Emergent Occasions*

In the *Devotions* Donne creates a work that is both profoundly individual and intimate, recounting the progress of the author's own illness, his near encounter with death, and profoundly universal, recounting the movement of Everyman from life to death. It is surely progressive, in that it records the progress of human life, and just as surely cyclical, both in its smaller structure and in its movement from health to sickness and sickness to health, in a drama of body and of spirit. Donne's finely shaped prose reflects these forward thrusting and returning movements, as he creates sentences that portray not only the intellectual but also the spiritual and emotional content of his experience, and sections of the text that reveal both its progressive and its cyclical qualities. In the *Devotions,* Donne adheres to patterns of meditation based on themes from daily life, on the nature of the world and the nature of man, on sickness and death and their meaning, on biblical texts and events, and he adapts these to his own experience, even as he reinterprets that experience to conform to the biblical contexts. Such use of traditional patterns and such meaningful and personal interaction with them are evidence that Donne is indeed part of the tradition of meditation defined by Martz and Lewalski. The *Devotions* is not only a formal meditation that grows out of theological and literary patterns; it is also a representation, expressed in the smallest and largest of its units, of evolving consciousness and spiritual pilgrimage.

In its method, the meditation on event and experience, in its subject, the consideration of time and of eternity and their intersection, and in its rhetorical strategy, a returning to points already made to force further revelations from them, Donne's *Devotions* is analogous to Eliot's *Four Quartets.* James Olney's description of the exploratory, meditative action of *Four Quartets* might be applied with equal appropriateness to Donne's *Devotions:* "Our consciousness . . . formally expands in its questioning and meditating and discovering. It is precisely this expanding, evolving consciousness that the poem both contains and expresses, both is and means."[23] In patterns of thought and patterns of rhetoric, in patterns of meditation on the conditions of his sickness and in patterns of prose, Donne enacts the process of discovery, leading to an understanding that, although at the center is ruin, our sickness may be health and our health sickness. Donne and Eliot both engage in a process in which they do not simply move forward, from sickness into health, but rather, as Eliot put it at the end of *Little Gidding,* "arrive where we started / And know the place for the first time."

III

ELIOT
Four Quartets
The Pattern in Revision

It should by now be evident that in suggesting that we may fruitfully compare a group of twentieth-century poems on identity, awareness, and literature with a seventeenth-century prose meditation on sickness and death, I am not simply ignoring obvious generic and historical differences; nor of course am I confining the discussion to purely formal questions but looking rather at what Ann Imbrie calls "a function of attitude," or what I would call generative impulses.

The differences between Donne and Eliot are undeniably important: the firm grounding of Donne in theological principles and assumptions in contrast to Eliot's tentative progression toward a philosophical and spiritual position; the relentless energy of Donne's prose in contrast to the much less intense formulations and reformulations of Eliot's verse; the single-mindedness of Donne, coupled with his dazzling mental gymnastics, in contrast to the eclecticism of Eliot as he progresses toward a high-church view informed by Eastern philosophy. These differences of course separate Donne and Eliot, yet the two are linked by meditation: they share an approach that is not merely thematic, or attitudinal, but methodological. As we have discerned in Donne a meditative structure that is both linear and cyclical, that consists in progressive contemplation, or even excavation, of a point, a returning that involves a going deeper, so Eliot, like Donne, uses incremental thinking as a mode of inquiry and of organization. Particularly prominent in *Four Quartets* is the statement of an idea in a form apparently final but subject to successive reformulation, the movement of verse that is both retrospective and progressive.

This mode, which I take to be an essential element in the meditative practice of Eliot and Donne, is structural and organizational, a mode by which the text is constructed. It is not of course unique to Donne and Eliot, but it is something of which Donne's heavy rhetorical patterning shows him aware and something that Eliot comments on explicitly. In his tercentenary essay on Lancelot Andrewes, Eliot quotes with approval a critical account of Andrewes's technique:

> He does not expatiate, but moves forward: if he repeats, it is because the repetition has a real force of expression; if he accumulates, each new word or phrase represents a new development, a substantive addition to what he is saying. He assimilates his material and advances by means of it. His quotation is not decoration or irrelevance but the matter in which he expresses what he wants to say. . . . The prayers are arranged, not merely in paragraphs, but in lines advanced and recessed so as in a measure to mark the inner structure and the steps and stages of the movement.[1]

This account of the short, meaningful, highly functional and expressive units of Andrewes's sentences would do nearly as well as a description of *Four Quartets*, in which statement and restatement are the characteristic modes of inquiry and expression. This aspect of Eliot's approach, meditative, incremental, a matter of method reflected in style, is well described by D. A. Traversi:

> The poet puts forward what are presented as personal thoughts and emotions . . . and builds a meditative discourse around them. He introduces them, develops and then drops them, seems to switch to other concepts, apparently unrelated, and then returns to the original themes, which emerge generally enriched, more subtly rendered, in the process. Ideas and feelings exist, in fact, in a constantly shifting and developing web of relationships. They lead by the end of the series to conclusions which we could not have foreseen at the beginning . . . but which are seen, by the time we have finished reading, to belong to a logical and consistent whole.[2]

What Traversi describes is a process less schematic, less clearly defined, perhaps more subtle or at least less clearly organized than the meditative process of Donne, but nevertheless linked to it by the method of incremental inquiry and presentation. As Eliot puts it in *Little Gidding,* "the purpose is beyond the end you figured / And is altered in fulfillment."[3]

The use of repetitive but incremental form so characteristic of Eliot's poetry is not restricted to the small rhetorical structures of each work but extends also to the larger units of *Four Quartets*. Just as Donne's work is made up of cycles within a narrative cycle, a repeating structure of meditation, expostulation, and prayer that occurs twenty-three times within the work, so Eliot's work is composed of smaller and larger units that are both cyclical and progressive. Like Donne's *Devotions, Four Quartets* may be seen as a unified whole; it also consists of individual quartets, each with five movements. As Martz and Lewalski have found clear meditative structures in the work of Donne, so Helen Gardner, F. O. Matthiessen, D. A. Traversi, and others have outlined the repeated structure found in each of the *Four Quartets,* seeing a five-part form in which lyrical and abstract, statement and metaphor alternate, following a generally similar pattern in each poem.[4]

Each quartet begins with a philosophical position or problem set in the context of the landscape or place that gives the poem its name; there follows a second section in which a single subject is handled in two boldly contrasting ways, first in a lyric and then in a colloquial passage; the third movement of each poem is darker, more somber, each a descent into something like the underworld.[5] The fourth section is briefer, lyrical, often in metered and rhymed verse; the fifth is a recapitulation and resolution of the themes of the poem. In choosing the designation "quartets," Eliot deliberately invited the notion of musical structure appropriate to the articulation and development of themes, the pattern of thesis, antithesis, and resolution that one finds in his verse.[6] Moreover, the five-part structure of each quartet might be compared to the extended five-part quartets of Bartok or the late Beethoven, to which Eliot turned his attention in the time before he began work on *Burnt Norton.*[7]

While each of the four poems is a quartet with five movements, the four taken together also make up a single work, a whole that might itself be described as a single quartet. In so describing *Four Quartets,* one should acknowledge that the poems were written over a period of six years and that Eliot's initial intention was not to write a sequence of four. Five years elapsed between the writing of *Burnt Norton* (which grew out of *Murder in the Cathedral*) and *East Coker;* even in 1940, according to John Hayward, Eliot intended "three quatuors"; only in the course of the composition of *East Coker* did the plan of a series of four emerge.[8] But this method of composition, joining parts to make a whole, was characteristic of Eliot. As he said in 1953, "That's one way in which my mind does seem to have worked throughout the years poetically—doing things separately and then seeing the possibility of fusing them together, altering them, and making a kind of whole of them."[9] And the result was something that Eliot considered a unity, that he chose to title as a group, and that he took pains to integrate in the writing of *Little Gidding.*[10]

Eliot: *Four Quartets*

Like Donne's *Devotions, Four Quartets* traces an arc of expression through a series of repeating cycles. It treats the large theme of time in relation to eternity, personal experience in relation to more general experience, and the problems of articulating that experience; these themes are expressed repeatedly within each poem, but that expression becomes progressively clearer within the course of the four poems.[11] In the musical or meditative structure of *Four Quartets,* the first two poems state and develop the theme — the relation between past and present, our attempts to grasp the shape and meaning of reality — whereas the third, a brooding movement in a minor mode, seems to annihilate all that they propose. *Burnt Norton* gives us a vision of the past, the rose garden, with its echoes in the present, and the ambiguous possibilities of redemption: the past may be unredeemable or conquered only through time. In *East Coker* that past is more closely identified with "ashes," "flesh, fur and faeces," with images of bodily death; Eliot suggests that the past is not so much instructive as deceptive. In *The Dry Salvages,* whatever patterns of human life may have seemed valid in *East Coker* are obliterated by the images of flux: "this thing is sure, / That time is no healer: the patient is no longer here." Out of the bleak darkness of *The Dry Salvages* comes the brilliant resolution of the fourth movement, *Little Gidding,* the triumph of celestial fire over earthly water, the shaping force of eternity invading the shapelessness of time.

In the practice of meditation outlined by Louis Martz, the composition of place, the mental image of the subject to be contemplated, is the initial and crucial step. Appropriately, each of the quartets bears the name of a place of particular significance to Eliot, yet one that can be made to bear larger and more general meaning. *Burnt Norton* is named after a manor house in Gloucestershire that Eliot visited in the late summer of 1934 or 1935.[12] East Coker, a village in Somersetshire, is the origin of Eliot's ancestor Andrew Eliot, who left England for America circa 1669, and of Sir Thomas Elyot, whose *Boke of the Governour* (1531) is quoted in section 1; it is also an image of the human past more generally. The Dry Salvages, a group of rocks off Cape Ann in Massachusetts, was familiar to Eliot from his summers as a child; the poem opens with reference to a great river, like the Mississippi, which flows by Eliot's birthplace, St. Louis, but generalized to a more pervasive natural force. Little Gidding, a manor house with chapel in Huntingdon that was the seat of an Anglo-Catholic religious community under the leadership of Nicholas Ferrar, to whom George Herbert, on his deathbed, sent his poems, was the place in which King Charles I, fleeing the parliamentary forces, sought refuge; visited by Eliot in May of 1936, it becomes a locus for religious discovery, pilgrimage, and illumination more generally conceived.

The common theme of *Four Quartets* and the *Devotions*, the relation between time and eternity, is seen by Donne in an explicitly religious, explicitly Christian context, a biblical and Trinitarian view of reality, whereas for Eliot the question, although it ultimately has religious implications and although its resolution has strongly Christian elements, is more largely philosophical and literary, less clearly narrative and personal. While Donne's understanding of the relation between time and eternity is strongly schematic (as expressed in Prayer 2, for example),[13] Eliot's sense is both perplexing and paradoxical. His questions, which at first sound secular, progressively become more explicitly theological.[14] Donne's presentation, though rhetorically dramatic and flamboyant, is essentially more stable, since it takes place within an established theological context. But for Eliot the whole effort is to *determine* the context, to *find* the pattern, to question whether a pattern exists that will make sense of the whole. Indeed, the movement of *Four Quartets* in general may be seen as the articulation of ideas, motifs, visions, at first in fragmentary and imperfect form, emerging at last in *Little Gidding* as a unified and adequate vision.[15] As James Olney puts it, "The mode of the *Quartets* is not to discover truth and to present it, but to pursue and to create it, and not to create it outside the pursuit but within it."[16]

I have asserted that Donne's *Devotions* and Eliot's *Four Quartets* both embody a meditative pattern based on smaller and larger cycles, on a mingling of the progressive and the cyclical, and that such structures reflect a mode of discovery. I want now to follow in some detail through each of the *Quartets* in succession the movement from less to more perfect forms and articulations, the images that are elaborated and repeated, and the patterns that are developed and varied.

The first poem of *Four Quartets, Burnt Norton,* begins in a world of echoes, memories, and possibilities, connecting past and future in a way that is both theoretical—

> What might have been is an abstraction
> Remaining a perpetual possibility
> Only in a world of speculation

— and actual, remembered; it blends the philosophical and the lyrical or imagistic in a way characteristic of Eliot. Eliot considers the most abstract questions but does so in the context of an actual garden that he visited, one that becomes our garden as well. At first Eliot appears to place us all outside its walls:

> Footfalls echo in the memory
> Down the passage which we did not take
> Towards the door we never opened
> Into the rose-garden.

Yet this place is clearly our common psychic property, with strong hints of Eden, or of the mythic garden we carry in our imaginations, as we go "Through the first gate, / Into our first world." Tinged with memories like the world at large as Donne or Herbert would have seen it, the garden carries hints of some presence, some larger coherence of which we are incompletely aware, a pattern waiting to be discovered. The children playing in the shrubbery give an image of primeval innocence, while the "dignified, invisible" presences suggest our first ancestors.[17] The first section then presents a relatively optimistic version of the relation between time and eternity: eternity, intersecting with time, leaves traces for us to glimpse: "What might have been and what has been / Point to one end, which is always present."

The second section of *Burnt Norton* presents a far more complexly schematic picture: it stresses the analogy between the little world of man and the cosmos, a principle that was lovingly, even obsessively, elaborated in the Renaissance;[18] it juxtaposes the two realms with a forcefulness reminiscent of Mallarmé, whom Eliot quotes, and of the metaphysical poets:

> The dance along the artery
> The circulation of the lymph
> Are figured in the drift of stars.

But while Eliot articulates the relationship between the cosmic structure and the earthly embodiment of it, he also stresses difficulties and contradictions. To understand time we must transcend it, yet our understanding is grounded in particular moments of time, and the attempt at clearer vision in itself strains our resources:

> To be conscious is not to be in time
> But only in time can the moment in the rose-garden,
> The moment in the arbour where the rain beat,
> The moment in the draughty church at smokefall
> Be remembered.

In the final line of the section—"Only through time time is conquered"—Eliot points to the resolution that will be articulated in *Little Gidding* and *The Dry Salvages*. But for the moment the issue remains problematic, as the speaker is torn between the demands of human existence and the transcendent consciousness.

For Donne eternity intersects time through divine purpose and action: "Every thing is *immediatly* done, which is done when *thou* wouldst have it done. Thy purpose terminates every action" (Exp. 19). Eliot also employs the Christian imagery of incarnation: that fixed point about which all else revolves is "the bedded axle-tree" of the opening, which conflates the manger of Christ's birth and the bloody cross of his crucifixion, the specific point at which, for both Donne and Eliot, eternity intervenes in time. But by contrast, Eliot's poem emphasizes the human agency in the perception of meaning; such radical intersection is seen in the joining of two points of time that take us beyond time and that are seen by the speaker rather than simply created by divine force.[19]

Like Donne, perhaps even more explicitly, Eliot confronts us with paradox. As Meditation 14 stripped away time and place to show the nothingness of human happiness, so Eliot sets opposites against each other, denying them both—"Neither flesh nor fleshless; / Neither from nor towards." But in contrast to Donne's emphasis on the radical dependency of human life, Eliot's denial of all known categories works toward a visionary moment, a glimpse of the transcendent reality left by the expulsion of opposites.[20] Using the images of rising and falling, Donne depicts an inverse relationship between earthly and heavenly success; Eliot denies the earthly categories to insist that when all is gone the cosmic form persists.

> Neither movement from nor towards,
> Neither ascent nor decline. Except for the point, the
>   still point,
> There would be no dance, and there is only the dance.
>   (*Burnt Norton* 2)

Eliot: *Four Quartets*

And like Donne, who used rhetorical patterning to convey meaning, who perceived that "the *Heavens* are not the lesse constant, because they move continually, because they move continually one and the same way," Eliot captures that moment of stasis in a mirroring rhetorical device (epizeuxis) that makes his sentence stand for a moment suspended: "only through time time is conquered."

As Donne's *Devotions* tends to move through patterns of questioning and resolution in the sequence of meditation, expostulation, and prayer, so each quartet is a dialogue between abstract statement and concrete image, between vision and loss of vision, between comprehension and confusion.[21] The fleeting vision of *Burnt Norton* 2 is succeeded by a dark journey paralleled in each of the *Quartets:* in *Burnt Norton,* into the dim light of the London underground; in *East Coker,* into a darkness that begins with the language of Milton's *Samson Agonistes* and expands to encompass the cosmos and the world of man; in *The Dry Salvages,* to the intellectual vacancy of the journey by rail or ship that allows the subconscious to emerge. In *Little Gidding* the journey to the underground fuses the experience of Dante in Hell, struggling to catch "the sudden look of some dead master / Whom I had known, forgotten, half-recalled," with that of Eliot himself, pacing the streets of London, surveying the damage in his capacity as air-raid warden during the Blitz: "Over the asphalt where no other sound was / Between three districts whence the smoke arose."

This journey into the depths is in each poem followed by a brief lyric section before the final section of resolution. The images of *Burnt Norton* 4 are at once simple and striking yet potentially rich and complex, as light and dark, human death and divine intervention are juxtaposed. The very simplicity of Eliot's language suggests a larger context for time and the bell, the black cloud and the sun, but the nature of that context appears only gradually.

> Time and the bell have buried the day,
> The black cloud carries the sun away.
> Will the sunflower turn to us, will the clematis
> Stray down, bend to us; tendril and spray
> Clutch and cling?
> Chill
> Fingers of yew be curled
> Down on us? After the kingfisher's wing

> Has answered light to light, and is silent, the light is still
> At the still point of the turning world.
> *(Burnt Norton* 4)

In this passage metaphors refuse to stay metaphors but acquire a force of their own, giving the images representing the passing of the day an almost animistic quality, a potentially religious significance: the sunflower, associated with the soul, follows the sun; the kingfisher, the royal bird emblematic of Christ, answers light to light; the yew in the churchyard symbolizes death and eternity; time, the bell, and the black cloud assume power over the forces of day and light. While these images take on an active role, human beings, normally dominant, are not only passive but dead, underground, awaiting the ministrations of yew, clematis, and sunflower. And as in a seventeenth-century shaped poem (like Herbert's "Easter Wings," for example), this passage goes through a cycle of deprivation (culminating in "Chill") and rebirth.

The power of words and language to articulate, to comprehend or control reality, a major concern of *Four Quartets* that Eliot shares with Donne, emerges in *Burnt Norton* 5. In the course of this section, as in *Four Quartets* generally, words move from time-bound to timeless. At first frail, limited, impotent,

> Words strain,
> Crack and sometimes break, under the burden,
> Under the tension, slip, slide, perish,
> Decay with imprecision, will not stay in place,
> Will not stay still.

These are simply the ordinary words of our lives, barely adequate for communication; but there is also the Word, the Logos, the pattern that gives shape to the rest, the word that God speaks in time.[22]

> Words, after speech, reach
> Into the silence. Only by the form, the pattern,
> Can words or music reach
> The stillness, as a Chinese jar still
> Moves perpetually in its stillness.

Remarkably silent, a form standing in dramatic contrast to the "Shrieking voices / Scolding, mocking, or merely chattering" that oppose it, the Word of the end of section 5a suggests Christ in the wilderness ("The Word in the desert / . . . most attacked by voices of temptation") but also the power of divinely ordered language, of the Creative Word to establish order.

Eliot's poems, like Donne's *Devotions,* are shaped by such echoing words, by phrases and images used in the beginning and returned to at the end with new and enriched meaning. The conclusion of *Burnt Norton* recalls the opening — "the hidden laughter / Of children in the foliage" — and points toward the final vision and resolution in "Quick now, here, now, always." This Janus-like line suggests not only the energetic speed of playing children but also life and eternity, for *quick* bears the meaning of *alive,* and the *here* and *now* of time are juxtaposed with the *always* of eternity. Although *Burnt Norton* ends in a minor key ("Ridiculous the waste sad time / Stretching before and after"), the positive has been articulated. The poems that follow represent the struggle between the view that life is shapeless and meaningless, that language and thought are unable to comprehend or articulate it, and its converse. The elements of the meditation have been laid down; they reappear in shifting configurations in the next three quartets.

Whereas *Burnt Norton* emphasizes the world of memory, the return to "our first world," the recollection of Eden and the laughter of the children in the garden, *East Coker* emphasizes the cyclical sequence, the rise and fall, the generation of all life:

> In my beginning is my end. In succession
> Houses rise and fall, crumble, are extended,
> Are removed, destroyed, restored, or in their place
> Is an open field, or a factory, or a by-pass.
> Old stone to new building, old timber to new fires,
> Old fires to ashes, and ashes to the earth
> Which is already flesh, fur and faeces,
> Bone of man and beast, cornstalk and leaf.
> (*East Coker* 1)

Like *Burnt Norton, East Coker* contains images of the past, but rather than the individual memory or re-vision of a universal past grounded in a specific place, it recalls a communal life encompassing us all. In *East Coker* the past is really past, the dead (though we may see them dancing) are really dead, unlike those mysterious presences in *Burnt Norton:* "The dancers are all gone under the hill" (*East Coker* 2), and we too will join them in the endless cycle of generation and death. Yet the poem is neither melancholy nor hopeless, but, rather, reconciled to the cyclical nature of life that Eliot emphasizes: "Feet rising and falling / Eating and drinking. Dung and death." If *Burnt Norton* was the poem of air, *East Coker* is the poem of earth, depicting a rural community, closely allied to nature, quite literally part of the soil:

> Lifting heavy feet in clumsy shoes,
> Earth feet, loam feet, lifted in country mirth
> Mirth of those long since under earth
> Nourishing the corn.
> (*East Coker* 1)

The diction and the images are far more practical, basic—indeed, earthy—than those of the other three poems. Here memory is not simply a fleeting glimpse but an ongoing pattern that, "if you do not come too close, / On a Summer midnight, you can hear . . . / And see." Eliot's language recalls the world-weary preacher of Ecclesiastes: there is a time for living and for dying, for all things in their season, and as in the biblical text, Eliot's lines convey a detachment that precludes either optimism or pessimism:

> there is a time for building
> And a time for living and for generation
> And a time for the wind to break the loosened pane
> And to shake the wainscot where the field-mouse trots.
> (*East Coker* 1)

The notion of appropriate cycle and sequence articulated in section 1 is handled in a sharply divergent fashion in the rather florid verse of section 2a, which, like the comparable section of *Burnt Norton*, repeatedly juxtaposes opposites to make the point of unseasonableness and conflict. As he will in *Little Gidding*, Eliot uses images of the natural world to depict the unnatural, here as conflict and contradiction, there as brilliant resolution:

> What is the late November doing
> With the disturbance of the spring
> And creatures of the summer heat,
> And snowdrops writhing under feet
> And hollyhocks that aim too high
> Red into grey and tumble down
> Late roses filled with early snow?

Once again Eliot's characteristic alternating—of concrete and abstract, attempted statement and reaction, modification or comment—suggests that the statement made, the form first glimpsed, is inadequate. Accordingly, Eliot goes on to suggest that the pattern so clearly seen in the dancing figures, images of matrimony, concord, and rhythm, is only illusory. There is no knowledge to be gained from the past; the pattern of the dance and the patterns of language are alike misleading; and the point is made in determinedly prosaic verse:

> There is, it seems to us,
> At best, only a limited value
> In the knowledge derived from experience.
> The knowledge imposes a pattern, and falsifies,
> For the pattern is new in every moment
> And every moment is a new and shocking
> Valuation of all we have been.
> (*East Coker* 2)

Thus the vision of stability and permanence we had thought was being offered to us, something more palpable and valid than the fleeting images of *Burnt Norton,* is firmly rejected. This is one of a long sequence of rejections of formulations to be replaced by subsequent articulations and perceptions in which "We are only undeceived / Of that which, deceiving, could no longer harm."

The central third section of *East Coker,* like that of *Burnt Norton,* is a vision of darkness, encompassing and consuming all; beginning with the voice of Milton's Samson, it proceeds to contemporary London, *Hamlet,* the Psalms, *The Tempest,* St. John of the Cross, the Gospel of John, *A Midsummer Night's Dream,* and St. John of the Cross again. Its multiple and copious references demonstrate yet another way, beside the vision of the ancient village, in which Eliot's persona is indebted to the past. This use of antecedent texts as the context for one's own discovery and as a source of one's own language links Eliot to Donne while it differentiates him; for whereas Donne's texts are patristic and biblical, Eliot's are eclectic, ranging from the mundane and worldly—the captains and merchant bankers—to the mystical way of negation, but remaining in the minor mode throughout.

Eliot, like Donne, articulates in words the ways in which time is intersected by eternity, but his very language also represents a conjunction of two moments in time. That is, his use of quotation and allusion creates a rather odd and anachronistic mixture of the modern and the late Renaissance: he recalls Sir Thomas Browne ("For the world, I count it not an Inne, but an Hospital, . . . not to live but to die in"), as well as Milton, in the Latinate use of the word *prevents,* meaning to come before ("we shall / Die of the absolute paternal care / That will not leave us, but prevents us everywhere" [*East Coker* 4]).[23] Eliot makes lavish use of his predecessors, often quoting from several at once; yet he varies their phrasing, thus altering the past in the very act of connecting with it. This collage of direct and modified quotations creates in Eliot's poetry the very intersection of past and present articulated in his criticism, as in "Tradition and the Individual Talent," where he speaks of the present reshaping the past, not only in that new works alter the shape of the canon, but as allusion and quotation rewrite earlier texts.[24]

East Coker, like the other poems of *Four Quartets,* moves toward resolution, yet resolution achieved within the framework of paradox. The lyric fourth section, like the opening of the second section, is sharply oxymoronic — "the wounded surgeon," "the dying nurse" — and almost metaphysical in its approach. Although the sickness Eliot describes is more of the spirit than of the body, this section articulates a vision like Donne's in the *Devotions:* "To be restored, our sickness must grow worse."[25]

The precise and complex expression of section 4 prepares for the return to the central issue of language as a shaping force and the articulation, as in *Burnt Norton,* of the inadequacy of words to that task. But the voice of *East Coker* 5 is far more personal than that of *Burnt Norton* 5, reflecting, if not an anxiety of influence, then certainly an awareness of the overwhelming greatness of one's predecessors. In these final lines it is the determinedly middle-aged poet that speaks, as Eliot, adapting a Renaissance commonplace, characterizes himself as a pygmy following a race of giants.

> And what there is to conquer
> By strength and submission, has already been discovered
> Once or twice, or several times, by men whom one cannot hope
> To emulate —

The timeless moment is gone, replaced by a long sequence of figures we cannot match, articulated in a series of phrases that make our debt and our weakness progressively obvious.

> there is no competition —
> There is only the fight to recover what has been lost

And found and lost again and again: and now, under conditions
That seem unpropitious.

If the mood of "For us there is only the trying. The rest is not our business" recalls the resignation of the midpoint of the *Devotions,* Eliot's method nevertheless differs sharply from Donne's obsessive attention to logic, rhetoric, and detail. The studied indifference of the final lines of *East Coker* instead approach mysticism, taking us into the depths, out of this world into what sounds like death and whatever lies beyond:

> Here and there does not matter
> We must be still and still moving
> Into another intensity
> For a further union, a deeper communion
> Through the dark cold and the empty desolation.
> 					(*East Coker* 5)

Like *Burnt Norton, East Coker* concludes with images that recall its beginning and with Mary Stuart's motto, "In my end is my beginning," the mirror image of the phrase with which the poem opens. The symmetrical placing of these two mottoes enables Eliot to move from the philosophical position that one contains in nuce all one's future being to the defiant affirmation, the principle of faith, that the end is only the beginning. Although the mood of *East Coker* is resigned and philosophical rather than fearful or paradoxically affirmative in the face of doubt, such use of mirroring rhetorical forms and of a structure progressive as well as cyclical recalls the symmetry of Donne's *Devotions.*

Although the end of *East Coker,* with its mention of "the wave cry, the wind cry," prepares us for the watery depths of *The Dry Salvages,* this third quartet so contrasts in mood and texture with the others that some critics have judged it, as Eliot did *Hamlet,* "obviously a failure."[26] In the continuum of *Burnt Norton* and *East Coker,* it represents a further movement downward: whereas *Burnt Norton* allows us to sense unseen but dignified presences and to hear the excited quick and quickening laughter of children in the leaves and *East Coker* permits us to glimpse the ancient, mysterious ceremonies of our ancestors, "Holding eche other by the hand or the arm / Which betokeneth concorde," *The Dry Salvages* rejects the very notion of such supernatural presences, patterns, or meanings. Coming after the first two poems, the opening lines of *The Dry Salvages* sound startlingly prosaic, and the setting, the muddy Mississippi, is damned with unconvincing praise. "I do not know much about gods," the poem begins, and then for the numinous, the evocative, the mysterious, it substitutes the ordinary, the physical, "the river / [as] a strong brown god." The river described by Eliot is the necessary, the irreducible part of our natures, a "reminder / Of what men choose to forget," as well as an image from his own past.

This poem, which has much to do with the loss of human structure, with intellectual or spiritual conceptions, nevertheless allows us to feel the forceful rhythm of this "strong brown god—sullen, untamed and intractable," an immanent rather than a transcendent deity.[27]

> The river is within us, the sea is all about us;
> The sea is the land's edge also, the granite
> Into which it reaches, the beaches where it tosses
> Its hints of earlier and other creation.

The Dry Salvages expresses two contrasting attitudes: on the one hand it negates previously articulated conceptions of existence, especially in section 2, which asserts that none of these categories of thought or language has the power to shape our experience or make it comprehensible: "There is no end, but addition: the trailing / Consequence of further days and hours." But it also points to something much more fundamental and inescapable, the basic rhythm of life that underlies our experience:

> The tolling bell
> Measures time not our time, rung by the unhurried
> Ground swell, a time
> Older than the time of chronometers, older
> Than time counted by anxious worried women
> Lying awake.
>   (*The Dry Salvages* 1)

Written during the darkest hours of World War II, when London suffered under the Blitz, Eliot's poem defines not only his own situation ("the failing / Pride or resentment at failing powers") but also that of society at large, purposeless and doomed, "In a drifting boat with a slow leakage."[28] But what is represented as an image of destruction, the enemy of human order, is also a preserver of something more basic than that human order. That image of preservation comes through not only in debris, refuse, things that survive, but also in language, words recurring to create the beginning of a pattern. While articulating flux, Eliot asserts and uses form, in the repetition (anaphora, parison) of "Time the destroyer is time the preserver"; the alliteration of "cargo . . . cows and chicken coops"; the alliterative word play of "The bitter apple and the bite in the apple," which recalls the imagery of Genesis and the first two quartets. While *The Dry Salvages* depicts irreducible disorder and loss, that which we would like to suppress, it does so in the cyclical motif of internal rhyme ("It tosses up our losses"); and while it rejects human order, the poem nevertheless contains a vast variety of rhythmic lines and modes—an imitation of terza rima, a modified sestina, markedly rhythmic sections, four- and five-stress lines, internal and end rhyme, and verbal patterning of all kinds. In his use of the figures of rhetoric to establish order in the midst of chaos, stasis in the midst of flux, Eliot's method once again recalls Donne's ("this minute I was well, and am ill, this minute" [Med. 1]). *The Dry Salvages* develops opposing poles of stability and change, juxtaposing images of flux and motion—the river, the sea, the citation of Heraclitus in section 3—with images of surprising permanence, "the ragged rock in the restless waters," which "On a halcyon day . . . is merely a monument," but "in the somber season / Or the sudden fury, is what it always was" (*The Dry Salvages* 2).

Because *The Dry Salvages* is the darkest point, the antithesis within the sequence, the glimpses it offers of something more elevated are largely parodic, not in the sense of being inadequate or absurd, but rather in playing a sequence of notes in a new key.[29] The visionary images, for example, are essentially superstitious, like the references to spiritualism and fortune-telling in section 5; the invocation of the Virgin in section 4—

> Lady, whose shrine stands on the promontory,
> Pray for all those who are in ships, those
> Whose business has to do with fish

—may sound like a pedestrian imitation of Psalm 107;[30] and the poem closes with what sounds like a pun:

> We, content at the last
> If our temporal reversion nourish
> (Not too far from the yew-tree)
> The life of significant soil.

What is vital, the lines seem to insist, is not human life, activity, or creativity but the soil—the most basic element of earth, that which we are when we are nothing, when we have lost whatever spark it was that gave us life; our highest function is to become fertilizer for the omnipresent yew tree of an English cemetery. The final line is the more striking in that it comes suggestively close to but avoids a more likely phrase — "the life of significant toil"; but this suggestion, that human activity creates meaning, is precisely what *The Dry Salvages* questions.

Yet the symbols of this section, traditionally linked with death, also have their converse. Eliot's language is masked, consisting of words that seem allusively close to other more positive words: the process of death and return to dust is "our temporal reversion," our reversion in time, which, in the movement of *Four Quartets,* is hoped to be also temporary. The soil does in fact nourish life; nature's cycle of birth and death does go on (it is "older than the time of chronometers," *The Dry Salvages* 1); the yew is planted in graveyards because it is an evergreen of exceptionally long life, hence an image of eternity. And *The Dry Salvages,* though it seems to negate everything positive articulated in the other three poems, also anticipates the resolution of *Little Gidding.* It looks backward, quoting the images of quickness and light that we glimpsed in *Burnt Norton* ("The wild thyme unseen, or the winter lightning"), and anticipates the final resolution of *Little Gidding:* "The hint half guessed, the gift half understood, is Incarnation" (*The Dry Salvages* 5).

Little Gidding, the final movement of *Four Quartets,* resolves through paradox and complexity what has gone before. In this poem Eliot turns not to a river or to ominous rocks in the eternal sea, the large, generalized symbols of Romantic literature, but to a civilized place with explicitly religious associations. In a shrine of Christianity, of Anglicanism, of royalism, a place "where prayer has been valid," where purposes quite different from one's own are revealed by a process of reenactment, the questions of our relation to the patterns of the past receive a less hopeless answer than before.[31]

Since *Four Quartets* queries the power of language to comprehend and control reality, it is appropriate that *Little Gidding* not only articulates the idea of linguistic control but that the poem itself is the most highly organized and brilliantly wrought of the *Four Quartets.* Whereas the other poems tend to represent the meditative process, the ongoing attempt at understanding, in a series of statements, many of them absolute and often at odds with one another, *Little Gidding* insists on paradox, from its opening lines forcing together oxymoronic terms that indicate something extraordinary and highly charged.[32]

> Midwinter spring is its own season,
> Sempiternal though sodden towards sundown,
> Suspended in time, between pole and tropic.
>   (*Little Gidding* 1)

These lines focus with particular intensity on the great paradox of the Incarnation, which occurs within time and is yet beyond it: "This is the spring time / But not in time's covenant." Like those of earlier poems, the formulations of *Little Gidding* are incremental representations of understanding, but the vision achieved here is transcendent. Eliot uses traditional images of the soul's growth—sap, springtime, budding—and of divine visitation—pentecostal fire—but in transforming the blossom (a frequent image of the human spirit) into a "transitory blossom / Of snow," Eliot shows that the kind of regeneration or vision he means is not simply natural.[33] He brings before us again the four elements—earth, air, water, fire—and sets their qualities—hot, cold, moist, dry—in opposition. He forces together Anglo-Saxon and Latin—"Sempiternal though sodden towards sundown," "the dumb spirit" and "pentecostal fire"—to create a series of dazzling oxymora:

midwinter spring
sempiternal / sundown
pole / tropic
frost / fire
glare [brightness] / blindness
melting / freezing
zero / summer
windless cold / heart's heat
flames the ice

    Whereas the opening of *Little Gidding* stops time, the second part of section 1 is about process, figured as a journey. It begins in a series of conditionals, addressing the reader and moving him into the experience of the poem through spatial references that combine apparent explicitness with ultimate vagueness: "Taking the route you would be likely to take / From the place you would be likely to come from." The journey has its own duration, expressed by present participles—"taking," "starting," "knowing." But most of all, this journey leads us into the past, as our ordinary actions intersect with past actions and events and as our progress, far from unique, recapitulates the pattern of earlier journeys that inform our own.

As in the mimetic prose of the seventeenth century, the very structure of Eliot's lines creates this journey: his rhetorical patterning, the anaphora of "If you came," "If you came," "You would find," "It would be," reenacts a repetitive yet progressive action, as the modern pilgrim retraces the steps of Charles I who "came at night . . . a broken king." And whereas the attempts in the earlier poems to appropriate the meanings of the past fail because those meanings are no longer relevant, the past is here discovered not as we seek it but as we make our own journey. "Tradition," Eliot once said, "cannot be inherited, and if you want it you must obtain it by great labour."[34] The meaning of experience for which Eliot's personae have so often struggled is revealed as a surprise, a gift, or, to use the religious terminology toward which Eliot himself tends, a matter of grace and revelation.

>And what you thought you came for
>Is only a shell, a husk of meaning
>From which the purpose breaks only when it is fulfilled
>If at all.
>   (*Little Gidding* I)

Although the final line implies the possibility that the anticipated vision will never occur, the passage also suggests a kind of power in the pattern, a meaning or revelation that may emerge in the reenactment of patterns that seem unpromising. The notion is related to that of George Herbert's prayer in "The Altar," "That, if I chance to hold my peace, / These stones to praise thee may not cease."[35] Meaning is found neither by active searching and analysis nor by a mindless adherence to form, but, in contrast to "we had the experience but missed the meaning" of *The Dry Salvages*, it can emerge from apparently sterile or lifeless patterns: "What you thought you came for / Is only a shell, a husk of meaning." The action of the conscious mind is subordinate to the purpose that overtakes us:

>You are not here to verify,
>Instruct yourself, or inform curiosity
>Or carry report. You are here to kneel
>Where prayer has been valid.
>   (*Little Gidding* I)

In *Little Gidding*, the hints, guesses, and inadequate attempts of the first three poems assume more definitive shape. Whereas we earlier might have glimpsed the past only dimly, or have been mindlessly bound by it, Eliot now depicts meaningful communication in the images of pentecostal fire.

> And what the dead had no speech for, when living,
> They can tell you, being dead: the communication
> Of the dead is tongued with fire beyond the language of the living.

These tongues of fire, recalling those that appeared over the disciples' heads on Pentecost, a sign of their transformation from learners and followers to apostles, are a potent manifestation of the Holy Spirit, as well as an image of diverse possibilities of expression. And, as transformed by Eliot, they are a powerful image of the vitality of the past in our lives.

Section 2 begins by summing up the images of the first two poems ("the burnt roses"; "Dust in the air suspended" [*Burnt Norton*] and "The wall, the wainscot and the mouse" [*East Coker*]); it moves on to the images of *The Dry Salvages* (death, water, and earth), the final stanza showing succession, if not redemption, as "Water and fire succeed / The town, the pasture and the weed." The section remarks memories and remnants, even as it declares endings, and it proclaims the termination of all possible attitudes toward life—hope and despair. Just as the small and large cycles of Donne's *Devotions* bring us to where we began, to ruin at the center, to the radical instability of human life, to being shipwrecked within the care of a merciful God, so *Four Quartets* comes to its end in the images of its opening, images now richly resonating through the sequence of four poems.

Whereas Eliot previously gave us a series of statements needing to be reconciled with one another, in *Little Gidding* the conjunction has already taken place. In the dark journey of section 2b, as Eliot treads the streets of Kensington after an air raid, his encounter with "some dead master" parallels Dante's meeting with his tutor Brunetto Latini in the *Inferno*, and the fires of London touch the fires of hell. Eliot's verse is a tissue of allusions through which he comes to understand his own experience: Dante's vision of uncertainty, as he comes to himself "in the middle of the journey of our life . . . within a dark wood where the straight way was lost," is captured in time and place, tied to Eliot's own disorientation in the bombed landscape of London.[36] Like Dante, Eliot represents a place where the spiritual and the secular intersect, creating a point without reference points where another dimension becomes apparent:

> In the uncertain hour before the morning
> Near the ending of interminable night
> At the recurrent end of the unending.

Whereas Donne relies primarily on biblical and patristic texts, Eliot joins the voices of several dead masters to create his own. In *Little Gidding* section 2b, while emulating Dante's terza rima, Eliot also borrows from Mallarmé; from Herrick ("Last season's fruit is eaten / And the fullfed beast shall kick the empty pail" recalls "The Hock-Cart"); from Milton ("bitter tastelessness of shadow fruit"); from Pope ("Then fools' approval stings, and honour stains" has the diction and the structure of half a heroic couplet); from the Bible ("refining fire"); from Shakespeare ("where you must move in measure, like a dancer" recalls Octavius Caesar, who "kept / His sword e'en like a dancer";[37] and the figure who "faded on the blowing of the horn," the all clear, recalls the ghost of Hamlet's father at the crowing of the cock). This journey to the underworld frees the persona to move on to the place where, quoting Julian of Norwich, "All shall be well and / All manner of thing shall be well."

Little Gidding, like the other poems of *Four Quartets,* moves from the very particular context of the poet's time and place toward universal meanings, as actions transcend themselves by their intersection with other actions which they parallel. The recollection of Charles I seeking refuge at Little Gidding merges with a number of figures of suffering, martyrdom, and even frustration. The "three men, and more, on the scaffold," analogous to Christ who died with two "malefactors" (Luke 23:33), may be Charles and his supporters;[38] the one "who died blind and quiet" may be Milton; but the language also raises other associations — Samson, whom Milton celebrated, and blind Homer, whom he imitated. Yet the individualizing details are finally subordinate to the emerging pattern: "See, now they vanish, / The faces and places, . . . / To become renewed, transfigured, in another pattern" (*Little Gidding* 3).

Whereas the beginning of *Four Quartets* was marked by disjunctions, patterns gone awry or misunderstood, meanings lost or no longer valid, the conclusion of *Little Gidding* displays what Dr. Johnson would have called *discordia concors,* a violent yoking of opposites, as Eliot brings together sharply disparate images or experiences. In the brilliant opening of section 4, Eliot juxtaposes positive images — the dove descending, sign of the Holy Spirit at the baptism of Jesus (John 1:32), and the tongues of fire of Acts 2 — with the flame of incandescent terror — the V–2 rockets descending on London. Like the power of God in Donne's *Devotions,* the fire of *Little Gidding* is both creative and destructive, purgative and inspiring. Illumination and release, "The one discharge from sin and error," are achieved through death: one is redeemed "from fire by fire," saved from the fires of hell by the purgatorial fire imaged in the poem.[39] The insight and the method here are analogous to Donne's depiction of the emergence of life from death, faith from doubt, and to his use of a single word or image with radically diverse meanings ("give me, *O Lord,* a *feare* of which I may not be *afraid"* [Prayer 6]), but Eliot's formulations are even more shocking and flamboyant than Donne's, as he depicts the purging power of the Judaeo-Christian God with a sharply secular image of torment — the shirt of Nessus that Medea sent to Hercules in fury of disappointed love and jealousy.

> Who then devised the torment? Love.
> Love is the unfamiliar Name
> Behind the hands that wove
> The intolerable shirt of flame
> Which human power cannot remove.

In contrast to the metaphysical paradoxes of *East Coker* — the striking but more usual "wounded surgeon" and "the sharp compassion of the healer's art" — this deeply disturbing image joins Medea's act of bitter revenge and her love, clearly Eros, with the love of God. But such forced juxtaposition is of a piece with Eliot's insistence in this poem on the conjunction of opposites, as well as on the absolute divergence of our possible pathways.

While the conclusion of *Little Gidding* resonates with images from the previous poems, it also transcends and departs from them, defining a situation that is at once stasis and process. As Donne returns to origins at the end of the *Devotions,* finding even in returning health an intimation of illness, so Eliot also returns to the beginning: "When the last of earth left to discover / Is that which was the beginning" (*Little Gidding* 5). Eliot recalls the cyclical quality of *East Coker* in

> We die with the dying
> . . . . .
> We are born with the dead:
> See, they return, and bring us with them.

Mary Stuart's motto in *East Coker* returns as the poet's own, in phrases that preserve the rich ambiguity of *end*, with its theological and Aristotelian overtones:

> What we call the beginning is often the end
> And to make an end is to make a beginning.
> The end is where we start from.

The ongoing concern with language as a tool for ordering reality is expressed as a perfectly harmonious dance, one less earth- and time-bound than that of *East Coker*. Eliot, like Donne, uses and reuses images, phrases, and experiences, bringing us by the end of his work to where we were at the start, but enabling us to see it anew. In *The Dry Salvages* "we had the experience but missed the meaning"; here we "arrive where we started / And know the place for the first time."

Both Donne and Eliot use meditative form to shape their work; both probe an experience in incremental, repetitive phrases; both work from individual perceptions and glimpses to a larger whole. In each instance, the meaning emerges through a familiar pattern or sequence of actions, as Donne lives out the sickness of sin, as Eliot wrestles with eternal questions in particular places. In comparing the meditative process at work in *Four Quartets* and in Donne's *Devotions*, we see the persistence of a mode of inquiry and representation that shapes a work, but we also see a way of marking differences in temperament, in belief, in understanding between the world of Donne and the world of Eliot.

In the voice of the familiar compound ghost, in the voices of "the dead poets and artists," Eliot not only discovers his own voice; he also finds the meditative method of inquiry and discovery that shapes his work. But whereas Donne creates a cycle through narrative and rhetorical symmetry, Eliot works through theses, antitheses, and syntheses to shape philosophic finality and the impression of an aesthetic whole. Whereas Donne's sense of the transcendent deity and the theological grounding of experience becomes the context for his own particular narrative, which represents the fate both of John Donne and of Everyman, Eliot's vision is in a way more particular, not only to the spiritual and literary concerns of Eliot himself, but also to England: "Here, the intersection of the timeless moment / Is England and nowhere. Never and always." Whereas Eliot returns at the end of his poem to the images of the earlier poems, gathering them all up into a final vision, Donne's concluding images return to the uncertainty of the opening, to the instability of health, to the ruinous nature of mankind. Eliot, fascinated by language, is able to mold at last a paradoxical, unified vision composed of the mystical—"a condition of complete simplicity / (Costing not less than everything)"—and the beatific ending of *The Divine Comedy*—"And the fire and the rose are one"—to present a state in which human understanding and articulateness seem to triumph; the patterns imperfectly understood emerge at last to give clarity and meaning:

> And every phrase
> And sentence that is right (where every word is at home,
> Taking its place to support the others,
> The word neither diffident nor ostentatious,
> An easy commerce of the old and the new,
> The common word exact without vulgarity,
> The formal word precise but not pedantic,
> The complete consort dancing together)
> Every phrase and every sentence is an end and a beginning,
> Every poem an epitaph.

The experience defined and articulated by *Four Quartets* is not only less passionate, and certainly more literary, but also less clearly individualized and narrative than that of Donne's *Devotions*. Donne gathers the intensely emotional experience of his work around a series of overlapping and personally focused questions: Am I sick or well? Will I live or die? Will I be saved or damned? In contrast to Donne's intensely realized voice, Eliot's questions are more broadly philosophical: Do we have any freedom to act? Is our life determined? In what context shall we view events? Is there a pattern, a shape, a coherence, a meaning to life? If so, can we perceive that pattern? And, having found it, can we express it in language? Donne, ardent in belief and alarmed lest he slip into unbelief, gives us finally a more existentially poised ending, in which his power to fail and God's power to save are eternally balanced and in which that balance is rhetorically expressed.

Although one would be hesitant to describe Eliot's work as more optimistic than Donne's—so very moderate, so complexly qualified are his affirmations—it is nevertheless true that the ending of the *Four Quartets* is, within the terms of Eliot's discourse, finally more positive than the radically conditional ending of the *Devotions*. For all the boldness of

Eliot's fusion of opposites, his insistence on unity, and for all the skill with which he unites much of the preceding poetic material in the last section of *Little Gidding,* his conclusion is syntactically quite simple and his strategy essentially additive. (The most frequent conjunction, *and,* occurs in lines 2, 4, 10, 17, and 21 of the section.) Eliot's essentially positive vision relies heavily on the present tense, even in his final allusion to Julian of Norwich and the beatific vision of Dante. By contrast, Donne's concluding vision, though determinedly affirmative, places its hope in the future; it is also much more precariously balanced and syntactically more complicated than Eliot's, depending heavily upon qualifiers, upon dependent clauses, upon conditionals and petitions. Whatever confidence Donne expresses in his central main clause is radically dependent upon the fulfillment of these petitions.[40] For all the negativism of many of Eliot's pronouncements, the outcome of his meditation is, in comparison to Donne's, remarkably coherent and satisfying, a successful rhetorical and philosophic whole. Eliot's final confidence grows out of his own vision, gained with difficulty over the course of four poems and many years; Donne's, out of the divine faithfulness in which he struggles to believe.

The more one delineates similarities between Donne and Eliot, the more one needs to qualify and remark differences; the more one articulates differences, the more marked the connections. As is apparent from his essays on Andrewes and the metaphysical poets, Eliot was not only an admirer of seventeenth-century writers but a writer whose notion of the poetic craft, the nature of composition, and the relation between composition and one's understanding of the world was in part shaped by them, so much so that his pronouncements on the nature of their work (though by no means always accurate or consistent) are often a useful description of his own.[41] Eliot made of the world of Donne and his contemporaries a more ordered and orderly place than it was because it satisfied a need of his own. But not only did he borrow phrases and concepts from these writers, so abundantly evident in *Four Quartets,* he also adopted a similar methodology, a process of incremental inquiry and dramatic representation. For both Donne and Eliot, meditation is a way of exploring and reshaping or restructuring reality.[42] For both of them time is something that intersects with eternity, for Donne by explicit divine intervention, for Eliot by the intersection of moments of time that create the moment of eternity, a moment of "midwinter spring," "suspended in time," "between pole and tropic," "the intersection of the

Eliot: *Four Quartets*

timeless moment [which] / Is England and nowhere. Never and always." In Donne and Eliot, generic links obtain, not in the rigidity of external forms, but in the poet's understanding of his project, in the shaping of his inquiry, in his method. Eliot's final articulation of the process of spiritual pilgrimage in *Little Gidding* expresses as well his relation to his seventeenth-century forebears:

> We are born with the dead:
> See, they return, and bring us with them.

IV

BROWNE
Religio Medici as Normative Autobiography

Like Donne's *Devotions upon Emergent Occasions* and Eliot's *Four Quartets, Religio Medici* and *Walden* move from the personal to the universal, from an individual's account of his experiences to their ultimate, cosmic context. And, as in Donne and Eliot, this sense of writing in time and of a particular place, yet sub specie aeternitatis, is related to the rhetorical strategies of Browne and Thoreau, even to their use of syntax and metaphor. But while *Religio Medici* and *Walden* share some of the meditative qualities of the *Devotions* and the *Four Quartets,* they are more accurately characterized as what might be termed *normative autobiographies;* each work presents a self that is both particular and universal; each offers an account that, for all the disclaimers about its idiosyncrasies and its limitations, is nevertheless set forth as exemplary.[1] Although these works, like the *Devotions* and *Four Quartets,* represent discovery, they are concerned as well with making the reader share that experience; they are revelatory and celebratory even more than exploratory.

Like Donne and Eliot, Browne and Thoreau share a subject matter as well as an approach to that subject. Both are in a sense "metaphysical" writers, and both, I would argue, as a consequence, stretch the limits of ordinary prose. By calling their texts metaphysical I mean not simply that they handle weighty philosophical themes but that, like the English metaphysical poets of the seventeenth century, Browne and Thoreau deal simultaneously in two levels of reality, the mundane and the universal; these are writers who, in Sir Thomas Browne's own phrase, see light as the shadow of God and who—I would say therefore—attempt to push readers to see through their prose a level of reality that prose can never express, who use it to the full even as they demonstrate its inadequacy. Despite important differences in the degree of particularity in dealing with the natural world and with theology, both Thoreau and Browne propound the view that man is "that great and true *Amphibium,* whose nature is disposed to live . . . in divided and distinguished worlds."[2] Both insist on a dual, or paradoxical, view of reality, sometimes by making explicit statements, sometimes suggestions. "Who can speake of eternitie without a solœcisme," says Browne, indicating the craftsman's awareness of the phenomenon to which I refer, the literal inability of human grammar, rooted in time, to encompass the infinite, "or thinke thereof without an extasie?" (*Religio Medici* 1.11), suggesting the goal at which he aims, the breakthrough into another realm. *Walden* likewise is dotted with sentences that indicate Thoreau's concern with expression as a means to the ineffable, with his penetrating the dead metaphor of "men labor under a mistake" to find the truth beneath, with his illuminating realization about his beans — "this was not the light in which I hoed them."[3]

In bringing together *Religio Medici* and *Walden,* I shall consider the extent to which metaphysics affects style and structure, syntax and method, not vaguely and generally, but literally and directly, in the construction of particular sentences, in the elaboration of general conceptions. Thus I shall be asking not only whether the works of Browne and Thoreau are similar in effect but also in origin; and conversely, what relationship exists in each work between conceptual genesis and mode of expression. I shall argue that both writers have constructed their prose not only to convey a particular meaning but to allow for, indeed to force the realization of, another kind of meaning that contrasts with or even contradicts the first.

To be sure, I am not the first to suggest parallels between Browne and Thoreau: Thoreau's fondness for sixteenth- and seventeenth-century English literature is well known, and, as has been noted, Thoreau undertook a good deal of reading in Chalmers's *Works of the English Poets* in his days as an undergraduate at Harvard; he even copied into his college commonplace book the sentence from Browne, "We carry with us the wonders we seek without us: there is all Africa, and her prodigies in us."[4] But while the question of influence has been considered, that of comparability of method has not, for it is not only the language that is similar, or the thought, but the method of articulating that thought, the reasoning by analogy to reach the ineffable. Richard Poirier argues in *A World Elsewhere* that "for all the attention paid to *Walden,* to its echoes of English literature of the seventeenth century, and to the author's capacity for word play, no one has sufficiently demonstrated its truly dazzling inventiveness and originality."[5] I would put it another way: there has been too little investigation of the possibility that whatever similarities may exist between Thoreau and Browne are not simply the result of imitation but of similar techniques of composition that proceed from the worldview of each.

Both *Religio Medici* and *Walden* were written by young men, or perhaps one should say, by men arrived at the age of self-importance—the early thirties—who felt the need to explain themselves.[6] And both works, despite modest disclaimers, define not only the nature of the author but of man in general; they are normative rather than merely descriptive. Although Browne begins cautiously enough, "I dare, without usurpation, assume the honourable stile of a Christian" (1.1), and although he confesses himself "naturally bashfull" (1.40), his subsequent declarations, even of tolerance, show him very firm in his own opinions, and his judgment on the mass of his fellow men, the multitude, is harsh and aloof: "It is no breach of Charity to call these fooles" (2.1). Such sublime assurance also marks Thoreau, who, while apparently regretting his limitations—"Unfortunately, I am confined to this theme by the narrowness of my experience" (3)—is supremely confident in his own attitudes: "I have lived some thirty years on this planet, and I have yet to hear the first syllable of valuable or even earnest advice from my seniors. They have told me nothing, and probably cannot tell me any thing, to the purpose" (9). There is more of pretense, of rhetorical calculation, in Thoreau's protestations of humility, more of awesome and breathtaking underestimation of his own effrontery in Browne, yet the basic similarity between these two young men who thank God that they are not like other men remains striking.

Readers have always found *Religio Medici* a remarkably personal, idiosyncratic work. One of its earliest readers, Sir Kenelm Digby, found that Browne spoke too much of himself;[7] present-day critics continue to take issue with Browne's tone, finding *Religio Medici* too personal, too glib, too easy in its declarations of faith.[8] Browne would seem to forestall such criticism by stating in the preface that *Religio Medici* is a "private exercise directed to my selfe, . . . rather a memoriall unto me then an example or rule unto any other" and that "there are many things delivered Rhetorically, many expressions therein meerely Tropicall, and as they best illustrate my intention; and therefore also . . . many things to be taken in a soft and flexible sense, and not to be called unto the rigid test of reason" (To the Reader). Yet a private work, in the process of publication, must surely lose some of its claim to privacy, and Browne, in publishing *Religio Medici,* changed it very little from the unauthorized first edition.[9] Moreover, Browne's progressive definition of his faith in relation to the faith of Christianity, of Protestantism, and of Anglicanism places his work and his belief in a larger, and public, context.[10] In addition, its title directs our attention to a further representative quality: the faith of this physician is to be understood in relation to that of physicians generally, as well as in relation to the generally held view of the religious beliefs of physicians.[11] The need to negotiate between the particular and the general, the perceived and the actual, has direct consequences not only for large rhetorical choices but even for the structure of Browne's opening sentences.

Like Donne's *Devotions upon Emergent Occasions,* Browne's *Religio Medici* has a dual structure — the official, formal, external division into parts and sections and the less formal yet powerful motivating force of the work. *Religio Medici* consists of two sections, the first part, which deals with the virtue of faith, and the second, which treats "that other Vertue of Charity" (2.1). Yet this structure is much clearer in retrospect than it is in one's reading, for unlike Burton's *Anatomy of Melancholy, Religio Medici* has no synopsis, no overview proffered at the beginning. Indeed, it is not even clear at the outset what the subject of the first part is, as Browne begins simply, "For my Religion." Rather we have a progressive sense of Browne's self-revelation, as he displays his belief, and then, more briefly, his charity. F. L. Huntley and Raymond Waddington have made excellent arguments for relating the two books of *Religio Medici* to the two tables of the Law, the book of faith corresponding to the love of God, and the book of charity corresponding to the love of neighbor, these two commandments, in the words of Jesus, comprising all the law and the prophets.[12] But clear though this structure may be in retrospect, in an important sense our experience of Browne's text is quite different: for as we read we encounter a series of meditations, a series of discrete statements that, taken together, constitute a *confessio* rather than a rationally comprehensible treatise on faith. Browne, as a matter of strategy, chooses not to announce his division of the text but rather to proceed informally, giving us the initial impression that his faith is all, not merely a part of the picture.[13] The force of modern reactions to *Religio Medici* may have to do not only with the relatively extreme fideistic position Browne adopts (he restates with enthusiasm the dictum of Tertullian: "Certum est quia impossibile est") but also with the difficulty of ascertaining Browne's agenda. In *Religio Medici* Browne defines his religion not simply by theological principles but by the active experience of believing, as he stretches his faith to the limits as an act of devotion.

Critics have noted, and not infrequently commented negatively on, Browne's apparent lack of spiritual depth: Stanley Fish calls him "the bad physician"; Joan Webber asserts that "Browne pulls the sting from pain";[14] some find that he articulates all too easily what others have struggled with. The ingenuous tone and the naiveté of voice are there, as Browne congratulates himself on his humility (2.8); as he rejects that "triviall and vulgar way of coition" as "the foolishest act a wise man commits in all his life" (2.9); as he announces with regard to his aesthetic sense, "I can looke a whole day with delight upon a handsome picture, though it be but of an Horse" (2.9). Browne, like most of us caught talking to ourselves, may be a little embarrassing, but his innocence is neither so simple in origin nor so negative as it might first appear. In evaluating the voice of *Religio Medici,* one must recognize the genre — personal meditations, set down, as Browne tells us, at a time and place when "I had not the assistance of any good booke" (To the Reader).

But the persona of *Religio Medici* is also a deliberate construct, a representative self in the act of discovery. Browne's persona is exemplary, and his text hortatory. *Religio Medici* has the self-approving quality of inner monologue, of a man talking to himself about himself, yet judging what he finds there worthy of praise, not for himself, but as a sign of divine providence and beneficence. Dr. Johnson's acid remark, that "surely, a man may visit France and Italy, reside at Montpellier and Padua, and at last take his degree at Leyden, without any thing miraculous," is of course apt, but it misses the point — that Browne articulates the personal discovery of a more general truth.[15] When he writes, "Now for my life, it is a miracle of thirty yeares" (2.11), Browne is not so much self-congratulatory as he is engaged in discovering the miracle of divine providence, which, he argues, rather than Fortune, rules human life. And significantly, Browne creates rhetorical and syntactical structures that allow, even force, his readers to participate in that process of discovery.

Browne's critics have been puzzled — or put off — by his insistence on taking on more of belief than seems necessary, by his assertion that "me thinkes there be not impossibilities enough in Religion for an active faith" (1.9). As Anne Drury Hall notes, Browne performs the latitudinarian move of reducing the essential elements of faith to a very few, but he also, conversely, rejoices in his ability to believe, indeed to believe things not only above but contrary to reason.[16] This approach, I would argue, is less a sign of naiveté than of careful strategy, for as Michael Wilding and Achsah Guibbory have suggested, Browne, who for years was thought not to be a champion in the wars of truth, has in fact chosen his ground very carefully: he affirms the virtue of tolerance toward Catholics but also, by implication, toward Anglicans; he finds charity in his heart for all — except the multitude, easily dismissed as "fooles." In the presentation of himself as a believer, Browne draws a position that is, according to his lights, broad in its tolerance but also heroic in belief, so that not only the Puritans of his day but also a committed Anglican like Browne may be seen as a "true warfaring Christian," one for whom a religious and political position of tolerance can have something of the air of a crusade.[17] But in contrast to the grimness of midcentury sectarians, there is almost a quality of *sprezzatura* to Browne's religious faith, what Jonathan Post has called the comic mode of *Religio Medici*, as he displays the ease with which he, like a spiritual athlete, can believe.[18]

In Donne and Eliot the process of meditation and of discovery is represented by the characteristic structural and rhetorical patterns of repetition and incrementality. In Browne and Thoreau likewise modes of syntactical and rhetorical organization grow from their understanding of the self in the universe. The two chief rhetorical patterns in *Religio Medici* are circularity, a returning with ever-increasing precision to a subject, and a sequence of analogies that ultimately leads to a rhetorical and conceptual breakthrough. Browne's mode of discovery in *Religio Medici* is cumulative and additive; he moves in a series of circles that return to the same point but that bring additional information with each circuit. Not only Browne's organizational scheme but also his unifying concept is circular and iterative: "But to difference my self neerer," he says, "& draw into a lesser circle" (1.5); he sees himself as moving within "the great wheele of the Church" (1.6); this figure relates him to God, "a sphere whose center is everywhere and whose circumference is nowhere" (translation of Browne's note to 1.10). In fact his method is both cyclical and progressive, for as he moves he returns to those subjects already treated; he reveals ever more about subjects apparently dismissed. Browne's transitional sentences convey a kind of enumerative and discarding action, a progression from one part of his argument to the next: "As for those wingy mysteries in Divinity" (1.9); "That other attribute wherewith I recreate my devotion" (1.13); "This is the ordinary and open way of his providence.... There is another way full of Meanders and Labyrinths" (1.17).

Browne's prose style, representing the process of discovery and self-presentation, uses a combination of hypotaxis and parataxis to track that exploration, to depict a course both direct and hedged about with circumstances. After the initial prepositional phrase "For my Religion," Browne interrupts with a dependent clause that suspends meaning until a series of objections has been met and allows us to rest only briefly before setting off again on a further series of qualifications.[19] And in accordance with the mimetic character of this opening, each new point leads to further qualifications: "For my Religion, though there be severall circumstances that might perswade the world I have none at all, as the generall scandall of my profession, the naturall course of my studies, the indifferency of my behaviour, and discourse in matters of Religion, neither violently defending one, nor with that common ardour and contention opposing another; yet in despight hereof I dare, without usurpation, assume the honorable stile of a Christian" (1.1). Browne opens with a series of clauses that combine forward motion with suspension, hesitation, and modification; his prose is paratactic in its use of coordinating conjunctions to connect parallel phrases; yet the forward motion of the whole — the definition of the exact nature of his faith — is both sustained and kept in suspension by the very precision, the ongoing modification of the description of context.

As one can see from the scheme below, in the first units parallels are not rounded out but elongated; that is, the second or third phrase in a series is always longer than the first, and one series concludes by leading to another, which leads to another:

For my Religion,
    though there be severall circumstances that might perswade
        the world I have none at all,
            as the generall scandall of my profession,
            the naturall course of my studies,
            the indifferency of my behaviour,
                and discourse in matters of Religion,
            neither violently defending one,
            nor with that common ardour and contention
              opposing another;

Browne: *Religio Medici*

> yet in despight hereof I dare, without usurpation,
>   assume the honorable stile of a Christian:
>
> not that I meerely owe this title to the Font,
>   my education,
>   or Clime wherein I was borne,
>
> as being bred up either to confirme those principles . . .
> or by a generall consent proceed in the Religion of my
>   Countrey.

Although this passage is complex and its forward motion frequently interrupted, its effect is both energetic and satisfying. The suspension of meaning and the extension of parallelism provide a rhythmic pattern that arouses expectation in the first half of the paragraph and delays fulfillment until the second; the final sense toward which the passage moves is that of victory over obstacles.

Having made us feel the tension of opposition, the force of the negation of all the possible bases for his faith, Browne proceeds to affirm and again to reinforce with parallelism his positive reasons for calling himself by the name of Christian. This not so surprising conclusion has to some seemed overstated, but Browne's rhetorical structure is calculated to make us realize the importance and the providential nature of his choice. In the second segment the structure is less complex and more satisfying, full of doublets, but lacking the unexpected extensions of the first half:

> But having, in my riper yeares,
>   and confirmed judgement,
>   seene and examined all,
> I finde my selfe obliged by the principles of Grace,
>   and the law of mine owne reason,
>   to embrace no other name but this.

This time the "neither" that follows the affirmation is not a contradiction but a reinforcement:

> neither doth herein my zeale so farre make me forget
>   the generall charitie I owe unto humanity,
>   as rather to hate then pity Turkes,
>   Infidels,
>   and (what is worse)
>   Jewes,

> rather contenting my selfe to enjoy that happy stile,
> then maligning those who refuse so glorious a title.

This section, with the circular patterns in which Browne sets off to tackle a problem and concludes by resolving it, is a microcosm of the whole work. In subsequent sections, he proceeds cyclically, retracing his steps, refining his definition, returning to points already treated to state them even more precisely.

If my description of this process of discovery and revelation seems to recall Eliot's meditative method, one should note that Browne is more self-assured, more circular in his motion, Eliot, more tentative and linear. Browne organizes his material in a series of concentric circles that bring him to the heart of the matter, the precise nature of his faith, and its relationship to the Church of England. He proceeds through a series of discriminations—"But because the name of a Christian is become too generall to expresse our faith" (1.2); "Yet have I not so shaken hands with those desperate Resolutions" (1.3); "As there were many Reformers, so likewise many reformations" (1.4)—that lead finally to the following climax: "But to difference my self neerer, & draw into a lesser circle: There is no Church whose every part so squares unto my conscience, whose articles, constitutions, and customes seeme so consonant unto reason, and as it were framed to my particular devotion, as this whereof I hold my beliefe, the Church of *England,* to whose faith I am a sworne subject" (1.5). The cyclical sequence by which Browne finds himself a member of the established Church of England represents for him a providentially guided choice through a difficult maze, hence the sense both of drive and of complexity in his prose. The claims that he makes for himself and for his faith become more extreme in subsequent sections, but this early affirmation is also worth pondering, for Browne presents his belonging to the Anglican church, long dominant but in 1642 seriously challenged, not as a matter of course but of right reason and devotion; by offering this conclusion at the end of a syntactical sequence that first delays, then provides gratification, he makes that point the more persuasively.

In *Religio Medici,* then, the presentation of the faith of this particular physician becomes representative, paradoxically, of that of his Church and his country; the idiosyncratic personal statement becomes the exemplary, the hortatory, representation of religious faith as it is and as it ought to be. This effect is produced, not by apodictic statements applicable to others, but rather by a series of personal statements so enthusiastically delivered as to have a kind of moral force. Browne's treatise carries a double message: the assertion on the one hand of its limitations and its idiosyncrasies and, on the other, the strong suggestion that his religious practice is admirable enough that others ought to adopt it as well. If the enthusiasm with which he presents his own experience seems disproportionate to the novelty of it, or insensitive to the pain and complexity of human existence, I would argue that he represents the discovery of something for him perhaps unique but not unique to him. His concern is less with the display of a personal self, although the creation of a persona is an important feature of his text, than with the celebration of divine grace.

As in the sequence by which he finds himself within the Church of England, Browne's celebratory rhetorical treatment of the human condition is a sequence of ever more dramatic statements of the truth that he perceives:

> For the world, I count it not an Inne, but an Hospitall, and a place, not to live, but to die in. The world that I regard is my selfe, it is the Microcosme of mine owne frame, that I cast mine eye on; for the other, I use it but like my Globe, and turne it round sometimes for my recreation. Men that look upon my outside, perusing onely my condition, and fortunes, do erre in my altitude; for I am above *Atlas* his shoulders. The earth is a point not onely in respect of the heavens above us, but of that heavenly and celestial part within us: that masse of flesh that circumscribes me, limits not my mind: that surface that tells the heavens it hath an end, cannot perswade me I have any; I take my circle to be above three hundred and sixty, though the number of the Arke do measure my body, it comprehendeth not my minde: whilst I study to finde how I am a Microcosme or little world, I finde my selfe something more than the great.
> (2.11)

Like the passage examined earlier, this one is resolutely paratactic, moving from one phrase to another with little subordination. It is the prose of discovery, but a discovery forced upon the reader by ever more striking statements, as one perception is replaced by a sharper vision. Browne's prose, like Donne's, also combines the apparatus of reason with the experience of wonder, as he examines the world as a kind of binary system: "not an Inne, but an Hospitall, and a place, not to live, but to die in."

As frequently in Browne, the matter here at issue is limits, what the human mind or spirit can reach, what contains it. But unlike Donne, whose sense of self is often ruthlessly limited—the persona whose thoughts can go everywhere is confined to a sickbed, his release from illness may well come through death—Browne constructs a series of clauses that deny human limitations: "that masse of flesh that circumscribes me, limits not my mind: . . . I take my circle to be above three hundred and sixty." Characteristically, the central metaphor is that of a globe or circle: "The world that I regard is my selfe, it is the Microcosme of mine owne frame, that I cast mine eye on; for the other, I use it but like my Globe, and turne it round sometimes for my recreation." Browne describes circles in the globe, in the universe, in the circumscription of the flesh; he does so in a series of circling phrases that keep returning to the center that is the self, the only thing that is unbounded: "Men that look upon my outside, perusing onely my condition, and fortunes, do erre in my altitude; for I am above *Atlas* his shoulders"; "whilst I study to finde how I am a Microcosme or little world, I finde my selfe something more than the great." The passage is resolutely self-centered, self-involved, as Browne uses the figure of epistrophe to return again and again to *us:* "The earth is a point not onely in respect of the heavens above us, but of that heavenly and celestial part within us: that masse of flesh that circumscribes me, limits not my mind." And Browne uses *conduplicatio* to lace the passage with the most relevant pronoun, *my:* "Now for my life"; "The world that I regard is my selfe, it is the Microcosme of mine owne frame, that I cast mine eye on." Browne moves from the apparent naiveté of self-appraisal in "I am above *Atlas* his shoulders" to the more general description of human capacity: "There is surely a peece of Divinity in us, something that was before the Elements, and owes no homage unto the Sun" (2.11).

In *Religio Medici* as a whole, Browne takes us through the sequence of things in which he believes; these do not amount to the formal articles of a creed or orthodox public confession but rather reflect the particular emphases of an Anglican Christian of the mid-seventeenth century. Stating that there are "two bookes from whence I collect my Divinity; besides that written one of God, another of his servant Nature" (1.16), Browne takes special delight in divine patterning in the world of nature, in which he finds nothing amiss ("there are no *Grotesques* in nature" [1.15]); "I cannot tell by what Logick we call a Toad, a Beare, or an Elephant, ugly, they being created in those outward shapes and figures which best express the actions of their inward formes" (1.16). While he dismisses as superstition certain miracles revered in the Roman Catholic Church ("I cannot conceive why the Crosse that *Helena* found and whereon Christ himself died should have power to restore others unto life; I excuse not *Constantine* from a fall off his horse, or a mischiefe from his enemies, upon the wearing those nayles on his bridle which our Saviour bore upon the Crosse in his hands" [1.28]), he carefully regards and affirms biblical ones, even though his reason would give cause to doubt. For example, he concludes after a list of difficult propositions, "yet doe I beleeve that all this is true, which indeed my reason would perswade me to be false; and this I think is no vulgar part of faith to believe a thing not only above, but contrary to reason, and against the arguments of our proper senses" (1.10). Yet Browne also avoids too literal a reading of Scripture, finding St. John's description of the heavenly city in Revelation, for example, too gross and material to do justice to spiritual reality. He expresses his belief in witches, as forming a link within "the Ladder and scale of creatures" (1.30), yet he prudently finds that not all that appears to be witchcraft is actually so but rather results from special knowledge of natural phenomena (1.31). Browne's concerns, with literal reading of Scriptures, with miracles, with witchcraft and demonology, with the relation of these issues to the growth of natural science and observation, clearly reflect the shared concerns of his own time; but his argument proceeds from these questions to the even more basic point of his work, his prevailing sense of the spirit that informs matter.

In a dramatic and central section located at the heart of part 1 Browne moves from professed doubt about "these particular and divided spirits" to a ringing affirmation of belief in a divine spirit immanent within the world. Browne begins with the tentative statement—"there may be (for ought I know) an universall and common Spirit to the whole world. It was the opinion of *Plato,* and it is yet of the *Hermeticall* Philosophers" (1.32)—but the passage moves to increasing specificity and affirmation:

> However, I am sure there is a common Spirit that playes within us, yet makes no part of us; and that is the Spirit of God, the fire and scintillation of that noble and mighty Essence, which is the life and radicall heat of spirits, and those essences that know not the vertue of the Sunne, a fire quite contrary to the fire of Hell: This is that gentle heate that brooded on the waters, and in six dayes hatched the world; this is that irradiation that dispells the mists of Hell, the clouds of horrour, feare, sorrow, despaire; and preserves the region

> of the mind in serenity: whosoever feels not the warme gale and gentle ventilation of this Spirit (though I feele his pulse) I dare not say he lives; for truely without this, to mee there is no heat under the Tropick; nor any light, though I dwelt in the body of the Sunne. (1.32)

There is an intellectual and theological point here: Browne clearly distinguishes between a kind of world spirit, a demiurge, about which he remains skeptical, and the spirit of God, about which he has no doubts. But there is also a crucial rhetorical movement from uncertainty to certainty, and a rhetorical technique that is cumulative as well as discriminatory: Browne's initial skepticism does not hinder but rather leads to the incorporation of a rich variety of sources; the metaphorical descriptions of the Hermeticists, about which Browne admits doubt at the beginning of the passage, nevertheless form part of the description of the Spirit of God, which in Genesis moved upon the face of the waters.[20]

Browne's rhetoric here is characteristically balanced, reflecting what Murray Roston has called "an achieved equilibrium of spirit."[21] This passage on the nature of divine immanence puts forward a proposition, yet qualifies it; it uses a balanced structure to state both sides of the issue: "There is a common Spirit that playes within us, yet makes no part of us"; it uses consecutive phrases and clauses to build a progressively more dramatic and powerful sense of what Browne seemed in doubt of at the beginning of the passage; whatever spirit there may be in the world (in the opinion of Plato and the Hermetic philosophers), there is most assuredly a divine spirit, its existence emphasized by anaphora and its nature described in terms of Platonic and Hermetic imagery: "*This is that* gentle heate that brooded on the waters, and in six dayes hatched the world; *this is that* irradiation that dispells the mists of Hell" (emphasis mine).

By the end of the passage Browne has gone from apparently doubting the existence of this spirit to finding it more real than anything else we know, identifying it with life, light, and heat: "whosoever feels not the warme gale and gentle ventilation of this Spirit (though I feele his pulse) I dare not say he lives; for truely without this, to mee there is no heat under the Tropick; nor any light, though I dwelt in the body of the Sunne." Each of the concluding clauses covers the same intellectual territory—it affirms the existence of this divine spirit—but its additive force is rhetorically significant, for each clause represents a fresh assertion, a fresh instance of discovery, a realization that the immaterial is more real than the material, the spiritual than the physical.

The dramatic emphasis on the powerful presence of spirit in matter seen in this passage is central to *Religio Medici,* and it paves the way for an understanding of man living in a world that is spiritual as well as physical; as Browne says so famously: "Thus is man that great and true *Amphibium,* whose nature is disposed to live not onely like other creatures in divers elements, but in divided and distinguished worlds; for though there bee but one world to sense, there are two to reason; the one visible, the other invisible" (1.34). The conception leads also to the second of Browne's primary approaches, the use of analogy as a tool of thought and rhetoric. Since a divine spirit pervades reality, Browne is able to speak of physical reality as an emblem of the spiritual: "In briefe, conceive light invisible, and that is a Spirit" (1.33). He sets up an analogy between the comprehensible and the incomprehensible, like a mathematical equation that remains forever open-ended, and by that process he moves both through reason and beyond reason.

The habit of analogical thinking is characteristic of Renaissance thought, but Browne typically uses it to point beyond itself, to the incomprehensible. It is this use of analogy to defeat analogy, of reason to defeat reason, and of language to display the limitations of language that links Browne with Thoreau. Both of them are fond of metaphor, but both make clear that metaphor points to something beyond itself. Both use words that look literal, ordinary, but that open up to extra-ordinary meanings, that turn out to be verbal or conceptual puns. In *Religio Medici* 1.10 Browne rejects technical philosophical terminology, which he clearly finds inadequate to the purpose, in preference for metaphor, which he represents as both a means of understanding and a means of confounding his understanding: "I had as leive you tell me that *anima est angelus hominis, est Corpus Dei,* as *Entelechia; Lux est umbra Dei,* as *actus perspicui:* where there is an obscurity too deepe for our reason, 'tis good to set downe with a description, periphrasis, or adumbration; for by acquainting our reason how unable it is to display the visible and obvious effects of nature, it becomes more humble and submissive unto the subtilties of faith: and thus I teach my haggard and unreclaimed reason to stoope unto the lure of faith." Browne here gives Platonic metaphor place over Aristotelian terminology, but he does not simply ignore the rational process. The statement *"Lux est umbra Dei"* is based on a clear analogy: light is to God as shadow is to light.[22] But it is an analogy that breaks down in the contemplation of it. Light and shadow are both comprehensible to the human mind, but the notion that these opposites are in fact part of an orderly gradation, that God is as much brighter than light as light is than shadow, causes the mind to founder. This is an equation encompassing the finite and the infinite, revealing at once that, as Nicholas of Cusa pointed out, nothing is relative to infinity, and yet forcing us toward an understanding based on relationship. Browne's method is to lead us to the limits of human understanding—to make us comprehend as much as we can, and to acknowledge—in the *O altitudo!* of which he was so fond—the incomprehensibility of the whole.

I have been arguing that Browne's prose reenacts the discovery of sacred truth, not that what Browne discovers is unique to him but that he appropriates it dramatically to himself and that he forces that discovery upon his reader.[23] The process is represented especially brilliantly in a number of passages to which I want to turn next, passages in which Browne's syntactic and rhetorical strategies are essential to the sense of wonder and realization that characterize *Religio Medici*. In the first of these passages, Browne reenacts a meditation on the attributes of God, characteristically using reason to defeat reason, to produce an acknowledgment of the infinite superiority of the Deity:

> In my solitary and retired imagination, (*Neque enim cum porticus aut me lectulus accepit, desum mihi*) I remember I am not alone, and therefore forget not to contemplate him and his attributes who is ever with mee, especially those two mighty ones, his wisedome and eternitie; with the one I recreate, with the other I confound my understanding: for who can speake of eternitie without a solœcisme, or thinke thereof without an extasie? Time we may comprehend, 'tis but five dayes elder then our selves, and hath the same Horoscope with the world; but to retire so farre backe as to apprehend a beginning, to give such an infinite start forward, as to conceive an end in an essence that wee affirme hath neither the one nor the other; it puts my Reason to Saint *Pauls* Sanctuary. (1.11)

Browne gives us here an instance of his meditations, a deliberate recalling of God and his attributes. He does not, as in the examples cited by Louis Martz, recreate that meditation in full detail but provides for us an encapsulated version of the course it takes and its results. Browne emphasizes the personal realization of a preexisting truth: "I remember I am not alone, and therefore forget not to contemplate him and his attributes who is ever with mee."

Critics have remarked what they consider Browne's leisurely style, his excessively poised and balanced manner,[24] but though this passage is stately in pace, it is also efficiently functional, for it enacts step by step the process it describes, driving the mind of the reader backwards and forwards with increasing power until it surrenders to God's own self-summary: "*I am that I am*" (1.11). His balanced style represents both the use of reason and the inadequacy of it: "With the one I recreate, with the other I confound my understanding." The verbs of the passage describe opposite activities: "recreate" implies not only relaxation and enjoyment but a kind of expansive activity, literally a creation anew, whereas "confound" points to the quintessentially contrasting motion of destruction, bringing to disorder, the opposite of *fundare,* to establish, fix, or confirm. This contrast is reinforced by condensation and by a balancing of clauses and phrases of equal length against each other: "With the one I recreate, with the other I confound my understanding." As one verb leads to another, Browne leads us through a process of exultation to a pleasurable surrender.

Browne next moves to a set of rhetorical questions that point to literal truths: "For who can speake of eternitie without a solœcisme, or thinke thereof without an extasie?" Because what is beyond time cannot be enclosed within tenses, eternity overwhelms our grammar; what is beyond space can only be reached if, in the literal meaning of ecstasy, we stand outside ourselves. But in this question, as in the previous statement, Browne prepares our minds for an elastic and extravagant movement, one that becomes even more extreme in the next sentence. "Time we may comprehend," he begins, taking as his starting point a premise that not every reader would grant.[25] But even the potential weakness of this point strengthens Browne's argument, for if we cannot comprehend time, which is "but five dayes elder then our selves," surely we cannot grasp eternity—precisely his point. Yet Browne forces us to make the effort, in an almost physical sense, for the internal movement of the sentence is even more exhausting than the logic of the whole. With "but to retire so farre backe," our minds move backwards; but with the logical consequence of that statement—"as to apprehend a beginning"—we immediately think of an opposite motion, for a beginning is necessarily the beginning of something that moves forward, not backward. Similarly,

Generating Texts

"to give such an infinite start forward, as to conceive an end" not only encourages but impels us sharply forward, as Browne in one breath tells us that there is an infinite distance to be traveled and then immediately brings us up short against the end. As if running headlong into a stone wall were not sufficiently confounding, Browne denies the whole process in the concluding phrase and clauses—"in an essence that wee affirme hath neither the one nor the other."

This motion of the mind is also reinforced by the rhythms of the prose. Browne begins with an almost metronomic movement in the quite evenly balanced clauses:

>   with the one I recreate,
>   with the other I confound my understanding:
>   for who can speake of eternitie without a solœcisme,
>   or thinke thereof without an extasie?

The evenness of length of the elements and the parallelism of structure make the motion easy. But the next sentence embodies a more complicated motion; having set up an expectation of regularity, Browne inserts somewhat longer units in place of the anticipated shorter ones and so makes us move faster through a sentence whose sense is increasingly complicated:

>   Time we may comprehend,
>   'tis but five dayes elder then our selves,
>   and hath the same Horoscope with the world;
>   but to retire so farre backe as to apprehend a beginning,
>   to give such an infinite start forward, as to conceive an end
>   in an essence that wee affirme hath neither the one
>   · nor the other;

Not only is the last infinitive complex ("to give . . . the other") the longest of the whole sentence; it also breaks the parallelism by adding an unexpected modifying clause: "in an essence that wee affirme hath neither the one nor the other." The effect is like casually asking a singer with just enough breath to make it to the end of a phrase to sing one phrase more. And the additional notes are not the whole and half notes with which the sentence began but a rapid series of eighths and sixteenths. Not only is the tempo faster, but the pattern of stress has become far more complicated. Whereas the early clauses approximate a stately poetry, the later ones are increasingly disordered and disturbed.

> Tĭme wĕ mărỹ cómprĕhénd,
> 'tis bŭt fíve daýes éldĕr thén oŭr sélves,
> aňd háth the sáme Hóroscópe wìth the wórld;
> bŭt tŏ rětíre só fařre bácke ăs tŏ ápprĕhénd ă bĕgíňning,
> tŏ gíve sŭch ăn íňfiňĭte stárt fórwărd, ăs tŏ cŏncéive ăn énd
> >> in ăn éssence thăt wée affirme hăth néither the óne
> >>> nŏr the othĕr;

Browne's own language reinforces this sense of acceleration and deceleration, of shifts of tempo. This complicated sequence comes to a halt in the ever-mysterious, self-enclosing self-definition of God—"*I am that I am*"—of which Browne notes, "'Twas a short one"; and his own phrases and clauses become brief with puzzlement—"to confound mortalitie, that durst question God, or aske him what hee was"—before being released again in the incomparable flow of time into eternity: "Saint *Peter* speakes modestly, when hee saith, a thousand yeares to God are but as one day: for to speake like a Philosopher, those continued instances of time which flow into [a] thousand yeares, make not to him one moment; what to us is to come, to his Eternitie is present, his whole duration being but one permanent point without succession, parts, flux, or division" (1.11). In this final section Browne's prose is once again divided into small, freely flowing units, as if in imitation of the "one permanent point without succession, parts, flux, or division." The sudden release of energy after the halting, self-confounding balancing of the opening of the paragraph is the imitation of a spirit released into that divine eternity, no longer trapped in the puzzlement of human reason.[26] This passage, however brilliant, is not self-indulgent rhetoric but rhetoric focused and directed, representing the discovery of a particular vision of reality.

Such an orchestration of rhythm, tempo, and balance, such a use of statement to defeat statement may be seen again in the penultimate section of *Religio Medici,* part 1, which begins: "Againe, I am confident, and fully perswaded, yet dare not take my oath of my salvation; I am as it were sure, and do beleeve, without all doubt, that there is such a City as *Constantinople,* yet for me to take my oath thereon, were a kinde of perjury, because I hold no infallible warrant from my owne sense to confirme me in the certainty thereof" (1.59). Stanley Fish has described such passages as essentially meaningless virtuoso exercises, written to call attention not to the subject but to the writer's technique (367). But brilliant as this passage is, its ultimate function is to call attention not to Browne's doubt but to a radical uncertainty in the nature of things, to demonstrate that sense, the basis of most of our knowledge, can finally yield only uncertainty, to show that eternity defies ordinary logic, and to go on from there to establish confidence on the basis of paradox.

In this dazzling process of persuasion and transformation Browne first chips away at our confidence with short units and repetitions in which each assertion is balanced by a negation: "I am confident, and fully perswaded, yet dare not take my oath of my salvation." The double assertion of the first clause ("confident, and fully perswaded") somehow makes the subsequent negation twice as forceful. The sequence, moreover, makes us particularly dubious of the next positive statement, even before we have time to think that nothing could be less reassuring than "I am *as it were* sure." In continuing, "and do beleeve, without all doubt," Browne clearly does protest too much, but even these gestures do not prepare us for a man who questions the very existence of Constantinople. In his refusal "to take my oath thereon," he demonstrates that sense, normally that by which we know, can in fact never lead to certainty.[27] Appropriate to its meaning, the paragraph has an hour-glass structure, descending to nothing at its center and then rebuilding on the basis of faith and paradox: "When an humble soule shall contemplate her owne unworthinesse, she shall meete with many doubts and suddainely finde how little wee stand in need of the precept of Saint *Paul, Worke out your salvation with feare and trembling.*"

For all the praise of Browne as a rhetorician, and even the criticism of him as a kind of verbal trickster, the most stunning statement of this whole section is in fact not Browne's but Christ's: "*Before Abraham was, I am*" (John 8:58); the rest of the famous paragraph is only the dramatic working out of this eradication of tenses; and while the effect of the prose is electrifying, its rhythmic motion is even, almost deceptively pedestrian. In short, it is the idea that is exciting, not merely the rhetoric that so superbly embodies it and gives full play to its intellectual challenges. Thus, however adept Browne is, he is not the originator of a self-serving scheme but a participant in an ordered framework with dimensions far beyond himself, as he makes clear at the start: "*Before Abraham was, I am,* is the saying of Christ, yet is it true in some sense if I say it of my selfe, for I was not onely before my selfe, but *Adam,* that is, in the Idea of God, and in the decree of that Synod held from all Eternity. And in this sense, I say, the world was before the Creation, and at an end before it had a beginning; and thus was I dead before I was alive, though my grave be *England,* my dying place was Paradise, and *Eve* miscarried of mee before she conceiv'd of *Cain*" (1.59).

The two sentences of this brilliant section are sharply diverse in structure: the first consists of units of uneven length, beginning with a long introductory unit and followed by shorter ones, as Browne progressively explains his point and in so doing realizes the difficulty of his explanation. The second, by contrast, flows evenly in smooth, extended parallels. But whereas difficulty of concept was expressed in the first sentence by uneven pacing, it is conveyed in the second even more strongly by the discrepancy between what Browne seems to feel and the means he chooses to express himself. The sentences roll out as if they contained no difficult matter, with the matter growing more difficult all the time, as Browne moves to ever more specific and personal instances of his point, from existence before creation, to annihilation before creation, to death preceding life, to the specifying of that death and birth in time and place. The passage also plays dramatically on the paradox of spirit and matter, juxtaposing our working assumption—that the only true life is physical life—with the principle of faith—that the true life is the life of the spirit. Our sense of shock derives from our persistent habit of thinking in physical terms only, whatever our belief, and from Browne's deliberate paralleling of oppositions—end with beginning, dead with alive. The sentences climax in the continued reversal of time—grave preceding dying, miscarriage preceding conception—and in the intensification created by a radical foreshortening of time and a shocking juxtaposition of distant places. Paradise, the place of life, birth, hope, creation, becomes the place of projected and eternal death; our general mother becomes the destroyer of all subsequent life; finally, in a kind of submerged pun, the conception of God—his idea of the world—is contrasted with the conception of Eve—the human misconception or miscarriage by which the divine creation was nearly lost. Such prose is in itself a paradox: Browne's sentences are extremely orderly, grammatically clear, beautifully structured, but their effect is to undermine all conceptions of order—not by imitation of chaos, but by stretching order to the limits to show its inadequacy to deal with the eternal. Browne states the truths of faith as clearly as they can be stated, but the result is a breakdown of human logic, for his matter is not just doctrine but paradox: "Who can speake of eternitie without a solœcisme, or thinke thereof without an extasie?"

The recreation, in its dual sense, of devotion so abundantly present in *Religio Medici* is for Browne "the debt of our reason wee owe unto God, and the homage wee pay for not being beasts" (1.13). Browne aims at both the recreation and the confounding of our understanding, at delight in the mind's working and at recognition of its limitations, and ultimately at its surrender to the mysteries of faith. In this effort rhetoric is both a powerful tool and an ultimate and deliberate failure, but it is a failure that, like much else in Browne's work, opens up a perspective beyond itself, as the good physician teaches his readers to see what can be seen and to revel in what cannot. Browne's style is both energetically climactic and paratactically balanced, giving an impression of moderation and control as well as of exuberance. Browne is the advocate of belief and the embracer of difference, the accomplished stylist whose sentences open up unexpected ranges of reality as he shifts us from the physical to the spiritual, from the ordinary and literal meanings of a phrase to the extraordinary, revealed in profound puns: "At the sight of a Crosse or Crucifix I can dispence with my hat, but scarce with the thought or memory of my Saviour" (1.3); "(though I feele his pulse) I dare not say he lives" (1.32).

Both Browne and Thoreau created texts in which the presentation of the self becomes a model for discovery and for conduct, texts that provide not only explicit statements but mimetic forms that lead the reader through a similar discovery, whether in the ever more brilliant restatement of a point by Browne or in the revelation of an unsuspected meaning of a word by Thoreau. As we shall see in the next chapter, by taking up the notion of physical phenomena as the key to deeper meaning, and adopting the method of analogy, Thoreau was to advance from the principle articulated by Browne, that "*Lux est umbra Dei*," to find for himself that "the sun is but a morning star" (333).

V

THOREAU
Walden
The Rhetoric of Time Illumined by Eternity

LIKE SIR THOMAS BROWNE, for whom "the world that I regard is my selfe, it is the Microcosme of mine owne frame, that I cast mine eye on," Henry David Thoreau meditates upon the self. And like Browne, Thoreau assumes that his readers have some interest in that self, that what he tells us about it will pertain also to the life of other men. When Thoreau proposes in *Walden,* not "to write an ode to dejection, but to brag as lustily as chanticleer in the morning," like Browne who finds his life "a miracle of thirty yeares," he points out that "if I seem to boast more than is becoming, my excuse is that I brag for humanity rather than for myself."[1] But the central point of connection between these two writers is the shared sense of the cosmic, the metaphysical implications of everyday actions, and the linguistic and rhetorical means by which that conception is represented.

The notion that life is to be seen sub specie aeternitatis is dramatically articulated by Thoreau: "Why should I feel lonely? is not our planet in the Milky Way?" (133). As this pair of questions demonstrates, this perception is a revelation not only for the writer but for the reader. Indeed, Thoreau's prose sequence makes his reader reenact this revelation, for he begins with a question rooted in the personal, the homely diction of everyday life, and moves without warning to the universal. In Browne this forcing of the reader to cosmic or theological insights takes the form of ever more dramatic statements of a single truth: "Whosoever feels not the warme gale and gentle ventilation of this Spirit (though I feele his pulse) I dare not say he lives"; "And *Eve* miscarried of mee before she conceiv'd of *Cain.*" In Thoreau this attitude characteristically emerges as a sudden and unexpected perspective on reality, a new vista that opens up at the end of a sentence, a realization that we do not, as it were, live in a house with four sides, but that one side is open to another dimension, another world. Browne's revelations emerge in the dramatic statement of theological principles; Thoreau's, in the description of a natural event. Browne elaborates the paradoxes of a physical world permeated by spirit, or time by eternity; Thoreau reveals that truth glancingly, in an unexpected pun. But both use their rhetoric to surprise, to reveal, to force the reader to a new insight.

Thoreau addresses the issue of the extra dimension explicitly in his Conclusion: "We think that if rail-fences are pulled down, and stone-walls piled up on our farms, bounds are henceforth set to our lives and our fates decided. If you are chosen town-clerk, forsooth, you cannot go to Tierra del Fuego this summer: but you may go to the land of infernal fire nevertheless" (320). For all its matter-of-factness, its grounding in concrete detail, Thoreau's prose is actually a minefield of surprises. For the New Englander, the ordinary reader who thinks he has his life mapped out and that foreign travel is precluded by civic responsibilities, Thoreau offers the ultimate surprise; if the South American land of fire is excluded, the eternal one may not be: "The universe is wider than our views of it" (320). And although these rhetorical fireworks are particularly marked in *Walden*'s concluding chapter, the quick shift to the other dimension, to the other meaning of language, is absolutely characteristic of *Walden,* even, I would argue, its most essential feature. From the earliest pages Thoreau both articulates the approach and practices the technique, as he shifts from the literal to the transcendental, the mundane to the cosmic, with a brilliant metaphysical pun: "We might try our lives by a thousand simple tests; as, for instance, that the same sun which ripens my beans illumines at once a system of earths like ours. If I had remembered this it would have prevented some mistakes. This was not the light in which I hoed them" (10).

Whereas Browne tends to assert ever more brilliantly and explicitly his awareness of man as amphibium, the duality of his nature, and the metaphysical within the physical, Thoreau allows it to emerge, bit by bit, in unexpected glimpses. Already by the third paragraph of *Walden* Thoreau makes clear the surprisingly wide range of his audience and his intention, as he writes ostensibly to the fellow citizens whose impertinent inquiries he has recorded: "I would fain say something, not so much concerning the Chinese and Sandwich Islanders as you who read these pages, who are said to live in New England" (4). In the course of this sentence the reader is subjected to uncertainty about the place—

China, the Sandwich Islands, Concord—but even more radically about the nature of the activity: "concerning ... you who read these pages, who are said to live in New England." Such a sentence may suggest at first merely a doubt about the audience and its location and then, much more troubling, the doubt about the verb itself, whether it means simply to reside, as one first supposes, or more basically and radically, to exist at all, or to live in any positive sense.[2] Although Thoreau describes Concord (or perhaps England and America) as a "part of the world [where] it is considered a ground for complaint if a man's writings admit of more than one interpretation" (325), from the very beginning his words demand that we notice more than one meaning. When Thoreau says that he requires of every writer "some such account as he would send to his kindred from a distant land," he seems to refer not only to a traveler writing home to his family but also to the extent to which we are all kin to one another. And Thoreau defines himself as such a traveler, one who is "at present ... a sojourner in civilized life again" but who has "travelled a good deal in Concord" (3, 4).

Walden, like *Religio Medici,* is a normative autobiography: it describes a self that is exemplary as well as idiosyncratic. Both Browne and Thoreau apologize explicitly for the focus on the self: Thoreau says, "I should not talk so much about myself if there were anybody else whom I knew as well" (3); Browne describes *Religio Medici* as "a private exercise directed to my selfe, ... rather a memoriall unto me then an example or rule unto any other" (To the Reader, 1). Yet these statements are formal apologias rather than accurate descriptions of texts that construct vigorously individualistic yet representative personae. Browne's apologies for the idiosyncratic and personal nature of the text occur largely in the preface, whereas in the body of *Religio Medici* Browne simply undertakes to talk about himself. Focus on the self is an even more pervasive concern for Thoreau, who spends a fair amount of time pointing to the fact that he is describing himself, as well as pointing to the specificity and the idiosyncrasy of what he is doing.[3]

Just as Browne makes liberal use of the first person pronoun, which becomes one of the recurring and unifying features of his work, Thoreau also emphasizes the first person as a basic and determinative element: "In most books, the *I,* or first person, is omitted; in this it will be retained; that, in respect to egotism, is the main difference. We commonly do not remember that it is, after all, always the first person that is speaking" (3). Thus, Thoreau is at pains to be explicit about his undertaking, pointing out to us the nature not only of his own work but of all self-representation, indeed of all writing. Thoreau on the one hand seems to move to placate those readers who find him merely crankily or obsessively egocentric: "I will therefore ask those of my readers who feel no particular interest in me to pardon me if I undertake to answer some of these questions in this book . . . I should not talk so much about myself if there were anybody else whom I knew as well" (3). Yet, like Robert Burton, he can switch quickly out of the apologetic mode. In establishing a persona at the opening of "Economy," Thoreau represents himself as a reader, and also as a writer, with expectations and demands: "I, on my side, require of every writer, first or last, a simple and sincere account of his own life, and not merely what he has heard of other men's lives" (3). Thoreau speaks of the "narrowness of my experience" (3), yet he clearly also expects some commonality of interest: "As for the rest of my readers, they will accept such portions as apply to them" (4). While Browne emphasizes the duality of the self, its being both body and spirit, as a microcosm of the greater physical world, Thoreau represents the self also as a microcosm of the greater communal world, and he stresses that in writing his experience he lays out a pattern that others may follow, not by going to Walden Pond, but by living, as he put it, "deliberately."

Analogous to Anne Drury Hall's account of *Religio Medici* as a combination of the epistolary and meditative modes, one might describe *Walden* as a blending of essay and meditation. Whereas Browne's work seems so self-contained that not every reader has detected the epistolary quality to which Hall draws attention, Thoreau makes it clear that certain inquiries about his experiences and motives have preceded the writing of *Walden*. This assertion is in part a rhetorical ploy, a way of establishing his reason for writing. But I would not go so far as to see this statement simply as pretense; it is perhaps partly a holdover from *Walden*'s origins in lyceum lectures.[4] Both works begin with a kind of negotiation of the grounds of discourse, a setting up of the terms of the text. Browne begins, as if in medias res, "For my Religion." Thoreau begins as if in the middle of a protracted dialogue with inquisitive neighbors: "I should not obtrude my affairs so much on the notice of my readers if very particular inquiries had not been made by my townsmen concerning my mode of life, which some would call impertinent, though they do not appear to me at all impertinent, but, considering the circumstances, very natural and pertinent" (3).[5] Thoreau's linguistic play on the matter of pertinence, meaning relevance, and impertinence, meaning an inappropriate intrusion to another's affairs, shows the distinctive quality of his prose: *Walden* is marked by a sense of humor and wit that offers surprising flashes of insight, a word play that is based not on superficial resemblances but genuine links and probing questions. This quality is also the metaphysical wit found in Browne, the ability that Dr. Johnson discerned in poets to discover occult resemblances in things apparently unlike, the kind of wit described by the seventeenth-century theorists Gracián and Tesauro, for whom the wit of human poets was a perception of the work of a witty creator.[6] Thus the most marked quality of Thoreau's prose is also one that he shares with Browne.

I have argued that in his emphasis on the self and the representation of it as exemplary, in the revealing of intimate details to an expanding audience, in the awareness, not only stated but recreated in the text, of a dimension beyond the physical, Thoreau is linked to Browne. There are also ways in which Thoreau's technique, while analogous to Browne's, modifies and extends it, sometimes in explicitness of approach, sometimes through a more suggestive, allusive quality. Like Browne, Thoreau rejects the notion of life as simply limited to the terrestrial realm, and his use of the double meaning of light—as physical light but also as that quality by which we see, not only with our eyes but with our minds— makes the point brilliantly. For both Browne and Thoreau, the natural world is not simply a set of physical phenomena but something infused with a deeper significance. Browne inherits this view from the rich and flourishing tradition of Christian Platonism: "Thus there are two bookes," he writes, "from whence I collect my Divinity; besides that written one of God, another of his servant Nature, that universall and publik Manuscript, that lies expans'd unto the eyes of all."[7] Thoreau's awareness of this tradition owes a good deal not only to his reading of seventeenth-century poets—Herbert, Vaughan, even Browne himself— but also to his intellectual friendship with Emerson, whose ideas of the Oversoul derive, among other sources, from the Cambridge Platonist Ralph Cudworth.[8] Thoreau expresses this sense of the larger cosmic world partly in explicit declarations: "Olympus is but the outside of the earth every where" (85). But, like Eliot and in contrast to Donne, Thoreau is less explicit in matters of theology: whereas in Browne the spirit that we must feel to be alive is the divine Spirit, in Thoreau the cosmic dimension is less specifically located; it is pervasive, frequently alluded to, sometimes under such phrases as "an old settler" or the notion of Walden being "the work of a brave man surely, in whom there was no guile" (193); many of the biblical phrases and concepts occurring in *Walden* remain as what Eliot would call "hints and guesses."

For Thoreau, living at Walden Pond is itself an act of meditation: "I went to the woods because I wished to live deliberately, to front only the essential facts of life" (90), he says, and one of the chief indicators of the meditative nature of the experience is the precision with which he describes his surroundings and his actions—the exact amount, to the half cent, spent in building his house, feeding himself, and planting his crops; the precise depth, length, and width of Walden Pond, the qualities of its water in relation to that of other ponds, the dates at which it broke up in successive years. Such detail is so extreme that it could suggest either a kind of obsession with fact or a Franklinesque interest in the minutiae of daily life; yet neither of these seems a likely explanation in the case of Thoreau, who objects that "our life is frittered away by detail" (91).[9] But in a manner that would not be out of place in the focus on the senses, the composition of place described by Louis Martz, the physical in *Walden* leads to a metaphysical discovery; the very concentration on the surface of life leads to a vision of something else beneath. When Thoreau says, "I did not read books the first summer; I hoed beans" (111), he suggests the latter activity not as an alternative to instruction but as a higher mode of it, for the physical activity links him to a more universal meaning: "But while we are confined to books, though the most select and classic, and read only particular written languages, which are themselves but dialects and provincial, we are in danger of forgetting the language which all things and events speak without metaphor, which alone is copious and standard" (111).

Indeed, from the very beginning of *Walden,* the measured pace of Thoreau's prose suggests both the method and the result of his inquiry, the progressive deliberateness of his search, the means by which the physical is joined with the spiritual:[10]

> When I wrote the following pages, or rather the bulk of them, I lived alone, in the woods, a mile from any neighbor, in a house which I had built myself, on the shore of Walden Pond, in Concord, Massachusetts, and earned my living by the labor of my hands only. I lived there two years and two months. (3)

> I was seated by the shore of a small pond, about a mile and a half south of the village of Concord and somewhat higher than it, in the midst of an extensive wood between that town and Lincoln, and

about two miles south of that our only field known to fame, Concord Battle Ground; but I was so low in the woods that the opposite shore, half a mile off, like the rest, covered with wood, was my most distant horizon. (86)

Thoreau's diction here is resolutely plain, predominantly Anglo-Saxon: he offers bits of information in series of heavily punctuated modifying phrases that give a sense of completeness, of precision, of exhaustive attention to each detail. In both passages Thoreau describes a sphere of experience strictly limited, defined by "the narrowness of my circumstances"; yet the very circumscription of the picture leads to the sense that there must be something more than meets the eye, although what that might be remains indeterminate. It is the more remarkable that out of details and rhythms so pedestrian should come the vision of Walden as the "earth's eye," "God's Drop," and of Thoreau's activity as a way of probing the ultimate meaning of existence; through the principle of analogy Thoreau shares with Browne, the physical is joined with the spiritual.

But one should also note the great variety of *Walden:* this kind of heavily weighted, deeply evocative and significant prose is of course not its only mode. Sometimes there is Thoreau the pragmatic reporter, tending to the advocate: "For more than five years I maintained myself thus solely by the labor of my hands, and I found, that by working about six weeks in a year, I could meet all the expenses of living" (69); this is the man who tried to persuade an Irish laborer to adopt his methods of subsistence farming. Sometimes there is a Romantic quality to the prose, as Thoreau, the reader of Wordsworth and Coleridge, links his vision of physical nature with native and classical mythology: "Sometimes I rambled to pine groves, standing like temples, or like fleets at sea, full-rigged, with wavy boughs, and rippling with light, so soft and green and shady that the Druids would have forsaken their oaks to worship in them; or to the cedar wood beyond Flint's Pond, where the trees, covered with hoary blue berries, spiring higher and higher, are fit to stand before Valhalla, and the creeping juniper covers the ground with wreaths full of fruit" (201). There are occasional stretches of mere reportage, the flatness of which some critics suggest Thoreau increasingly fell into later in life.[11] There is the dialogue in "Brute Neighbors" between the hermit and the poet, which resembles the dialogues of Izaak Walton's *Compleat Angler;* and of course there are the gnomic, apodictic passages that recall Emerson.

In this long and complex work there are varying degrees of intensity and a variety of methods, but I want to turn to the characteristic means by which Thoreau moves from the literal to the metaphorical, the rhetorical devices by which he represents the revelations that result from his deliberate life at Walden Pond. This movement is accomplished, as I have suggested, not merely by a process of assertion, although there are assertive passages in *Walden,* but by use of language and syntax that bring the reader to a different view of reality. I have already noted a few of the many passages in "Economy" that increasingly raise the suspicion and finally lead to the awareness that Thoreau's reference is ambiguous, multivalent, in passages that take the metaphorical sense of the familiar phrase and make it suddenly literal, or that turn the literal, suddenly, to the visionary. And as I have suggested, although there is a greater variety of styles and a firmer grounding in concrete detail than in *Religio Medici,* these methods, though not constant, are among the most characteristic and essential qualities of *Walden.*

Typical of this linguistic depth is the opening paragraph of the second chapter, "Where I Lived, and What I Lived For":

> At a certain season of our life we are accustomed to consider every spot as the possible site of a house. I have thus surveyed the country on every side within a dozen miles of where I live. In imagination I have bought all the farms in succession, for all were to be bought, and I knew their price. I walked over each farmer's premises, tasted his wild apples, discoursed on husbandry with him, took his farm at his price, at any price, mortgaging it to him in my mind; even put a higher price on it, — took everything but a deed of it, — took his word for his deed, for I dearly love to talk, — cultivated it, and him too to some extent, I trust, and withdrew when I had enjoyed it long enough, leaving him to carry it on. (81)

This passage, like much in Thoreau, may at first appear straightforward enough, yet it leaves one with an odd suspicion that more than the ordinary is going on, that the passage as a whole is unstable. The paragraph is filled with simple and literal verb forms — *surveyed, bought, walked, tasted, discoursed, took, mortgaging, took, put, cultivated, withdrew* — many of which admit of more than one meaning: for example, Thoreau may survey with his eye, or with instruments, as he did to earn his living. This second, less literal group of meanings is suggested by the opening linking of the seasons of the year with the phases of human life and by Thoreau's em-

Thoreau: *Walden*

phasis on the dominance of imaginative activity: "In imagination I have bought all the farms in succession." The meanings become concentratedly uncertain when Thoreau mingles what must or may be done physically—"I walked over each farmer's premises, tasted his wild apples, discoursed on husbandry with him"—with actions that are clearly mental or imaginary—"took his farm at his price, at any price, mortgaging it to him in my mind." The duality of meanings becomes even more explicit in the word play of "took his word for his deed," in which deed may mean both an action and the title to a piece of property; or "cultivated it, and him too to some extent," which joins the action of agricultural and social cultivation; and "walked over each farmer's premises," suggesting the physical property, but also the principles on which his life is based.

My point is not that everything in this section has a hidden or determinate meaning—quite the contrary; in fact a number of readers have been to my mind too eager to assign specific meanings to Thoreau's words and images.[12] Thoreau is certainly not writing an allegory, nor can he, in the mid-nineteenth century, depend on acceptance of a system of iconography. Rather, almost like the writer of a mystery, Thoreau arouses the suspicion that a surprise lurks around every corner, that each of his words may harbor a double meaning. The result is a text that sensitizes us to the possibility of meanings beyond those we have realized. The relation between time and eternity, between the cosmic and the mundane, is not a simple one, not a system of equivalences, but a matter of catching a glimpse now and then, just as Thoreau's words suggest, now and then, a meaning beneath the surface.

The passage that ends chapter 2 will illustrate what I mean: it seems at first to suggest a fairly clear system of correspondences, a relatively direct access to the realm of eternity: "Time is but the stream I go a-fishing in. I drink at it; but while I drink I see the sandy bottom and detect how shallow it is. Its thin current slides away, but eternity remains" (98). But the concluding images suggest not finality of vision but rather the necessity for vigorous action within an uncertain context: "My instinct tells me that my head is an organ for burrowing, as some creatures use their snout and fore-paws, and with it I would mine and burrow my way through these hills. I think that the richest vein is somewhere hereabouts; so by the divining rod and thin rising vapors I judge; and here I will begin to mine" (98). Thoreau's image suggests the possibility of discovery but also implies that he is only on the scent of something that Browne could revel in the possession of; hence his rhetoric, rather than being clearly celebratory, is suggestive and hortatory. Thoreau, having identified the place of discovery — "Where I lived was as far off as many a region viewed nightly by astronomers" (87–88) — must now awaken his readers to the opportunity for such discovery, through images of morning, a time of awakening, a time, as he says, when "there is least somnolence in us" (89).

Walden itself is a long series of wake-up calls in which, in the course of a sentence or a group of sentences, we are moved from a literal to a metaphorical reading or from a mundane to a cosmic: "One value even of the smallest well is, that when you look into it you see that the earth is not continent but insular. This is as important as that it keeps butter cool" (87). Thoreau takes us from physical facts — the relative proportion of water and land on the earth — to metaphysical implications, articulated the more sharply in relation to the physical fact: "This is as important as that it keeps butter cool." Often these results are achieved with a stroke of wit, reminding us that, as in the seventeenth century, a metaphysical consciousness was not a matter of gloomy solemnity but of insight, even of humor, that demonstrated the connection between the mundane fact — in this instance a piece of salted cod — and the eternal dimension: "Who has not seen a salt fish, thoroughly cured for this world, so that nothing can spoil it, and putting the perseverance of the saints to the blush?" (120).

Thoreau, then, uses words that, in association with each other, point to more than one meaning: he uses zeugma to juxtapose the passive and active, the literal and the metaphorical — "It makes but little difference whether you are committed to a farm or the county jail" (84); "I made no haste in my work, but rather made the most of it" (42); and he uses a modified form to juxtapose the pedestrian and the profound: "As if you could kill time without injuring eternity" (8). Thoreau uses a single verb in a literal and metaphorical sense: "Before we can adorn our houses with beautiful objects the walls must be stripped, and our lives must be stripped" (38); he enlivens clichés, moving from the proverbial to the literal: "It is not necessary that a man should earn his living by the sweat of his brow, unless he sweats easier than I do" (71). And most often, Thoreau uses deep, multiple puns, as in "I was determined to know beans" (161), a statement that has its literal meaning in the cultivation of seven miles of bean rows but that also in its negation of the idiom "not to know beans" refers to the most elementary knowledge. Thoreau expresses a determination to know *something*, but also to know the most *basic* of things, that which links him to a source of being: "I came to love my rows, my beans, though so many more than I wanted. They attached me to the earth, and so I got strength like Antæus" (155).[13] Although Thoreau can on occasion indulge in casual or whimsical word play (as in his description of James Collins's cat, which "took to the woods and became a wild cat, and, as I learned afterward, trod in a trap set for woodchucks, and so became a dead cat at last" [44]), his puns usually signify a vital link between two kinds of reality. When he describes his labor—"to make this portion of the earth's surface ... produce instead this pulse" (155)—Thoreau uses not only the technical name for beans and peas but also a word suggesting the very living quality of the earth itself.

We have been seeing in Thoreau's prose not simply the articulation of meaning but a rhetorical process by which the reader discovers that meaning, a mimetic sequence that recreates the persona's own mode of discovery. Besides his use of significant word play, his quick flashes of metaphysical wit, Thoreau also uses the structure of sentences and paragraphs to represent and recreate the experience of discovery. Sometimes series of short, unconnected syntactic units, statements and interrogatives force the reader to pause and digest each new bit before moving on to the next; often, as in Browne, these dramatically elaborate a single principle: "Thank Heaven, here is not all the world. The buck-eye does not grow in New England, and the mocking-bird is rarely heard here. The wild-goose is more of a cosmopolite than we; he breaks his fast in Canada, takes a luncheon in the Ohio, and plumes himself for the night in a southern bayou. Even the bison, to some extent, keeps pace with the seasons, cropping the pastures of the Colorado only till a greener and sweeter grass awaits him by the Yellowstone" (320). Sometimes, as in Browne's dramatic sequences, these groups of sentences are incremental, moving the reader to a deeper or more complex sense of Thoreau's point. Although Browne is much more likely to provide a lengthy Senecan period, and Thoreau, a series of individual sentences, the technique for representing an ongoing revelation is analogous.[14]

In addition to series of short sentences, Thoreau also uses longer syntactical units to represent the subtle process of discovery in a connected chain of events or observations:

Generating Texts

> In warm evenings I frequently sat in the boat playing the flute, and saw the perch, which I seem to have charmed, hovering around me, and the moon travelling over the ribbed bottom, which was strewed with the wrecks of the forest. Formerly I had come to this pond adventurously, from time to time, in dark summer nights, with a companion, and making a fire close to the water's edge, which we thought attracted the fishes, we caught pouts with a bunch of worms strung on a thread, and when we had done, far in the night, threw the burning brands high into the air like skyrockets, which, coming down into the pond, were quenched with a loud hissing, and we were suddenly groping in total darkness. Through this, whistling a tune, we took our way to the haunts of men again. But now I had made my home by the shore. (174)

In this quietly remarkable section a series of short, parallel modifying phrases, almost in imitation of the notes of the flute, represents the sequence of actions by which one element of the scene is linked to the next—the man playing the flute, the perch hovering around him, the moon traveling—not through the sky, but reflected in the water so that it too seems to be part of the magical, charmed scene below. The heavy punctuation emphasizes the discrete quality of each point, while the syntactical connections bind the passage unmistakably together. As Thoreau gives bits of information in a series of short prepositional phrases—"from time to time, in dark summer nights, with a companion," he recreates history in a way that charms us too, bringing the past experience of adventure, that of the younger man or boy who comes to the pond in the dark with a friend, together with the present experience of discovery. The moon of the present scene is united with the recollection of burning brands that rise in the air like skyrockets; the moment of illumination is brief, leaving the two of them, in imitation of the human condition, "groping in total darkness." Yet as at the ending of chapter 2, where uncertainty leads to action and potential discovery, where Thoreau senses "that the richest vein is somewhere hereabouts . . . and here I will begin to mine" (98), so here, if the pond is unmistakably a place of enchantment, of attraction, of burning brands, Thoreau's language suggests that discovery can occur even in "the haunts of men," a place not entirely devoid of the spirit, toward which, whistling a tune, Thoreau and his companion go.

Not only is this passage mimetic, imitative of the charmed scene and the hypnotic experience; it also raises subtle suggestions that are reiterated hundreds of times throughout the text of *Walden*. The passage persistently conveys the sense of a spirit within nature, not necessarily something grand and awe-inspiring, not explicitly present, but rather mysterious, as yet undefined, yet repeatedly felt. That sense is communicated in the following paragraph by the suggestion that Thoreau in his boat is "serenaded by owls and foxes," that he hears "the creaking note of some unknown bird close at hand," that he is "communicating by a long flaxen line with mysterious nocturnal fishes," that he feels "some life . . . of dull uncertain blundering purpose there, and slow to make up its mind." Thoreau of course describes a fish (perhaps with a little of the angler's frustration), but the second possible referent is the writer himself, trying to make out the outlines of something distinctly felt yet not clearly perceived. Thoreau concludes the paragraph by making explicit the link between the upper and lower worlds, the pond and the sky: he speaks of pulling the fish "squeaking and squirming to the upper air," as if the pond beneath were the lower air, simply an extension of our atmosphere. As he casts his line downward, his thoughts wander upward, "to vast and cosmogonal themes in other spheres," until the faint jerk on his line "interrupt[s] [his] dreams and link[s] him to Nature again."[15] The link between nature and the spirit is finally established in the last two sentences, where it is made clear that fishing is a meditative act: "It seemed as if I might next cast my line upward into the air, as well as downward into this element which was scarcely more dense. Thus I caught two fishes as it were with one hook" (175).

Although *Walden* most strikingly represents the revelatory process of discovery, Thoreau also uses mimetic structures to depict the ordinary life of humankind, the numbing sequence of activity that, in "Economy," he subjects to withering criticism:

> still living, and dying, and buried by this other's brass; always promising to pay, promising to pay, to-morrow, and dying to-day, insolvent; seeking to curry favor, to get custom, by how many modes, only not state-prison offences; lying, flattering, voting, contracting yourselves into a nutshell of civility, or dilating into an atmosphere of thin and vaporous generosity, that you may persuade your neighbor to let you make his shoes, or his hat, or his coat, or his carriage, or import his groceries for him; making yourselves sick, that you may lay up something against a sick day, something to be tucked away in an old chest, or in a stocking behind the plastering, or,

more safely, in the brick bank; no matter where, no matter how much or how little. (7)

In this passage Thoreau's general dictum—"The mass of men lead lives of quiet desperation" (8)—is borne out by parallel phrasing, alliteration, repetition, even rhyming of words. Apparently positive activities (*voting*) are juxtaposed with a series of obviously negative ones (*lying, flattering*) to show the futility of it all. The whole cascade of details incorporates echoes of *Hamlet* ("contracting yourselves into a nutshell of civility" recalls "I could be bounded in a nutshell"; and the contortions of human beings—"dilating into an atmosphere of thin and vaporous generosity"—resemble the many figures Hamlet pretends to find in the clouds); it recalls the Gospels (laying up for oneself treasures, whether in heaven or on earth).[16] The whole extended sequence of phrases and clauses, at once cumulative and fruitless, comes down to the final syntactical balance of meaninglessness: "no matter where, no matter how much or how little."

Thoreau's representation of discovery works, as I've been arguing, at the most basic level of phrase, sentence, and paragraph, in units that vividly reenact his perceptions. But these are not the only levels at which his text is carefully mimetic. Just as Thoreau often writes individual sentences that seem discrete and unconnected yet also function as part of a progressive revelation, so the chapters of *Walden,* while self-contained, are part of the ongoing process of discovery. It has been said that whereas Emerson's natural unit is the sentence, Thoreau's is the paragraph, rather than the chapter or the book.[17] But while this would imply that Thoreau, like Emerson, might have difficulty putting together a longer coherent work, *Walden* is evidence to the contrary. Although embellished with a good deal of detail and example as well as with remarks and exhortations to his fellow man, the book has a clear narrative structure. It no longer has the journal form from which it grew; rather, Thoreau condenses his two years and two months at Walden into one, creating not simply a circumstantial account but a coherent presentation of detail that lends itself to meditation.

The two hundred carefully shaped pages of text manifest a variety of organizational forms, both narrative and cyclical.[18] Just as we noticed in *Religio Medici* a duality of structure—the formal division into the two parts based on the two tables of the law and the less formal but equally important driving force of progressive self-definition operating within the cyclical return to *I* — so also in *Walden* one might find several interactive kinds of structure. A powerful force in the later part of the book, as has often been noted, is the cycle of the seasons, the movement toward spring in nature and awakening in man exemplified by the detailed description of the return of migratory birds, the breakup of ice on the ponds, the growth of vegetation. There is, moreover, a strong impulse toward balancing, not only in Thoreau's sense of the relation between the individual and society, in his observing details of nature and pondering their significance, but also in the larger juxtapositions of whole chapters.[19]

Thoreau outlines the principles of his undertaking in "Economy," then works these out more specifically in "Where I Lived, and What I Lived For"; two favorite modes of learning are contrasted in chapter 3, "Reading," and chapter 4, "Sounds," in which he presents one as an extension of the other.[20] Subsequent chapters are even more clearly antiphonal: "Solitude" precedes "Visitors"; "The Bean-Field" balances the human field, "The Village"; the water of "The Ponds" is set against the dry land of "Baker Farm"; "Higher Laws" is set against (although with some irony) "Brute Neighbors." Thereafter, the cycle of the seasons dominates *Walden,* in the movement from "House-Warming" to "Former Inhabitants; and Winter Visitors" to "Winter Animals"; from "The Pond in Winter" to "Spring" to Thoreau's final peroration, which points out that the illumination achieved, though powerful, is yet incomplete.

The chapters of *Walden,* then, like its individual sentences, represent moments of discovery or of meditation on particular themes, but they are also part of a well-orchestrated progression. Thoreau went to the woods "to live deliberately," "as deliberately as Nature" (90, 97); he describes in detail natural phenomena that gradually acquire more and more significance as he represents them in reiterated and increasingly resonant images. Walden Pond, which at first "does not approach to grandeur," eventually becomes something which, "lying between the earth and the heavens, . . . partakes of the color of both" (175–76). It is a body of water whose rising and falling occurs not in response to obvious periods of wet and dryness but by some mysterious principle; it is "my well ready dug" (183), "earth's eye; looking into which the beholder measures the depth of his own nature" (186); "a perfect forest mirror" (188), within which we may "mark where a still subtler spirit sweeps over it" (189); finally it is associated with divinity through language that recalls the suffering servant of Isaiah and the Creator of Genesis: "It is the work of a brave man surely, in whom there was no guile! He rounded this water with his hand, deepened and clarified it in his thought, and in his will bequeathed it to Concord" (193).

In the course of Thoreau's observations the pond is no longer simply a natural object, it is also an emblem. Such an assertion clearly links Thoreau with Browne, yet the differences must also be noted. For both Browne and Thoreau there are two books from which they collect their divinity, the written word, whether of Scriptures or of Indian philosophy, and the face of nature, in which they find meaningful patterns. Both, extremely skilled craftsmen, dramatize the experience of the discovery of those spiritual and natural meanings. Although Thoreau's view of the world resembles Browne's, he cannot assume that attitude in his readers, to whom he sometimes hints and for whom he sometimes elaborates. Whereas Browne in *Religio Medici* takes nature as his book, reading theological meaning in the physical world, the progressions of his paragraphs typically elaborate paradoxes that he shares with orthodox Christian doctrine but that he expresses with particular éclat. By contrast Thoreau tends to present a more elusive if insistent vision, something glimpsed through the phenomena he describes, suggested by his persistently ambiguous word choices. Describing the uniqueness of Walden, Thoreau writes:

> Successive nations perchance have drank at, admired, and fathomed it, and passed away, and still its water is green and pellucid as ever. Not an intermitting spring! Perhaps on that spring morning when Adam and Eve were driven out of Eden Walden Pond was already in existence, and even then breaking up in a gentle spring rain accompanied with mist and a southerly wind, and covered with myriads of ducks and geese, which had not heard of the fall, when still such pure lakes sufficed them. Even then it had commenced to rise and fall, and had clarified its waters and colored them of the hue they now wear, and obtained a patent of Heaven to be the only Walden Pond in the world and distiller of celestial dews. Who knows in how many unremembered nations' literatures this has been the Castalian Fountain? or what nymphs presided over it in the Golden Age? It is a gem of the first water which Concord wears in her coronet. (179)

In a sense this passage is less consistent, less controlled than anything Browne might have written, but it is also powerfully evocative and characteristic of Thoreau. He writes with a light touch, calling up unmistakably rich and powerful meanings, yet scarcely seeming to maintain a hold over them. The words *spring* and *fall* run through the passage as if by free association, each word having multiple meanings; the passage mingles classical and Judaeo-Christian references, linking Walden with Eden and with the Golden Age; it joins a sense of the pond's primal quality with an odd mercantile reference to obtaining a patent of Heaven for its name and function. Walden is placed in time in such a way as to make it almost eternal and yet unknown: "Who knows in how many unremembered nations' literatures this has been the Castalian Fountain?"

Perhaps the most remarkable thing about the passage is the uncertain, even iridescent quality of its language, the characteristic movement between the literal and the metaphorical: "Successive nations perchance have drank at, admired, and fathomed it, and passed away," Thoreau says, leaving indeterminate whether those nations have measured the depth of Walden with line and stone as he has, or whether they have understood it. "Not an intermitting spring!" next suggests the constancy of Walden, as something that, although its sources are unknown, never goes dry, something persisting throughout history. But the following sentence implies yet another meaning—"Perhaps on that spring morning when Adam and Even were driven out of Eden"—joining the eternity of myth with the long history of Walden. Walden Pond, though linked with an Eden that is associated with eternal spring, was even then "breaking up in a gentle spring rain"—as if winter had preceded that very first season.[21] At that point Walden was "covered with ... ducks and geese, which had not heard of the fall," presumably the Fall of Adam and Eve, and yet also of the autumn. Thus Walden, that supremely natural phenomenon, which "had commenced to rise and fall," is also associated with the theological construct, the Fall of mankind. When Thoreau concludes, "It is a gem of the first water which Concord wears in her coronet," he once again deals in two realms of experience, associating Walden with the distinctions of civilization, the highest grade of precious stones, yet also recapitulating the preceding paragraph, in which Walden was literally there from the very first, a part of the Golden Age, just a little west, perhaps, of Eden.[22] Thus Thoreau's language recalls, implies, strongly suggests, but does not insist on a realm shared with Browne.

A further instance of the way in which Thoreau's reading of nature, though clearly allied to the emblematic tradition, is nevertheless distinguishable from Browne's is found in one of the more flamboyant passages of *Walden,* Thoreau's description of the forms that appear in a bank of sand as the frost comes out of the ground. The more Thoreau warms to his theme, the more elaborate become the patterns he observes; he indulges in a complex and extended reading of nature, discerning not only forms but also letters:

> When I see on the one side the inert bank,—for the sun acts on one side first,—and on the other this luxuriant foliage, the creation of an hour, I am affected as if in a peculiar sense I stood in the laboratory of the Artist who made the world and me,—had come to where he was still at work, sporting on this bank, and with excess of energy strewing his fresh designs about. I feel as if I were nearer to the vitals of the globe, for this sandy overflow is something such a foliaceous mass as the vitals of the animal body. You find thus in the very sands an anticipation of the vegetable leaf. No wonder that the earth expresses itself outwardly in leaves, it so labors with the idea inwardly. The atoms have already learned this law, and are pregnant by it. The overhanging leaf sees here its prototype. *Internally,* whether in the globe or animal body, it is a moist thick *lobe,* a word especially applicable to the liver and lungs and the *leaves* of fat, λείβω, *labor, lapsus,* to flow or slip downward, a lapsing; λοβος, *globus,* lobe, globe; also lap, flap, and many other words,) *externally,* a dry thin *leaf,* even as the *f* and *v* are a pressed and dried *b.* (306)

As his meditation progresses, Thoreau sees ever more in the thawing bank, finding "in the very sands an anticipation of the vegetable leaf," and in the leaf the prototype of all organic shapes, whether vegetable or animal, or even mineral: "Even ice begins with delicate crystal leaves, as if it had flowed into moulds which the fronds of water plants have impressed on the watery mirror. The whole tree itself is but one leaf, and rivers are still vaster leaves whose pulp is intervening earth, and towns and cities are the ova of insects in their axils" (306–7). In this discerning of a single pattern throughout the natural and even the human world, and finding in that repetition evidence of system and meaning, Thoreau resembles Browne, who in the *Garden of Cyrus* finds reticulated patterns in everything from the skin of snakes to the brickwork of houses and the marching formations of the Roman legions. The notion of nature as emblem, as well as a fascinating field for investigation, the shifting attention now to the meaning of natural phenomena, now to the surface patterns of those phenomena—these are things Thoreau shares with Browne, whose works treat nature in varying degrees as the subject of observation and of emblematic meaning.

But this passage differs from what we might find in Browne, not so much in its detail as in its ecstatic quality, in the single-minded intensity with which it probes this particular spot, finding ever more meaning — in the shape of the bank as well as in the words themselves, which seem to have a kind of Adamic force and authority. The notion of pattern in nature is something that Thoreau shares not only with Browne but with the Victorines of the twelfth century.[23] Yet its elaboration here has also distinctly Romantic touches — the emphasis on the personal quality of the experience and the identification not of an omnipotent creator but an "Artist," whose work manifests excess and energy as much as order and plenitude: "I am affected as if in a peculiar sense I stood in the laboratory of the Artist who made the world and me, — had come to where he was still at work, sporting on this bank, and with excess of energy strewing his fresh designs about." Thoreau's images here, though extremely and progressively elaborate, are also arbitrary, a creation of poetic imagination rather than an article of belief to be taken with ultimate seriousness or held in common by a community of believers.[24] Curiously, we may finish the passage feeling that it is not excessively symbolic but excessively literal; it begins and ends with the material fact; it proceeds to read meaning into it and impose significance on it, often more significance than it will bear.

Yet in *Walden* as a whole Thoreau tends to touch such notes more lightly, incrementally building a sense of the meaning of the pond, the natural world, and his experience, rather than making them fully explicit in any one passage. By the time we get well into the text, certainly by the time we reach the end, we may be surprised and delighted by Thoreau's particular turns of phrase, but we will be well aware of the metaphysical dimension of his experiences. Indeed in the later chapters one experiences this quality like a persistent series of overtones that constantly enrich the meaning of the text: "A single gentle rain makes the grass many shades greener. So our prospects brighten on the influx of better thoughts. . . . We loiter in winter while it is already spring. In a pleasant spring morning all men's sins are forgiven. . . . All things must live in such a light" (314, 317).

Although Thoreau makes such meanings so prominent that we come to sense and expect them nearly everywhere, *Walden* concludes with a particularly dazzling peroration, one that depends on rhetorical methods very like those of Browne, one in which the use of analogy is both explicit and celebratory. Like *Religio Medici*, *Walden* comes full circle, as

Thoreau uses the images of discovery and travel with which the book began. Thoreau begins with the dominant metaphor of geography: "To the sick the doctors wisely recommend a change of air and scenery. Thank Heaven, here is not all the world" (320). Images of physical change become the vehicle for a more significant exploration, that of the self, with which *Walden* opened: "What does Africa,—what does the West stand for? Is not our own interior white on the chart?" (321). And, like Browne, Thoreau connects the process of discovery with the process of speech: "I fear chiefly lest my expression may be not *extra- vagant* enough, may not wander far enough beyond the narrow limits of my daily experience, so as to be adequate to the truth of which I have been convinced" (324). He continues: "I desire to speak somewhere *without* bounds; like a man in a waking moment, to men in their waking moments; for I am convinced that I cannot exaggerate enough even to lay the foundation of a true expression. . . . The volatile truth of our words should continually betray the inadequacy of the residual statement" (324–25).

For Thoreau, as for Browne, language is an essential means to truth, as one sees in the meditation on the sandy bank, on the shapes it embodies, on the words applicable to it, on the shapes of the words. But language is also, finally, inadequate: the best way to find the truth is to go as far as language will take us and to leap from that point in the direction we are pointed. Like Browne, Thoreau finds analogy an essential mode of understanding, as when he compares his view of an insect with the Deity's view of man: "As I stand over the insect crawling amid the pine needles on the forest floor, and endeavoring to conceal itself from my sight, and ask myself why it will cherish those humble thoughts, and hide its head from me who might perhaps be its benefactor, and impart to its race some cheering information, I am reminded of the greater Benefactor and Intelligence that stands over me the human insect" (332). But whereas Browne could assume and celebrate such a mode of thinking, Thoreau must make it here more explicit, reducing it to metaphor rather than to truth. Its explicitness, its elaboration gives it a very different status from the electric declarative quality of "*Eve* miscarried of mee before she conceiv'd of *Cain*."

Thoreau uses analogy even more strikingly to represent the process of understanding, the leap beyond conventional wisdom, in the concluding paragraph of *Walden:* "I do not say that John or Jonathan will realize all this; but such is the character of that morrow which mere lapse of time can never make to dawn. The light which puts out our eyes is darkness to us. Only that day dawns to which we are awake. There is more day to dawn. The sun is but a morning star" (333). Thoreau has traced in detail the coming of the spring, has recounted what he did by night and what by day, how he spent his mornings and his afternoons; finally those things are seen not only as important in themselves but as an emblem of something far more significant. In a book that is so much about time and so much about dawn, Thoreau points at last to "the character of that morrow which mere lapse of time can never make to dawn." Just as for Browne "*Lux est umbra Dei,*" so for Thoreau "the sun is but a morning star." Both Browne and Thoreau rely on analogy, taking the brightest body of our experience and reaching beyond it to something brighter, indeed bright beyond our imagination; both in effect use reason to point beyond reason.

But while affirming the striking similarity of these formulations, the habit of analogy and the gift for the dramatic statement, one must note the distinctions. Although Browne speaks of "humour[ing] my fancy" in his preference for "an easie and Platonick description" over the "Metaphysicall definitions of Divines," this analogy is actually quite exact, and its purpose is to make "our reason . . . more humble and submissive unto the subtilties of faith" (1.10); Browne's definition is clear in its logical relationships but breaks down through human inability to fathom the possibility it points to. By contrast, Thoreau's statement, in which the analogy is further submerged, is visionary rather than fideistic; it points us not toward an admission of inadequacy but toward a hopeful realization of the dawn. Thoreau's image is evocative rather than strictly logical; he recommends that "in view of the future or possible, we should live quite laxly and undefined in front, our outlines dim and misty on that side; as our shadows reveal an insensible perspiration toward the sun" (324–25). Browne's purpose is to recreate and confound his and our reason; Thoreau's is to alert us to the dawning of the day prefigured in *Walden* itself. His text is always moving in the direction of that potential revelation.

Part of the difference, of course, is that Browne in some measure looks from an age of analogy toward an age of increasing interest in scientific observation for its own sake, he being one of the transitional figures between the two, whereas Thoreau, for all his delight in the facts of nature, is a constant interpreter of those facts, one who looks with some longing back to the time when sermons might be found in stones.

Thoreau assumes his reader's familiarity with such Renaissance notions as man as microcosm or the house as the expression of its owner or inhabitant; but rather than expounding the religious or philosophical significance of these tropes as Donne or Marvell or Jonson might have done, he touches on them lightly and turns them to personal use: "For the most part it is as solitary where I live as on the prairies. It is as much Asia or Africa as New England. I have, as it were, my own sun and moon and stars, and a little world all to myself" (130). Two hundred years earlier, Browne wrote more explicitly and schematically: "The world that I regard is my selfe, it is the Microcosme of mine owne frame, that I cast mine eye on; for the other, I use it but like my Globe, and turne it round sometimes for my recreation" (*Religio Medici* 2.11). Both have the sense of the greatness of humankind, of man as microcosm, and of man as possessing the external world for his own contemplation, even his own amusement. But whereas Thoreau speaks fancifully—"as it were"— Browne insists on his point. Whereas Browne can engage in a dazzling series of statements, even drawing, in the view of some, too much attention to himself, Thoreau works allusively, evocatively, or at other times exhorting his readers to share a vision nearly lost.

It might seem that Thoreau is humorous and witty in the modern sense, making a somewhat superficial use of Renaissance conceits, whereas Browne is grandly rhetorical and ceremonial, witty in the metaphysical sense. But the author of *Walden,* I would argue, is not primarily an imitator of such metaphysical or baroque stylists as Browne but, rather, a latter-day apostle who seeks to impart something of their vision to his own contemporaries. Of the dual reality of life and the failure of others to grasp it, Thoreau wrote: "Men esteem truth remote, in the outskirts of the system, behind the farthest star, before Adam and after the last man. In eternity there is indeed something true and sublime. But all these times and places and occasions are now and here" (96–97). Thoreau's self-assumed task is to make his readers aware of the presence of eternity—by exhortation, by juxtaposition, by implicit and explicit reference; in so doing he presses his prose to its limits, saying what can be said, but also pointing beyond to what cannot be said. Thus, for all his "dazzling inventiveness," in Poirier's phrase, he is still the practitioner of an old craft, and the articulator of an old view of the cosmos, one who believes "that men are generally still a little afraid of the dark, though the witches are all hung, and Christianity and candles have been introduced" (130–31).[25]

VI

BURTON
The Anatomy of Melancholy
"I Have Overshot My Selfe"

IF GENERIC QUESTIONS are particularly vexed for Renaissance nonfiction prose, they are almost overwhelming for *The Anatomy of Melancholy*. The first, the unavoidable, question to be asked is, What kind of work is it? How shall we classify, categorize, even describe it? Under what genre can it usefully be considered? These questions may partake equally of the scholarly and the incredulous, for Burton's *Anatomy* seems to defy its categories, and the range of critical accounts of it is unusually large and daunting. Some may find it a classifying, ordering project, an encyclopedic effort, the work of someone who is trying to get things under control. Others, looking not only at the synopsis but at the text itself, argue that it is manifestly *not* under control, a judgment made on the basis of both style and structure, by virtue of Burton's additions, expansions, multiplications of examples, of the *Anatomy*'s contradictions in tone and method.

Questions about the nature and focus of the *Anatomy* abound. Is the subject, the method, or the author at the center? In Burton's own day the work was known as Burton's *Melancholy*, a designation by subject, not as Burton's *Anatomy*, its usual short title today.[1] Burton's text is on the one hand immensely personal and idiosyncratic; on the other, enormously dependent on authority. Does Burton cite authority simply for the sake of completeness, because it is there, because Renaissance authors habitually turned to authority as a first step in any inquiry? Does the citation of authority lend credence to Burton's proceeding or, as has been argued, does it undermine it? Are we intended to judge one source against another, to arrive at some kind of conclusion? Or are we intended to see that authorities contradict one another, leaving us in perplexity and amazement? If we cannot determine Burton's attitude toward his subject, what about that toward the reader? There is enough inconsistency in the presentation of Democritus Junior to the Reader to render doubtful almost any generalization that might be made. And even if we could arrive at such a judgment, the preface is but a small part of the work, leaving us to ask whether a persona is maintained throughout the work or only in the preface, a satirical introduction to a more scholarly text.

The question of genre has been answered quite straightforwardly, if somewhat prematurely, by those who point out that *The Anatomy of Melancholy* is a systematic dissection of a subject (as implied by the technical term *anatomy*), and a subject, as has frequently been noted, that was of great interest in the later sixteenth and earlier seventeenth centuries.[2] Others have simply labeled it "a handbook of hygiene." But whatever comfort we may find in the simple designation of this work as "a manual of hygiene" or "a systematic treatment" is largely of the past; more recent descriptions of the *Anatomy* are more complex, if not always more cautious.[3] Critical discussions of the *Anatomy* range from those that judge it a unified but complex work to those that judge it a testimony to the inadequacy of human powers of comprehension or an indication of the author's inadequacy. Some have stressed its encyclopedic qualities, the attempt to comprehend all human knowledge at the last possible moment; others, its analytical quality. It has been associated with satire, with the tradition of learned paradox, with works that classify and with those that collect.[4]

Without for the moment choosing among this wide range of critical opinion, I would suggest that its very existence points to the complexity of the *Anatomy*. And rather than attempting to determine the single category into which the work fits, we may do better to observe that Burton's *Anatomy* has a rather special relationship to genre itself, that it tests and modifies our sense not only of itself but of generic boundaries, and that its very indeterminacy is an important part of its effect. The most likely reaction to the *Anatomy*, I think, is that it doesn't fit, easily or helpfully, into any of the categories to which it might seem to belong or conform clearly to any description of it. Despite Rosalie Colie's impressively learned account of the traditions of paradoxes within which Burton writes, finally the conventional notions of paradox sound rather neater than Burton's sprawling and uncontrolled work. Even Devon Hodges's useful discussion of Renaissance anatomies as works that deconstruct their subjects fails to account for what other readers have found in Burton—a unity in disunity, a complexity of parts and whole.[5] Rather than conforming to a particular genre or a method, even a tradition of paradox, or certainly to the context of Christian humanism, Burton's text seems to challenge and undo rather than merely follow or conform to genre. Critical accounts of Burton's *Anatomy* resemble those of a group of blind men describing a very large elephant: it's not that they're untrue, but that they fail to do justice to the whole.[6]

Beyond the complex questions of genre and kind, even coming to terms with the structure of Burton's work is problematic. On the one hand *The Anatomy of Melancholy* has a large and carefully conceived formal organization: its three partitions are subdivided into numerous sections, members, and subsections; a synopsis precedes each partition. The partitions treat, respectively, the causes of melancholy, its remedies, and then the two major divisions: religious melancholy and love melancholy. But as we look more closely at that structure, several peculiarities appear: in its large features, the form is inconsistent, nonparallel; the third division deals with two particular aspects of the first and second.[7] Moreover, the synopsis, which ought to supply a helpful overview, in fact demonstrates the impossibility of such an overview. There is, at first glance, a binary scheme of division and classification: the causes of melancholy are either supernatural or natural, primary or secondary, inward or outward, general or particular.[8] But these neat subdivisions quickly proliferate into a bewildering multitude of specifics, making it nearly impossible for us to comprehend either the general outlines of the subject or its most salient points. Moreover, in that synopsis, the system of binary oppositions breaks down. For example, with regard to diseases, Burton considers their causes (subsection 1) or their definition, number, division (subsection 2); they are of the body or of the mind (there being reckoned to be three hundred of the former, Burton proposes to deal with the latter); they are epidemical or particular; in disposition or in habits: these habits may include dotage, frenzy, madness, ecstasy, lycanthropia, chorus *sancti viti,* hydrophobia, possession or obsession of devils, or melancholy. At this point we realize that something has gone dreadfully wrong with the scheme of categorization that was supposed to help us through this maze. Burton, the professional scholar, the practiced writer, seems unable to handle the basics of the outline form, for he mixes the largest of categories—dotage, frenzy, madness, ecstasy—with particular ailments—lycanthropia, chorus *sancti viti,* and hydrophobia. The synopsis, rather than enabling us to comprehend the subject, in fact demonstrates its nearly infinite complexity; it becomes an epitome of the text rather than a road map of it.

Despite its large and impressive structure, problematic in itself, *The Anatomy of Melancholy* is also a very personal and idiosyncratic work, so much so that a good deal of the discussion of it has centered on the persona of Democritus Junior developed in the preface. That persona is self-contradictory, deliberately shifting and volatile, alternately cajoling and insulting the reader: "Gentle Reader, I presume thou wilt be very inquisitive to know what Anticke or Personate Actor this is, that so insolently intrudes upon this common Theater, to the worlds view, arrogating another mans name, whence hee is, why he doth it, and what he hath to say? Although, as he said, *Primum si noluero, non respondebo, quis coacturus est?* I am a free man borne, and may chuse whether I will tell, who can compell me?"[9] Burton goes on: "Yet in some sort to give thee satisfaction, which is more then I need, I will shew a reason, both of this usurped Name, Title, and Subject." The persona here suggests that we may wish to know—though we may have no such wish; he then insists on telling us—though he tells us he need not. And then he explains that he tells us because we wish—though he does so not out of necessity but voluntarily—yet plainly, grudgingly. Although Bridget Gellert Lyons and Lawrence Babb point out the roots of such proceeding in the persona of satire, even the unsuspicious or untheoretical reader may here join with Stanley Fish in feeling some sense of victimization, or at least deliberately induced bewilderment.[10]

But beyond the persona of Democritus Junior there are also tensions and contradictions apparent in Burton's method, his attitude toward his material. In the *Anatomy*, Burton collected a vast amount of information and opinion, stacking into his text whatever authorities he could find for symptoms, causes, and remedies. Yet precisely what we are to do with that material remains in doubt, for he does not adjudicate among these sources and recommendations: sometimes he arranges them pro and con, but so fascinated is he with the process of finding them that he frequently fails to take note of their areas of disagreement. Burton adheres, as one would expect, to the method of gathering authoritative opinions (in the sense of "mine author saith") on his subject; but once the instances are assembled, he leaves us to determine the outcome ourselves.[11]

Such a combination of methods may well leave a reader undecided as to the essence of Burton's work, combining as it does the medical and psychological, prescriptive and descriptive aspects of the subject. In undertaking to study melancholy, Burton deals with one of the favorite

Burton: *The Anatomy of Melancholy*

maladies of his time, one that a number of other writers (most notably Timothy Bright) also dealt with, the current medical-psychological-spiritual crisis.[12] But melancholy, as Burton presents it, is on the one hand a disease, an abnormal state; on the other hand, it is the universal state of humanity. When Burton begins the first section of the work proper with the Fall of Man, we know he is dealing with more than a mere aberration, albeit a widespread one. Taking the robe of the satirist Democritus, Burton writes, "Never so much cause of laughter, as now, never so many fooles and mad-men" (1.37); and "thou shalt soone perceive that all the world is mad, that it is melancholy, dotes" (1.24). So at the heart of this work is the central paradox that the aberration, the ailment Burton treats, is in fact universal; not only has he, as he says, "anatomized mine own folly" (1.112) but that of all the world alike.

Finally, the studied indeterminacy of the *Anatomy* has generic implications. The delineation of the audience is, perhaps deliberately, unstable: Burton writes of melancholy "by being busie to avoid Melancholy" (1.6); in other words, he intends to cure himself. Yet among the many contradictory reasons for undertaking this project is a desire to "spend my time and knowledge, which are my greatest fortunes, for the common good of all" (1.8). But later on he warns those who are melancholy to avoid, above all things, reading his book; yet, characteristically, the advice comes rather late, toward the end of the First Partition, and was not added until the third edition.[13] It's also clear from the very general kinds of prescriptions offered in the sections on cures that Burton intends something closer to a survey of the literature, of medical opinion, rather than a practical handbook, of which many were available. Thus Burton writes of a disease that is not only widespread but universal and to an audience that dare not read it for fear of being infected; he writes ostensibly for the public good but chiefly to please himself.

The point in all this is not that Burton does not quite know how to organize his material nor to whom he wishes to write; the point is not only that the subject is overwhelming. It may well be, as Bamborough suggests, that the moment for encyclopedic knowledge had passed and thus that the work testifies to the impossibility of comprehending our experience, but there's also a sense in which Burton's method is quite dramatically at odds with itself. One may attempt to comprehend a subject either with general truths or with specific examples, but of course every specific example breeds the fear that one may have forgotten another specific example; thus the very descent into particulars, which ought to be the stamp of completeness, in fact suggests incompleteness. There's something of the sorcerer's apprentice here: the more divisions of the subject, the more divisions are needed for completeness. If the subject is infinitely various, we seem always to have a gogolplex of examples; if x would comprehend the topic, we have, Burton seems to fear, $x-1$.[14]

What I'm suggesting, then, is not that Burton got it wrong—he seems to have got it right enough to fascinate readers for the better part of four hundred years—nor even that it was not possible to get it right, though this may well be the case—but that Burton has used a strategy that undoes itself, an attempt at order that manifests disorder, a striving for completeness that testifies to incompleteness. There are significant ways in which Burton's uses of structure, tone, persona, and genre are discordant, incongruous, shifting. I'd like to suggest also that we have here not just a particular method, nor a failure of method, but a dynamic interaction with a method, a choice that is ongoing, in which both readers and author interact with the text. Moreover, one may see such interaction not only in the preface of Democritus Junior to the Reader, which has received a disproportionate share of the critical attention bestowed on Burton, but also in the main body of the *Anatomy*.

The Anatomy of Melancholy, structurally speaking, is not a mistake but a paradox. Burton's performance in this work is perhaps the opposite of the art that hides art, the flawless performance that looks perfectly easy. The *Anatomy* has all of the trappings of the academy—a complete and obtrusive structure, plenty of apparatus to suggest an impersonal and scholarly discourse, citations of authority, references, footnotes, quotations in Latin, and thousands of precedents. But for all this structure, Burton's text is incredibly messy, unwieldy, disproportionate, decentered, bewildering. The last word on melancholy is finally inconclusive; the citation of authority produces no unanimity. This is so much the case that some readers have suggested that Burton's purpose is to undermine and discredit authority.[15] But no man ever loved it more: Burton cites authorities enthusiastically for one position, and then, just as enthusiastically, for the opposing position. He finds support for the bizarre and unlikely—that his mother's remedy of "a Spider, in a nut-shell lapped in silke" would cure an ague (2.254)—and the totally obvious, as with his citation of Montaigne, Aristotle, and "his learned Country-man *Adrian Turnebus*" (1.4) to embellish the truism that it's good to be well-rounded.

Rather than constituting a campaign against authority or even a subtle undermining of it, Burton's work represents, in my view, a fascination with process, with detail, with discovery, rather than with conclusion or resolution. Not only does Burton use structure in conflicting and perplexing ways: he is also at once explicitly concerned with boundaries and notably transgressive of them. He sets up three partitions of his subject, then deviates from ordinary parallel structure. He begins with binary opposition, only to move into a myriad of detail. He juxtaposes an elaborate formal structure with equally elaborate and extended digressions: a Utopia in the preface, a digression of the miseries of scholars in partition 1, a Digression of the Air in partition 2, a long disquisition on the nature of love in partition 3, from which Burton himself awakes, deep into a discussion of lust and abuse of wives: "But what have I to doe with this?" (3.117). Repeatedly, he interrupts himself with such phrases as "I have overshot my selfe, I have spoken foolishly, rashly, unadvisedly, absurdly, I have anatomized mine own folly" (1.112); "But I rove" (3.28); "But this is not the matter in hand" (3.77); "But to leave all these phantasticall raptures, Ile prosequute mine intended Theame" (3.95); "But I am over tedious, I confesse" (3.103).

To some extent this locution becomes a way of organizing material, of forcefully returning to the subject from which he has strayed, a transition, as it were, by a writer who has diverged from his planned outline; but it is also Burton's way of calling attention to what he is doing. We are not simply reading what Burton and the numerous authorities he cites have to tell us about melancholy; we are watching Burton tell us what he has to tell us, about melancholy or any other subject he cares to pursue. Just as Democritus Junior tells us early on "Thou thy selfe art the subject of my Discourse" (1.1), so Burton himself and his method become the subject of interest, and such shifts and contradictions help define the essence of his text.

The Anatomy of Melancholy, then, combines an enormous and apparently impersonal structure with an idiosyncratic, intrusive, highly characterized voice. Burton, especially in the preface but also throughout his vast work, is a consummate showman, changing masks rapidly, not so much to deceive as to call our attention to the process of masking. Of himself he says, "I confesse all ('tis partly affected) thou canst not think worse of me then I doe of my selfe" (1.12). Of his book he says, "'Tis not worth the reading, I yeeld it, I desire thee not to loose time in perusing so vaine a subject, I should bee peradventure loth my selfe to read him or thee, so writing, 'tis not *operæ pretium* [worth while]" (1.12). But in the next sentence: "All I say, is this, that I have presidents for it . . . others as absurd, vaine, idle, illiterate, &c. . . . others have done as much, it may be more, and perhaps thou thy selfe" (1.12). He both assimilates his voice to that of Democritus (in the long passage of descriptive biography) and distances himself from it, as he claims, "'tis not I, but *Democritus, Democritus dixit*" (1.110).

Like Sterne a century later, Burton goes out of his way to strain the boundaries of his organization, to arouse expectations and to deviate from them, to set off in one direction and suddenly to veer off in another, to follow the lead of his subject and its vagaries rather than its formal divisions. Perhaps the most pronounced example of this tendency is in the Digression of the Air, which begins famously with an extended simile depicting extravagant (in Thoreau's sense) or extracurricular motion: "As a long-winged Hawke when hee is first whistled off the fist, mounts aloft, and for his pleasure fetcheth many a circuit in the Ayre, still soaring higher and higher, till hee bee come to his full pitch; and in the end when the game is sprung, comes downe amaine, and stoopes upon a sudden: so will I, having now come at last into these ample fields of Ayre, wherein I may freely expatiate and exercise my selfe, for my recreation a while rove, wander round about the world, mount aloft to those æthereall orbes and celestiall spheres, and so descend to my former elements againe" (2.33). As described in this suspended sentence, the hawk's large expansive motion, out of its normal circuit, yet returning to it, is the model of Burton's method; it's an image of purposeful wandering but also of free movement, just as Burton's digressions range widely yet function within the larger context.[16]

The Digression of the Air also literally and figuratively tests the limits of Burton's project: whereas the *Anatomy* as a whole treats a very large subject, melancholy, which afflicts the entire human race, this digression deals with an even wider subject, all of human knowledge; it moves from the partial to the whole. In this digression Burton undertakes to resolve all unanswered questions, beginning with the most fanciful and extravagant: "In which progresse, I will first see whether that relation of the Frier of *Oxford* be true, concerning those Northerne parts under the Pole (if I meet *obitèr* with the wandering *Jew, Elias artifex,* or *Lucians Icaromenippus,* they shall be my guids)" (2.33). He also pursues the old and new questions of geography, astronomy, botany, zoology, and geology; he ponders the migration of birds, the place of the terrestrial paradise, the numbers of stars, the nature of the universe and the nature of God until he realizes, "my game is sprung, and I must suddenly come downe and follow" (2.58). In this investigation not only the subject but also the method diverges strikingly from that of the rest of the work: whereas throughout the *Anatomy* Burton relies on accumulated knowledge and the citation of authority, he here resolves to go and find out for himself.

The Digression of the Air strains our sense of the nature of the work in another way: whereas the *Anatomy* in toto is a philosophical or (in the old sense) scientific exploration, within which Burton's personal comments, frequent as they are, seem digressive, the Digression of the Air is both avowedly personal and remarkably universal. It's precisely within the section that proposes to investigate all the large questions of human knowledge that Burton reveals the most detailed information about himself: the place of his birth, the name of his grammar school, the parish he serves, his patroness, his tutor at Oxford, the identity and residence of his older brother. By this means the universal is intimately tied to the particular, and the idiosyncratic becomes a pattern for the general.

Given the scholarly context in which he wrote, and looking at the contradictions and inconsistencies within his work, some scholars have come to the conclusion that Burton concentrated his organizational powers in the synopsis, in the dividing of the topic, but felt no need to create coherence or consistency between the subdivisions.[17] Once Burton has established the large structure of his work with the aid of Ramist dichotomies, the theory goes, the movement of individual passages is regulated by another principle altogether. But the manifest inconsistency within sections, I would argue, goes beyond mere unconcern, and derives rather from Burton's particular approach to his subject, from his fascination with specifics. Burton's usual habit of moving is from a principle to an example to a principle; but very often the second principle contradicts the first because the examples, which flow into each other, shift the ground of the argument. In reading the *Anatomy* one moves as with the tides, through huge swathes of examples, through long paragraphs punctuated by sudden shifts of topic or mood; these topics, if we check, do indeed bear some relation to the outline, but one is far more likely to be caught up in the specifics of the discussion than to have a sense of it as a larger whole.

Numerous examples of this antimethod might be found: perhaps one of the most startling is Burton's treatment of the permissibility of suicide, in which he lists, with his usual thoroughness, the reasons why suicide might be allowable, coming perilously close to endorsing it, only to conclude, briefly, with the orthodox position (1.434–38). Another striking instance is the discussion of the various excesses of diet that lead to melancholy: in the midst of very detailed advice about what one should eat and not eat (mostly the latter), Burton tells us, in effect, to eat what we like. The general thrust of the section is to advocate moderation in diet, but then Burton offers the bit of advice that undermines all advice: "When all is said *pro* and *con*, *Cardans* rule is best, to keepe that wee are accustomed unto, though it be naught, and to follow our disposition and appetite in some things is not amisse, to eat sometimes of a dish which is hurtfull, if we have an extraordinary liking to it" (2.27). Burton concludes with a statement that would seem to cast doubt on his whole enterprise, to call the reader a fool for even reading this book, for asking advice well into middle age: "I conclude, our owne experience is the best Physitian, that diet which is most propitious to one, is often pernitious to another, such is the variety of palats, humors, and temperatures, let every man observe and be a law unto himselfe. *Tiberius* in *Tacitus* did laugh at all such, that after 30 yeares of age, would aske counsell of others, concerning matters of diet: I say the same" (2.27). Without going so far as Stanley Fish to see this text as simply manipulative, one can certainly see it as radically unstable, shifting in its emphasis. Indeed, the passage I've just quoted precedes yet further contradictory advice: "These few rules of diet he that keepes shall surely finde great ease & speedy remedy by it" (2.27). Burton combines overwhelming citation of conflicting authority with the commendation of common sense, of that which needs no written authority. He documents the variability of human preference and temperament, the instability of human moods; he gives an abundance of good advice and announces that every man must choose for himself.

Bridget Gellert Lyons has suggested that Burton not only writes of melancholy but also represents the mad and melancholy subject.[18] But rather than finding in Burton's text a calculated representation of such disorder, I would suggest that, if there is a mad quality to Burton's proceeding, it consists in the intensity of his focus, the absolute concentration on whatever quality or problem concerns him at the moment. His work is not only encyclopedic, it is obsessive; but it is also whimsical, remarkably responsive to the subject. It is, quite literally, enthusiastic: Burton always loses sight of the forest for the trees, even for the ferns and moss on the ground, as he attempts to provide examples of the principles he cites.

Burton: *The Anatomy of Melancholy*

But this approach, I would argue, is precisely how Burton finds, rather than loses, himself, and how the *Anatomy* achieves its characteristic form. Just as Burton's prose is often sequential, end-linked with one phrase spinning off into the next, rather than being clearly part of a large overarching periodic or even paratactic structure, so also one idea leads to another. Often a passage as a whole will seem to be organized by free association, by a process that leads to a quite different position by the end of the section from that stated at the beginning. Burton's prose re-creates, if not the actual movement of his mind, at least a very convincing replica of the sequence of thought, with all its attendant contradictions. For example, in the discussion of idleness and leisure as a cause of melancholy (1.2.2.6), idleness is first "the bane of body and minde, the nurse of naughtinesse, stepmother of discipline, the chiefe author of all mischiefe, one of the seaven deadly sinnes" (1.238). Burton moves then from idleness to solitariness, whether enforced or voluntary, the state of students and members of monastic communities, for whom solitariness is "very irkesome," "most tedious" (1.242). But in the next paragraph, solitariness becomes increasingly positive, so that we soon find ourselves deep in the mood of Milton's *Il Penseroso,* which strongly resembles this passage: "most pleasant it is at first, to such as are Melancholy given, to ly in bed whole daies, and keepe their chambers, to walke alone in some solitary grove, betwixt wood and water, by a brooke side, to meditate upon some delightsome and pleasant subject, which shall affect them most" (1.243).[19]

Burton concludes the sequence with two oxymoronic Latin phrases, *amabilis insania* and *mentis gratissimus error,* which stress both error and delight; but in contrast to his initial negative statement, he now emphasizes delight, the pleasures of letting the mind run in idyllic daydreams. By mid-paragraph, what was lately an irksome nuisance is a veritable paradise, a heaven on earth, a state approved by the Church fathers; the monastery, two pages before likened to a prison, is something whose loss is to be regretted, no longer the seat of idleness and sin but the guardian of civilization. And then, just when we think stability has been reached, Burton's weather vane swings round again as he bethinks himself, recalling the original direction of his argument: "This solitude undoeth us, *pugnat cum vitâ sociali,* 'tis a destructive solitarinesse" (1.245). Although Burton reverts, at the last, to his original point, the section as a whole has moved by free association rather than logic.

It has often been observed that Burton, following humanist practice, feels no need to be true to the meaning in context of the passages he quotes. But it's not just a question of Burton's imposing a meaning on such passages or distorting an original context to make a point; on the contrary, the examples and illustrations he cites often alter the direction of his presentation. The passage just considered does not show a writer who chooses to present the pros and cons of his subject as prelude to a conclusive judgment, nor even one who is overwhelmed by his material, but rather a writer who enters into his material so fully and imaginatively that he follows it wherever it takes him, who offers a sense of completeness of process rather than of finality.

Burton's citation of authority, like everything else in his work, is, by modern standards, even by Ramist standards, excessive. If Burton knows it, he will report it. If a source exists, he'll cite it. Whatever the apparent structure of the synopsis, an attempt to impose order on the material, Burton's method within the text is to let the process of exploration and discovery deeply influence the method of presentation. Burton is, one might say, a genuine go-with-the-flow sort of writer. This is, of course, the process he describes in Democritus Junior to the Reader, with reference to his own prose style: "So that as a River runnes sometimes precipitate and swift, then dull and slow; now direct, then *per ambages;* now deepe, then shallow; now muddy, then cleare; now broad, then narrow; doth my stile flow: now serious, then light; now Comicall, then Satyricall; now more elaborate, then remisse, as the present subject required, or as at that time I was affected" (1.18).

This famous passage, in which Burton defines his mode of writing, is the one most quoted to exemplify what such critics as George Williamson and Morris Croll have called the loose Senecan style.[20] This style is associated with the essay rather than with oratory, with meditation or discovery rather than with formal presentation or persuasion. It is predominantly paratactic; that is, the units of a sentence are not heavily or normally subordinated; they tend rather to be of equal weight. We do not feel a good deal of formal patterning, a sense of a large and comprehensive design; we do not need to wait for the end of the sentence to know what its overall design is. Rather, this style uses a good many end-linked units; the method of composition is additive, with one idea or phrase flowing out of the one that precedes it. But as others have noticed, this style, or rather this group of styles, is not simply an absence of style: though not creating a grand design that can be sensed early on, it has a rhetorical and emotional force of its own.

Burton: *The Anatomy of Melancholy*

The self-defining sentence from Burton just quoted certainly has its own rhythm and beautifully functional structure. It uses a good deal of parallelism, creating both balance and contrast ("now deepe, then shallow; now muddy, then cleare," etc.); it gives us the feeling of almost endless contrast without any sense of disorder. Although Burton asserts that he merely follows his subject wherever it takes him, allowing his manner to accord with his matter, he also suggests a more active role, as he attends not only to the variety of his material but also to the variations of his own mood, for part of his subject is himself: "[So] doth my stile flow: now serious, then light; now Comicall, then Satyricall; now more elaborate, then remisse, as the present subject required, *or as at that time I was affected*" (emphasis mine). Subsequently, Democritus Junior depicts himself not only as following his material through its rich intricacies but also as conveying his reader: "And if thou vouchsafe to read this Treatise, it shall seeme no otherwise to thee, then the way to an ordinary Traveller, sometimes faire, sometimes foule; here champion, there inclosed; barren in one place, better soyle in another: by Woods, Groves, Hills, Dales, Plaines, &c. I shall lead thee *per ardua montium, & lubrica vallium, & roscida cespitum, & glebosa camporum,* through variety of objects, that which thou shalt like and surely dislike" (1.18).

Although Burton stresses the spontaneous responsiveness of his style, and although that is how it is likely to strike a reader, the subsequent editions of the *Anatomy* provide strong evidence of careful crafting, showing how Burtonian effervescence anticipates the calculated, self-conscious breeziness of Laurence Sterne. In his preface Burton cultivates a variety of moods and voices, alternating between a stance in which he takes no responsibility for what he writes and one in which his refusal to take any such responsibility becomes remarkably assertive, even aggressive or hostile. Burton begins: "I am . . . a loose, plaine, rude writer, *ficum voco ficum, & ligonem ligonem* [I call a fig a fig and a spade a spade], and as free, as loose, *idem calamo quod in mente* [what my mind thinks my pen writes], I call a spade a spade, *animis hæc scribo, non auribus* [I write for the mind, not the ear], I respect matter not words; remembring that of *Cardan, verba propter res, non res propter verba:* and seeking with *Seneca, quid scribam, non quemadmodum,* rather what, then how to write" (1.17).

About this disarming and apparently ingenuous statement several points must be made. It is of course a topos (witness the citation of Seneca and Cardan); Burton, making the rhetorician's oldest move, places himself in the company of Othello, who was rude in his speech, and Polonius, who used no art at all; he asserts his spontaneity with the help of learned authority. And the topos, as so often, has a certain measure of irony, an almost comic quality, for while it is true that Burton has shunned many of the flowers of rhetoric, "jingling termes, tropes, [and] strong lines," nevertheless, the line "I respect matter not words" in the preface to a text that runs to hundreds of thousands of words must bring a smile. In asserting that he writes as he thinks, Burton takes the dominant rhetorical position of his day, joining with the anti-Ciceronians, who affirmed the importance of what was said rather than how it was said. His statement marks a distinction between the oratorical and the meditative or exploratory mode, and it serves as an assertion of modesty.

To be sure, Burton respects matter, case histories, and learned opinion. But he also demonstrates an abiding fondness for the written word, having chosen to spend his life with it and to build his work, not just with large ideas, but with multitudes of examples, instances, terms, and phrases, having chosen to note in his own books particularly striking examples of language. The annotations in his copy of Dekker's *The Belman of London,* for example, consist of lists of words and phrases that he found especially interesting; Burton also recorded the language of the streets, the language of canting, the language of beggars—all suggesting his fascination with forms and levels of language.[21] He even went so far as to note in the back of an early edition the increasing bulk of his text.[22]

Burton's love of words recalls Francis Bacon's remark about men lying, not out of utility, "but [from] a naturall, though corrupt Love, of the Lie it selfe."[23] We read Burton not for what he tells us about melancholy, nor for consolation—perhaps for the piquancy of his anecdotes—but chiefly for the rich and various texture of his prose. For Burton, language is essentially macaronic, carnivalesque, celebratory, and inherently vital; what keeps his prose lively, amid the proliferation of instances and examples, is the deliberate mingling of English and Latin, formal and colloquial speech.[24] As Burton says, "'Tis all mine and none mine," "I have laboriously collected this *Cento* out of divers Writers.... *aliud tamen quàm unde sumptum sit apparet* [yet it becomes something different in its new setting]" (1.11).

The following passage, in which Burton articulates his stylistic position, will demonstrate the characteristic mingling of levels of language,

Burton: *The Anatomy of Melancholy*

authority and opinion, and the way in which ideas and examples germinate in his prose:

> He respects matter, thou art wholly for words, hee loves a loose and free stile, thou art all for neat composition, strong Lines, hyperboles, allegories; he desires a fine Frontispiece, entising pictures, such as *Hieron: Natali* the Jesuite hath cut to the Dominicalls, to draw on the Readers attention, which thou rejectest, that which one admires, another explodes as most absurd and ridiculous. If it be not point blanke to his humour, his method, his conceit, *Si quid forsan omissum, quod is animo conceperit, si quæ dictio, &c.* If ought bee omitted or added, which he likes or dislikes, thou art *mancipium paucæ lectionis,* an Idiot, an Asse, *nullus es,* or *plagiarius,* a trifler, a trivant, thou art an idle fellow; or else 'tis a thing of meere industrie, a collection without wit or invention, a very toy. (1.13)

In this elaboration of the basic principle that there's no accounting for tastes, Burton begins with a balance and opposition between the two views, between "he" (who respects matter) and "thou" (who art wholly for words). The pattern is stated twice, the second time with elaboration; in the third use of the pattern, the centrifugal force of the examples makes the sentence spin out of its orbit: there is no "thou" to answer to "he desires a fine Frontispiece." Burton finally counters with "which thou rejectest," but the first half of the equation has overwhelmed the second, and the parallelism is destroyed, both by the unlike phrasing—"he desires," "which thou rejectest"—and by the amount of space given to each. The second sentence continues this disrupted pattern, giving us not so much a balance of forces as a kind of dramatic encounter, as Burton builds up the niggling insistence of the one side, "If it be not point blanke to his humour, his method, his conceit," followed by the insult to the other, "thou art *mancipium paucæ lectionis,* an Idiot, an Asse." On the one hand the sentences here are carefully constructed to represent parallelism and opposition; on the other hand they convey a sense of great energy, vitality, and spontaneity. And that vitality is communicated not only by the syntax but by the movement between Latin and English, between the relatively elevated "'tis a thing of meere industrie," "a collection without wit or invention" and the colloquial "a very toy," "point blanke," "an Asse," "cut to the Dominicalls." The joy of careful construction is at least matched by the eruptive enthusiasm of epithet. This kind of energetic variation, this rich presentation of the subject, is repeated on every page of the *Anatomy*. Burton indeed respects matter, not words, but the matter that he deals with and loves is words, words, words, and the energy of his prose reflects and reenacts the excitement of that encounter, which for Burton is the center of his intellectual and psychic life.

Burton's ongoing involvement with the words of his text may be seen even more forcefully in his many revisions.[25] In Democritus Junior to the Reader, Burton apologizes for the roughness of the style: "Another maine fault is, that I have not revised the Copie, and amended the stile, which now flowes remisly, as it was first conceived, but my leasure would not permit" (1.16). But like so much else in the *Anatomy*, this spontaneous apology is carefully constructed: it occurs in a passage that was moved from its original place in the Conclusion (of 1621) to the preface (in 1624) and remained in that position thereafter. Burton not only retained the apology for roughness of copy and want of time in all subsequent editions, he also added to it, not by way of polishing, but by way of emphasizing the disjunctions and dichotomies in his work.

In 1624 Burton wrote of his book, "I confesse it is neither as I would, or as it should be" (1.16). In the same edition he brought in verses from the conclusion that profess embarrassment: "When I peruse this Tract which I have writ, / I am abash'd, and much I hold unfit." In 1628 he inserted after these two confessional sections an additional apology: "*Et quod gravissimum*, in the matter it selfe, many things I disallow at this present, which then I writ, *Non eadem est aetas, non mens*, I would willingly retract much, &c. but 'tis too late, I can only crave pardon now for what is amisse." While Burton cut, pasted, moved, and spliced and while he continued to lament the state of his work, the text of this apology either stayed substantially the same or grew. In 1621 Burton confessed in the Conclusion: "[I] was enforced as a Beare doth her whelpes, to bring forth this confused lumpe, and had not space to licke it into forme, as she doth her young ones; but even so to publish it, as it was written at first, once for all, in an extemporanean stile, *quicquid in buccam venit*, as I doe commonly all other exercises, *stans pede in uno*, as hee made verses, out of a confused company of notes, *effudi quicquid dictavit Genius meus*, and writ with as small deliberation, as I doe ordinarily speake." In 1624 Burton moved this section into the Preface and appended to it "without all affectation of big words, fustian phrases, jingling termes, strong lines, strains of wit." To a list of things absent from his prose Burton added in 1628 "brave heats, elegancies"; to "exornations," which had been put in in 1624, he added "hyperbolical." In 1632 the existing "strong lines" was further modified: "that like *Acestas'* arrows caught fire as they flew."

In short, a careful comparison of editions reveals that Burton did indeed revise his text. He obviously reread it with care, and although he hardly ever blotted out a line, he added a good many. It has been argued that Burton made a good many changes for stylistic reasons, that he was more in control of his text in the 1624 edition than in the 1621.[26] But without denying that Burton was a conscious stylist—one who cultivated the appearance of spontaneity—I find a good many cases of the text simply building on itself, of one example or phrase inviting another, even though the point has already been sufficiently made. By and large Burton tended not to polish his text, to control its extravagances, but rather to affirm them. It is often precisely where he has made his point most clearly, fully, and adequately, that Burton adds a phrase here, a word there, a full-fledged example to demonstrate yet again the truth of what he has been saying. For example, having expressed the wish in 1621 to "have revised the copie, and amended the stile," Burton went on in 1624 to add (by bringing in material from the Conclusion): "I should indeed (had I wisely done), observed that Precept of the Poet, *nonumque prematur in annum,* and have taken more care: or, as Alexander the Physitian would have done by *Lapis Lazuli,* fifty times washed before it be used, I should have revised, corrected, and amended this tract; but I had not (as I say) that happy leisure, no *Amanuenses* [or] assistants." Surely the point has been made; but in 1628, Burton adds an illustrative anecdote, a benign version of the story of the sorcerer's apprentice, to which he appends: "I have no such skill to make new men at my pleasure, or meanes to hire them; no whistle to call like the Master of a Ship, & bid them runne, &c. I have no such authority." Then in 1632, Burton adds, "no such Benefactors, as that noble *Ambrosius* was to *Origen,* allowing him six or seven *Amanuenses* to write out his dictats, I must for that cause doe my busines my selfe." In short, in this passage Burton does not change or even modify the sense, but he surely expands the examples by which he demonstrates his point.

As the cases I have cited illustrate, there are sections of the text, many of them, that are in fact constructed like a mosaic, out of series of additions to the original. Sometimes the additions are large chunks, a sentence or a paragraph; sometimes they consist of a single word or phrase. In the 1628 edition (1.32) Burton changes the word *heads* to *pates;* in 1624 he adds, "their habitations like Mole-hills, the men as Emmets," but he had already made the point sufficiently by comparing human cities to "so many Hives of Bees." If there is a general tendency in these revisions, it is perhaps a movement toward the more colloquial, but there is also a nearly irresistible impulse on Burton's part to modify the text itself. Burton seems to have been his own most responsive reader, one for whom lines already written call forth a sympathetic or elaborating response. There is an almost antiphonal quality to his text, a fact much more evident in the original editions, which, with the convention of italicizing quotation and the presence of marginal notes, give a sense of the exchanges between Burton and the authors he quotes, just as a study of the revisions gives a sense of dialogue between Burton and his own text.

I have been arguing that Burton's text is dialogic throughout, that he could not read his own prose without responding and adding to it, and that such ongoing responsiveness links him with Sterne. That link is seen both in the revisionary quality of Burton's text and in its cultivation of a persona. The conclusion of the preface, a long passage in which Democritus Junior bids farewell to the reader, alternately placating and insulting him, demonstrates especially dramatically the nature of Burton's revisions and his playful but intense interaction with text and reader. As in the revisions previously considered, Burton did not first create one impression that he later modified; rather, the contradictions were there from the beginning but were emphasized and sharpened by the additions. Burton initially acknowledges the danger of his project, noting that "I am sure some will object, [to it as] too phantasticall, *too light and Comicall for a divine, too Satyricall for one of my profession.*" And he takes shelter with Erasmus under the excuse "'tis not I, but *Democritus, Democritus dixit*" (1.110). But in his revisions Burton sharpens both the offensive matter and the apologetic phrases. In 1621 he had written, "If I doe a little forget my selfe, I hope you will pardon it" (1.110); but in 1624 he prefaced this sentence with the somewhat harsher "Take heed you mistake me not," and expanded the instances of those who, foolishly, took general satire for specific criticism. In 1621 he says of satire: "One may speake in jest, and yet speake truth"; in 1628 he acknowledges but does not soften his point: "It is somewhat tart, I grant it"; and adds "as he said sharpe sauces increase appetite" (1.111). In 1624 Burton adds to a mildly placating section a quotation from Terence, "*Si quis est qui dictum in se inclementius / Existimavit esse, sic existimet*" [If any one thinks he has been insulted, let him think so]; he prefaces the apologetic section of

1621, "No, I recant, I will not, I confess my fault, acknowledge a great offence," with the insertion in 1624: "If any man take exceptions, let him turne the buckle of his girdle, I care not. I owe thee nothing, I looke for no favour at thy hands, I am independent, I feare not" (1.112).[27]

Reading this section of Burton's text is rather like, as Hotspur says, living in a windmill (though not with garlic and cheese); both insult and placation come in rapid sequence.[28] The appearance of a helter-skelter shifting of moods is not alleviated but compounded by the additions to subsequent editions of the *Anatomy*. Rather than organizing his arguments in favor of satire or of criticism into one section and following them with ameliorating circumstances, as he might if he were trying to give his reader a balanced sense of such an enterprise, of the tension within such a work, Burton makes his persona shift repeatedly from one to the other, so that the reader, rather than being instructed, is buffeted by the apparent shifts in attitude. When Democritus at last concludes with apparent graciousness, "I presume of thy good favour and gratious acceptance (gentle reader) out of an assured hope and confidence thereof, I will beginne" (1.113), he takes a stance that the preceding paragraphs have done everything to lay open to question. Nor is the confession "I have overshot my selfe, I have spoken foolishly, rashly, unadvisedly, absurdly, I have anatomized mine own folly" an answer to these difficulties, since this confession is placed within the persona's (or the author's?) admission that it is hard *not* to write a satire. In short, we have frames within frames within frames, paradoxes like that in which the Cretan declares all Cretans to be liars, so that the conclusion concludes nothing, and the revisions cultivate and extend the ambiguity and ambivalence created in the original version of the text.

Burton's text, as we might gather from this section of the preface, is not presented to us ready-made, with conclusions neatly ordered: the reader is rather forced through a maze of what appear to be contradictory propositions, forced to take part in the construction of the text and the meaning it holds. Rather than simply leading us through his text, Burton encourages, even insists upon, our engagement with it. This is paradigmatically the case in Burton's presentation of Democritus, a persona that suits Burton's purposes in a variety of ways — in his anatomical and physiological interests (the original Democritus cut up animals to discover the source of melancholy) and in his satirical approach (his response to human folly was laughter rather than tears or invective). But Burton's presentation of his relationship to Democritus is both curiously indirect and extended, designed to imply a relationship without specifying what it is and constructed so as to mislead us about the nature of that relationship before finally resolving it; or rather to suggest a relationship, later denied but nevertheless established.

Instead of explicit statement, Burton offers us process: we may well be misled or confused by the name, he says (he himself would have been so deceived — into expecting satire or philosophy); and he asserts the distinction between his method and that of others, who may use the name of Democritus only *"to get themselves credit"* (1.1). For us fully to understand, he says, he must tell us who Democritus was. There follows an account of Democritus as "a little wearish old man, very melancholy by nature, averse from company in his latter dayes, and much given to solitarinesse, . . . wholy addicted to his studies at the last, and to a private life." What, interrupts Burton, has all this to do with me? The answer to this rhetorical question at first denies similarity and then underscores it.

Burton begins with a modesty topos: "I confesse indeede that to compare my selfe unto him for ought I have yet said, were both impudency and arrogancy. I doe not presume to make any parallell, *Antistat mihi millibus trecentis* [he is immeasurably ahead of me], *parvus sum, nullus sum,* [I am insignificant, a nobody, with little ambition and small prospects]" (1.3). But then Burton proceeds to rescue his reputation and even to assert equality (to Jovius if not to Democritus) by a series of analogies and classical references: "Yet thus much I will say of my selfe, . . . I have liv'd a silent, sedentary, solitary, private life, *mihi & musis* [for myself and my studies], in the University as long almost as *Xenocrates* in *Athens, ad senectam ferè* [practically to old age], to learne wisdome as he did, penned up most part in my study. For I have beene brought up a Student in the most flourishing Colledge of *Europe, Augustissimo collegio,* and can bragge with *Jovius,* almost . . . ; for 30 yeeres I have continued (having the use of as good Libraries as ever he had) a Scholler" (1.3). Once again Burton speaks through his predecessors, asserting a connection with Democritus even while denying a specific similarity.

Burton's extended account of Democritus' method abruptly concludes, "You have had a reason of the Name" (1.6). But what precisely is the reason? Despite disclaimers, the similarities are many: that Burton, like Democritus, is writing a treatise of melancholy; that Burton is in fact completing the treatise of melancholy that Democritus had begun but that is now lost; that Burton, like Democritus, is an anatomist, and one who will laugh at the follies of humanity. But Burton's telling us the story of Democritus rather than merely stating these connections has two functions: it reinforces the *humilitas* topos (he is really nothing like his famous predecessor; he is only borrowing his name); it also makes the point of similarity more strongly in that the reader discovers the connections rather than being told of them. Perhaps most important, it involves the reader in a process of discovery, in an interactive relationship with persona and text that is characteristic of Burton throughout. That relationship is dramatically evident in the Democritus Junior passage with its elaborate self-presentation; it continues throughout the text itself, in which Burton, or the material, may lead us in unexpected directions; and it anticipates Sterne's teasingly intricate relationships with his major characters.

Burton does not merely search through ancient authors and record what he finds, nor does he attempt to impose order on his subject; rather, he is extraordinarily responsive to its configurations. The whole work gives us an enthusiastic sense of participation, of involvement, but without final judgment or evaluation, for it seems to be the process as much as the result that interests Burton. Just as in the paradigmatic account of his style and method he not only follows the landscape but also conveys the reader through it, so Burton, like others of his period, collects what pleases him and shapes it according to his own plan, yet without rigidity or fixedness. His account of his method begins with a conventional apology: "I have read many Bookes, but to little purpose, for want of good method, I have confusedly tumbled over divers Authors in our Libraries, with small profit, for want of Art, Order, Memory, Judgement" (1.4). But later the process becomes more active, more purposefully reflective of the author's involvement: while denying originality, Burton represents himself as actively engaged in theft (1.8): "No newes here, that which I have is stolne from others"; "'tis all mine and none mine," he says, quoting Macrobius; "I have laboriously collected this *Cento* out of divers Writers, and that *sine injuriâ,* I have wronged no Authors, but given every man his owne." But increasingly the emphasis shifts to his own contribution, as he suggests the shaping mind and hand: "The matter is theirs most part, and yet mine, *apparet unde sumptum sit* [it is plain whence it was taken] (which *Seneca* approves) *aliud tamen quàm unde sumptum sit apparet* [yet it becomes something different in its new setting]." The mass of quotation might seem to justify the conventional position: "We can say nothing but what hath beene said, the composition and method is ours onely, and shewes a Schollar" (1.11); but throughout his text Burton shows himself much more than a scholar in the narrow sense, certainly much more than a recorder. He does not impose a particular order on his material in that he does not argue a particular point of view, yet we feel on every page the enthusiastic response of the scholar to his material. He does not so much shape it as sympathetically reflect its variety, its complexity.

Burton is engaged with his reader not only in the preface, in the shifting role of Democritus Junior, but also throughout the body of the text. But perhaps even more significantly, Burton is in dialogue with his own text. The record of the additions to his text, the points at which, step by step, in response to a principle or an example, he thought of or discovered another illustration or a more colorful turn of phrase, suggests precisely this kind of encounter, this kind of engagement with what he himself had written. Burton is a writer who couldn't let the matter rest, who couldn't stop revising, who couldn't resist just one more change, to whom his text was perhaps the liveliest being he encountered. That view is amply attested by the revisions of *The Anatomy of Melancholy*, carried out over six editions and seventeen years, revisions that increased the bulk of the text by nearly half.

Not only is Burton involved with his text in the ongoing process of revisions; he also forces the reader to a heightened degree of engagement by creating structures and expectations that later turn out to be inadequate or inappropriate. Burton's prose combines aspects of elaborate organization and remarkable chaos; it is unstable in tone and in method. But such instability is not, I have been arguing, evidence of failure: it is rather the most prominent feature of Burton's text, a structural and tonal variability with generic implications. There is, as I shall argue more fully in the following chapter, a similarity to Laurence Sterne, who liked Burton's *Anatomy* well enough to filch a good deal from it and who a century later wrote a work that similarly couldn't be let go of, that seems to unravel in the process of composition. Of the structure of Burton's *Anatomy* one may say as Tristram Shandy does about the ever-expanding, ever-regressive narrative of his own life: "My work is digressive, and it is progressive too,——and at the same time."[29] In other words, it is precisely in his digressions, in his wanderings from the clearly defined path (as in a handbook of hygiene) that Burton finds his true subject, as it is in the extensive comments and additions that he makes the subject his own.[30]

In his endless qualifications and modifications of his text, Burton has created a work that undoes itself, that gets unwritten as it gets written, a work that is about process at least as much as about progress. The result is the peculiar fascination that Burton's *Anatomy* has had for generations of readers—for Dr. Johnson, who, although he found *Paradise Lost* perhaps excessively long, rose two hours earlier than he wished to read *The Anatomy of Melancholy;* for Lord Byron, who mined it for easy erudition;[31] and for readers who find that the method, the sense of engagement between author and reader, draws us into a text that we might otherwise leave untouched. Although not yet so manipulative as Sterne, Burton, in giving us structures that don't fit, makes us aware of the limits he intends to transgress before he transgresses them; he calls attention to the inadequacy of the form and yet uses that form brilliantly. There is, as Anna K. Nardo has argued, a sense of play in such a book as the *Anatomy*,[32] and that play, I would submit, is generic. In digression, transgression, and cultivated spontaneity, Burton forces a redefinition of the genre of which *The Anatomy of Melancholy* partakes and pushes us toward a rethinking of the notion of genre per se. In so doing he anticipates the work of Laurence Sterne.

VII

STERNE
Tristram Shandy
The Deconstructive Text

IN CONTRAST TO the other pairings discussed in this volume, the connection between Sterne and Burton is relatively well established. The first to take note of it in print was the Reverend John Ferriar, who in 1798 published a volume entitled *Illustrations of Sterne* in which he detailed particular passages of *Tristram Shandy* taken almost verbatim from *The Anatomy of Melancholy*. Ferriar points out that Sterne, considered innovative in his own time, was in fact relying on unrecognized sources: "When the first volumes of *Tristram Shandy* appeared, they excited almost as much perplexity as admiration. The feeling, the wit, and reading which they displayed were sufficiently relished, but the wild digressions, the abruptness of the narrative and discussions, and the perpetual recurrence to obsolete notions in philosophy, gave them more the air of a collection of fragments, than of a regular work. Most of the writers from whom Sterne drew the general ideas, and many of the peculiarities of his book, were then forgotten."[1] While noting borrowings from a good many writers of the later Renaissance, including Bacon, Montaigne, and Bishop Joseph Hall, Ferriar devotes particular attention to Burton: "I had often wondered at the pains bestowed by Sterne in ridiculing opinions not fashionable in his time, and had thought it singular, that he should produce the portrait of his sophist, Mr. Shandy, with all the stains and mouldiness of the last century about him. I am now convinced that most of the singularities of that character were drawn from the perusal of Burton" (56–57).

Ferriar's assertion that Sterne took much from Burton is incontestable: most striking, and most amusing, is Sterne's denunciation of plagiarism (*Tristram Shandy* 5.1), which relies heavily on the complaint of Democritus Junior to the Reader (1.9), itself heavily indebted to Burton's predecessors. Ferriar finds the genesis of the first four chapters of *Tristram Shandy* in a passage from Burton on the ways in which "we are plagued and punished for our father's defaults" (65); he juxtaposes Sterne's and Burton's celebrations of the dignity of man (5.1), and the stories of the beggar pursuing an implacable kinsman (5.1). He traces the consolation for the death of Tristram's brother Bobby (5.3), which includes Cicero's philosophical triumph over grief and a meditation on the transiency of all things, to Burton; he finds a number of Walter Shandy's prescriptions for Uncle Toby in Burton's cures for love melancholy.[2] And Ferriar's substantial list has been augmented by the work of later scholars.[3]

There is no doubt that Sterne read Burton, Rabelais, Montaigne, and Swift with profit and delight: the delight is reflected on every page, and the profits too. But whereas Ferriar feels his task is completed when he has located Sterne's sources, which he notes with such phrases as "Sterne should have considered how much he owed to poor old Burton" (73), my concern is not with borrowing nor with the notion of influence, which might lead us to believe that we had explained an author by noting whom he had read and excerpted; I am rather concerned with similarities of attitude and method, with what seems to me an essentially similar approach to the process of composition, an approach that is finally generic. Sterne stole from Burton the bits that most appealed to him, the parts most congenial to his imagination and interests. Moreover, the very fascination with earlier texts and the ability to incorporate large chunks of them into one's own text, whether seriously or playfully, are qualities that Sterne shares with Burton, qualities that deeply influence his work. The attitude to the text itself, the way it is constructed, and the way it reaches out to the reader are things the two writers have in common.

Let me first acknowledge the evident differences between these two texts: the one is a novel, described, according to the custom of its age, as a "private history"; the other is a medical and psychological treatise; the one is undoubtedly comic and indubitably bawdy, despite, even in part because of, its denials of that fact; the other has a serious moral and religious basis and a formal methodology. But such an attempt at a simple and concise account raises questions. Readers have long felt that if *Tristram Shandy* is a novel, it is unlike any other novel: much critical discussion has been devoted to demonstrating just how it grows out of its own and earlier periods (its relation to the learned wit of the Renaissance, for example, or to other interrupted narratives of the eighteenth century).[4] A number of readers have also described it as the first modern novel, properly seen in relation to the works of Joyce and Woolf. Similarly, *The Anatomy of Melancholy*, though it has its origin in medical treatises on melancholy, is inadequately defined by that genre, as the various designations of it as Menippean satire, encyclopedia, or commonplace book would suggest.

Nor is the tonal contrast between these two works so absolute as would at first appear. As Richard Lanham points out, modern American critics have redeemed *Tristram Shandy* from the Victorians' charge of immorality and triviality by making it into a serious philosophical work, concerned with such issues as time, truth, the process of thought, and the process of writing per se.[5] Moreover, although a case can be made for the serious purpose of the *Anatomy* as a whole, and such readers as Patricia Vicari have seen it as essentially therapeutic, an edifice based on humanistic thought and religious conviction, it is anything but univocally somber in tone. There are anecdotes, ostensibly serious in intent but hilarious in effect, like that of the baker who gelded himself to test his wife's chastity, of which Burton says, "Such examples are too common" (3.306). The qualities that attracted Laurence Sterne to *The Anatomy of Melancholy* — its zest, energy, and humor — continue to attract readers who find in it not moral instruction but a cure for melancholy in the form of entertainment.

For both Sterne and Burton genre is an important issue; in both *The Anatomy of Melancholy* and *Tristram Shandy* generic nomenclature or even adequate description presents problems. I have outlined ways in which Burton's *Anatomy* challenges and trespasses on structural and generic boundaries, ways in which one aspect of his work operates in tension with another, a fact of its construction that has led to competing and radically conflicting accounts of its essential character. The same may be said of *Tristram Shandy:* to a degree unusual with the novels of its period, critics have seemed to feel that if they could just get the *kind* right, or satisfactorily determine the appropriate classification, whether generic or attitudinal, under which to approach *Tristram Shandy*, much else would fall into place.[6] But as with *The Anatomy of Melancholy*, it has been unusually difficult to assign a designation, precisely because generic play and generic mixing are at the heart of Sterne's undertaking. As Wayne Booth points out with regard to *Tristram Shandy*, there is little use arguing for the unity of a work that so many readers have felt lacking in unity;[7] similarly, it is perhaps wide of the mark to define the genre of a work whose very point seems to be to test notions of genre.

The aspect of *Tristram Shandy* that has so delighted modern readers and to some extent irritated or puzzled earlier readers is its concern with text as text, it being not so much a work of fiction as a work about fiction; like the work of Woolf, Mann, Nabokov, and Joyce, with which it has been compared, it is a writer's novel, one whose chief interest is in the problems of writing. Whereas Victorian readers reacted with categorical indignation to both generic play and sexual innuendo, more recent readers have preferred works marked by a self-conscious concern with the work of art.[8] The paradigm of altered expectations may be seen in the contrasting essays written by Sir Leslie Stephen and his daughter Virginia Woolf: Stephen expresses, at length, his "regret that a man of Sterne's genius should have descended so often to mere buffoonery or to the most degrading methods of meeting his reader's interest"; Woolf finds that "even his indecency impresses one as an odd kind of honesty."[9] To the objections of nineteenth-century critics who thought Sterne unworthy of a literary tradition marked by high seriousness,[10] Woolf responded that we don't so much disagree with the assessment of his morals or lack of high seriousness as find them unproblematic. Richard Lanham takes the point further, arguing that it is not that *Tristram Shandy* lacks a purpose but rather that its chief occupation, its purpose, is game, the pursuit of pleasure.

For both Burton and Sterne, the text is an object interesting in itself, complex in appearance and composite in nature; in both, the text is far more than narrative or scholarly exposition, and the apparent content is embedded in a good deal else that contributes to the effect of the text on us. I have already described the tension between the synopsis—the formal ordering system of Burton's text—and the often disorderly body of the work—the thing of disproportionate, contradictory, effusive growth, a body of material that seems self-perpetuating, that engages in a kind of inner dialogue that leads it beyond the rational bounds set by the divisions of the topic. But there are other physical features that attract our attention: like Sterne's text, Burton's is visually interesting, with its rich array of type faces demarking quotation and "original material," a distinction particularly hard to make with Burton. Any given page reveals a lively interaction between the author and the authorities cited within the body of the text or referred to in the plentiful marginal documentation and comment.[11] The *Anatomy* also includes a frontispiece, featuring a picture of the author, and "The Author's Abstract of Melancholy," first added in 1628; explanatory verses were added in the edition of 1632, and in 1638 the picture of the author acquired a skull cap.[12] Thus,

Generating Texts

Burton's text continued to speak to the reader and continued to grow and change with each successive edition.[13]

For Sterne, even more than for Burton, the text is an object to be seen as well as read. There are, famously, the two black pages to mark the death of Yorick; the marbled pages, of which Sterne invites us to ponder the moral—"motly emblem of my work!" (3.36); the blank page for the reader to sketch his own image of the Widow Wadman; the comic diagrams representing the forward progress of Tristram's narrative (6.40) and the representation of Trim's flourish (9.4); the blank pages for chapters 18 and 19 of volume 9, which are inserted later. There is also, as in Burton, the textual variety created by italicized names of characters, titles in Gothic script, the plentiful use of dashes in imitation of breathless conversation, the strings of asterisks for words that the narrator thinks proper to tantalize with the omission of, the juxtaposition of English and Latin text, as in the case of Slawkenbergius's tale or Ernulf's excommunicating curse. Even the ironic inclusion of Slawkenbergius's entire tale—because, according to Sterne's note, "As *Hafen Slawkenbergius de Nasis* is extremely scarce, it may not be unacceptable to the learned reader to see the specimen of a few pages of his original" (1.288)—resembles but goes beyond Burton's fondness for reproducing large chunks of sources.[14] Sterne's textual play extends to the length and divisions of chapters: the chapters range from a single question—"Is this a fit time, said my father to himself, to talk of PENSIONS and GRENADIERS?" (4.5)—to many pages, and the chapter divisions are made as obtrusive as possible.

While Burton from time to time called attention to the process of his work or the direction in which his text was going, Sterne's attention is even more marked. The concern with text as text evident on the printed page is reinforced by verbal attention to the technical matters of writing, by Tristram's running commentary on his narrative: "How my father went on, in my opinion, deserves a chapter to itself.—" (5.2); "Stay———I have a small account to settle with the reader, before *Trim* can go on with his harangue.—It shall be done in two minutes" (5.8); "This will be fully illustrated to the world in my chapter of wishes.———" (3.1); "Let us go back to the ******———in the last chapter" (3.14). Like Burton's transitional comments—"But I rove," "But what have I to doe with this?"—such remarks, ostensibly pointers to the subject, also draw our attention to the narrator himself. Perhaps the most sophisticated of these self-conscious maneuvers is Tristram's discussion of the authorship of "that remarkable chapter in the *Tristrapædia*, which to [the narrator] is the most original and entertaining one in the whole book." Tristram lays out possibilities that turn out to be impossibilities—that my father wrote the chapter upon sash-windows before the event—in which case the event would not have taken place— and then adjusts the fictional frame to demonstrate that the narrator is not only inside the novel but also outside it: "The second reason, which I have the honour to offer to the world in support of my opinion, that my father did not write the chapter upon sash-windows and chamber-pots, at the time supposed,—and it is this. ——That, in order to render the *Tristrapædia* complete,—I wrote the chapter myself" (5.26).[15] Tristram here moves from the role of a talkative, companionable narrator commenting on the story he is telling to that of a narrator playing generic games, calling our attention to the frame of the story, first by appearing inside the frame and then deftly slipping outside. Even more than in Burton, we do not so much listen to the narrative as watch the narrator construct and deconstruct his text; its transparent factitiousness becomes the chief point of interest.

Like Burton, who begins the *Anatomy* with a justification for his undertaking that points to roots in medicine, theology, and satire but that turns out to be multiedged and ambiguous, so Sterne also calls attention from the start to the nature of his book. But whereas Burton's persona Democritus Junior addresses the issue of character, title, and work directly, Sterne's narrator begins, famously, with what sounds like a conversational aside, rather than the formal opening of a narrative: "I wish either my father or my mother, or indeed both of them, as they were in duty both equally bound to it, had minded what they were about when they begot me." In other words, Sterne indulges in generic play and ambiguity from the very beginning of his work. He alerts us to the fictional quality of fiction itself in opening chapters that include not only Tristram's account—much interrupted and commented upon—of his own conception but also a discussion of the proper way to write a narrative history.[16] In these chapters Sterne shifts forms and occasions to create something like a sampler of kinds of discourse: the offhand remark, the colloquial comment, the learned dissertation (on the nature of the homunculus), the energetic encounter with the reader, the comment on the foregoing anecdote, general comment on the nature of the text, discussion of the theory of composition and genre, investigation of historical records, and shifting of interlocutors from male to female — all in four chapters occupying just six pages. Not until the fifth chapter does the narrator finally offer a conventional beginning: "On the fifth day of *November,* 1718, which to the æra fixed on, was as near nine kalendar months as any husband could in reason have expected, — was I *Tristram Shandy,* Gentleman, brought forth into this scurvy and disasterous world of ours." But even in this first apparently conventional sentence the public, declaratory tone is undercut, first by the reference to a husband's possible doubts about his wife's fidelity and second by the diction of "this scurvy and disasterous world."

The opening paragraph of the novel likewise mixes elevation of diction (the philosophical discourse of polite society) — "that not only the production of a rational Being was concern'd in it, but that possibly the happy formation and temperature of his body, perhaps his genius and the very cast of his mind" — with a quick descent to a more colloquial treatment of the subject: "Believe me, good folks, this is not so inconsiderable a thing as many of you may think it." Sterne reverts to the relatively formal — "you have all, I dare say, heard of the animal spirits, as how they are transfused from father to son, &c. &c." — and then again to the lively, and colloquial — "so that when they are once set a-going, whether right or wrong, 'tis not a halfpenny matter,--away they go cluttering like hey-go-mad."

In short, from the very beginning of his novel, Sterne engages in linguistic play, involving levels of discourse, frames of reference, shifting of tone, ellipsis, and interruption, all signaling to the reader the variety of effects Sterne is capable of. Besides providing a flamboyant display of the narrator's prowess (rather like a glitzy software demonstration), these opening paragraphs are also a test for the reader, a kind of complex grid that enables him to register reactions to the quickly and subtly shifting variety of Sterne's text.[17] The bravura opening of *Tristram Shandy* is both invitation and challenge, analogous in its character and its methods to the shifting attitudes and moods of Democritus Junior to the Reader.

Sterne's novel resembles Burton's preface not only in its unstable verbal texture but also in its approach to structure, in its deliberate and nearly constant deviation from expectations. Given generic expectations of external form, Sterne's "private history" of course has no Burtonian synopsis, but Tristram does offer at the conclusion of volume 6 a series of diagrams supposedly representing the line of his narrative.

Sterne: *Tristram Shandy*

I Am now beginning to get fairly into my work; and by the help of a vegitable diet, with a few of the cold seeds, I make no doubt but I shall be able to go on with my uncle *Toby*'s story, and my own, in a tolerable straight line. Now,

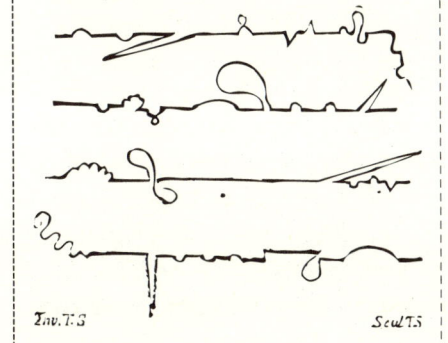

These were the four lines I moved in through my first, second, third, and fourth volumes.——In the fifth volume I have been very good,——the precise line I have described in it being this:

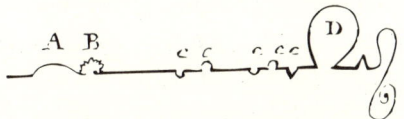

By which it appears, that except at the curve, marked A. where I took a trip to *Navarre*,—and the indented curve B. which is the short airing when I was there with the Lady *Baussiere* and her page,—I have not taken the least frisk of a digression, till *John de la Casse*'s devils led me the round you see marked D.—for as for *c c c c c* they are nothing but parentheses, and the common *ins* and *outs* incident to the lives of the greatest ministers of state; and when com-

In this passage Sterne mocks the notion of regularity, the assumptions that gravity and straight lines are to be sought after, that moral rectitude and regularity of composition are somehow one. But his method, if not his tone, is analogous to that of Burton, whose elaborations, additions, and above all, digressions, are central to his work. Burton has his synopsis, Sterne has diagrams, but for both, as Sterne puts it, "digressions, incontestably, are the sun-shine;———they are the life, the soul of reading" (1.22).

The presentation of self in Democritus Junior to the Reader is as inconsistent as the whimsical shifts of *Tristram Shandy,* and there are anticipations of the kinds of surprises we find in Sterne in the disproportions of Burton: he is the author who, after over one hundred pages of a preface in which he has both apologized to and insulted his reader, writes: "I presume of thy good favour and gratious acceptance (gentle reader) out of an assured hope and confidence thereof, I will beginne" (1.113). And once past the preface, no sooner does Burton begin his discourse proper than he finds it necessary to digress. Having ascribed the cause of human melancholy to sin, he announces, just a few pages into the body of his treatise: "Before I proceed to define the Disease of *Melancholy,* what it is, or to discourse farther of it, I hold it not impertinent to make a briefe Digression of the Anatomy of the body, & faculties of the soule, for the better understanding of that which is to follow" (1.139).

This digression, by the standards of *The Anatomy of Melancholy,* is relatively brief—twenty-three pages—and, duly considered, not a digression at all: Burton is correct in providing the basis in physiology and anatomy for the rest of his treatise.[18] But Burton's method is Sterne's in nuce, for as in *Tristram Shandy,* Burton discovers as he begins his discussion what else needs to precede a proper discussion of the subject; the digression is not a byway but a necessary element, an organic part of the whole. The difference, of course, is that Sterne is much more likely than Burton to emphasize his digressiveness, to call attention to the fact that he is moving through his subject by following sequences and intersections of ideas where they lead him. While Burton's proceeding at least has its roots in an orderly and scientific method, one that attempts to contain a vast subject—the notion that before he can treat melancholy, he must first treat the body and the soul—Sterne's is extravagantly whimsical and deliberately parodic.[19]

Whereas one senses in Burton's text a tension between his plan and its enthusiastic execution, Sterne's whole plan is plainly enthusiastic; he speaks of "this rhapsodical work" (1.13) and prides himself on the extent to which the apparently marginal is in fact central. The digressions are not, as a reader before Sterne might have thought, accidental or inadvertent; they are not digressions at all; they are the thing itself. The question posed by readers of *The Anatomy of Melancholy,* whether the major digressions of Burton's text—the Digression of the Air, the Digression of the Nature of Spirits, the Digression of the Misery of Scholars, and others—are departures from his plan or assimilated into the whole, is answered resoundingly by Sterne,[20] who begins with the assumption that his readers consider a digression a wandering from the main topic and proceeds, gleefully, to demonstrate that these digressions are after all very much to the point—though of course by then the point has been redefined:

> For in this long digression which I was accidentally led into, as in all my digressions (one only excepted) there is a master-stroke of digressive skill, the merit of which has all along, I fear, been overlooked by my reader,--not for want of penetration in him, — but because 'tis an excellence seldom looked for, or expected indeed, in a digression;---and it is this: That tho' my digressions are all fair,

as you observe, — and that I fly off from what I am about, as far and as often too as any writer in *Great-Britain;* yet I constantly take care to order affairs so, that my main business does not stand still in my absence. (1.22)

Sterne once again undermines the assertion of serious purpose with an escape clause, suggesting that all his digressions, "one only excepted," contain a "master-stroke of digressive skill." But of course we are not told which one lacks this skill, so that if we were to take this statement seriously we would be encouraged to examine each digression for this masterstroke. And if we were not to take it seriously, we would be thrown back on the notion that the jester who wrote this book is only digressing, laughing at us for seeking a serious purpose where none is, or perhaps for wasting our time with a text so clearly chaotic.

I have argued that Burton's structure, painstakingly laid out in his synopsis, is not precisely the "real structure" of his work but rather one that exists in counterpoint to it; and further that his forceful and pointed returns to his outline are evidence not of carelessness or an inability to manage his topic but rather of the tension between formal and organic structure, the synoptic outline and the associative, enthusiastic progress through the material that separates him from mere generic predecessors, from those who constructed more conventional anatomies. In this process Sterne has gone even further: digressions occupy a much larger proportion of his work; he calls attention to them in a way that on the one hand implies their transgressiveness and on the other hand impishly asserts their centrality. For example, he asserts the necessity of a digression to alleviate the seriousness of what has already been a pointedly giddy passage (1.22). He points out that the proper line of a narrative is mistakenly confused by "your men of wit and genius . . . with the line of GRAVITATION" (6.40). He elaborates on the necessity of digressions: "For, if he is a man of the least spirit, he will have fifty deviations from a straight line to make with this or that party as he goes along, which he can no ways avoid" (1.14). Like Burton, resolutely responsive to what he encounters, Sterne describes a process very like life itself, an ongoing encounter with experience that will change his text: "These unforeseen stoppages, which I own I had no conception of when I first set out;---but which, I am convinced now, will rather increase than diminish as I advance,---have struck out a hint which I am resolved to follow;---and that is,---not to be in a hurry;---but to go on leisurely, writing and publishing two volumes of my life every year" (1.14).

Not only does this process strongly resemble the quicksilver tones and modes of Democritus Junior to the Reader; it also calls our attention to the process of composition, to the text as text. Both Burton and Sterne engage in a good deal of discussion of the process of writing itself: Burton, as we have seen, emphasized the spontaneity of his writing, caring enough to edit and include the famous passages on hasty composition over the course of five editions. Sterne made a similar, and similarly disingenuous, claim of spontaneous construction when he asserted that he wrote the first sentence and trusted to Almighty God for the next (8.2), or when he declared of a detail, "But this is neither here nor there—why do I mention it?———Ask my pen,—it governs me,—I govern not it" (6.6). Sterne quite obviously cultivated the impression of spontaneity, performing a high-wire act in which he tempts us to believe that he does not know what he is doing or where he is going, daring us to believe that he can never again bring his narrative under control, and ultimately managing a virtuoso performance. There is the difference that Burton's text was subject to numerous and ongoing revisions, whereas Sterne published what he wrote quickly, adding new volumes rather than revising his text; toward the end of his life, he wrote in a race with death.[21] But this is a difference in the historical fact of composition more than in the effect the text has on the reader.

Sterne's method, I have been arguing, is analogous to Burton's, but it also intensifies a characteristic found in Burton. Burton follows the lead of his subject and his moods; Sterne deliberately tests his reader's patience with his resolve to follow his whims, to tell all: "I have undertaken, you see, to write not only my life, but my opinions also; hoping and expecting that your knowledge of my character, and of what kind of a mortal I am, by the one, would give you a better relish for the other: As you proceed further with me, the slight acquaintance which is now beginning betwixt us, will grow into familiarity; and that, unless one of us is in fault, will terminate in friendship.———*O diem præclarum!*———then nothing which has touched me will be thought trifling in its nature, or tedious in its telling" (1.6). The passage, which continues "if you should think me somewhat sparing of my narrative on my first setting out,—bear with me,—and let me go on, and tell my story my own way," is clearly tongue in cheek, serving to excuse even as it calls attention to a good deal of material that has no obvious or perhaps even possible relevance to the narration. If this were a tedious tale, one's heart might well sink on encountering a narrator who believes that

Sterne: *Tristram Shandy*

"nothing which has touched me will be thought trifling in its nature, or tedious in its telling." But as before, Sterne's digressiveness is not beside the point: it is the point, as is the teasing of the reader, the invitation to discern or disregard the relevance of this material, to join the narrator as partner rather than pawn in the game.

Sterne's discussion of narrative method, which repeatedly advocates digressiveness, also parodies the use of literary convention and critical authority, cited in support of his practice:

> I find it necessary to consult every one a little in his turn; and therefore must beg pardon for going on a little further in the same way: For which cause, right glad I am, that I have begun the history of myself in the way I have done; and that I am able to go on tracing every thing in it, as *Horace* says, *ab Ovo*.
>
> *Horace,* I know, does not recommend this fashion altogether: But that gentleman is speaking only of an epic poem or a tragedy; — (I forget which) — besides, if it was not so, I should beg Mr. *Horace*'s pardon; — for in writing what I have set about, I shall confine myself neither to his rules, nor to any man's rules that ever lived. (1.4)

Sterne's method here recalls in part Fielding's consultation of Homer, Vergil, and Aristotle on the subject of poetry and history in the prefatory chapters of *Joseph Andrews* and *Tom Jones;* but it even more closely parallels the shifting attitudes of Burton's persona. Tristram first pays elaborate allegiance to literary convention in his pretense of adopting Horace's method, then immediately admits that "*Horace . . .* does not recommend this fashion altogether" (1.4). Horace does not, of course, recommend it at all, but rather strongly advises against it. The joke continues as it becomes increasingly apparent that the narrator has paid very little attention to Horace — not being able to remember whether the dictum in question concerned epic or tragedy — whereas Sterne has given enough attention to this basic critical principle to be able to violate it flagrantly and precisely.

Sterne, like Burton, professes a thoroughness of methodology, implying that we cannot appreciate the complications, the consequences, until we have understood the causes, that we cannot understand the present without the past; but Burton's methodology is more genuinely and obsessively thorough, whereas Sterne's is more parodistic. Like Burton, Sterne consults learned authorities, but the effect is entertainment rather than genuine enlightenment: Burton quotes authorities on both sides of an issue and says, "Make up your own mind"; Sterne quotes Horace but acts contrary to his advice. In justifying his digression, Burton uses a common phrase of his period, "I hold it not impertinent"; Sterne adopts the mask of courtesy in the service of impertinence. In Burton's text pertinence means relevance to the subject, whereas Sterne proceeds from that meaning to a much more personal definition. Precisely in the assertion that everything is pertinent to his discussion, that "nothing which has touched me will be thought trifling in its nature, or tedious in its telling" (1.6), Sterne's narrator becomes teasingly impertinent in the modern sense.

Inclusiveness, like digressiveness, is not a departure from Sterne's design but inherent in it. Thus, for Sterne as for Burton the text is a composite, or, as Burton calls it, a *"Cento"* or "my macaronicon," a work composed of the works and fragments of others. For Burton the model is perhaps the commonplace book, a tissue of commentary on the particular topics of his synopsis;[22] for Sterne it may be an extravagant version of Locke's association of ideas.[23] Both writers use the principle of association, Burton more naturally, Sterne more flagrantly, to construct their texts. Burton proceeds from one idea to another, from one way of looking at an issue to another, tending to lose the original principle he was maintaining and moving over into another attitude altogether; Sterne demonstrates inevitable, whimsical, and unfortunate connections and sequences. *Tristram Shandy,* like the *Anatomy,* is made up of different kinds of texts, but Sterne, even more than Burton, calls attention to the process of construction, as he does to his transgressiveness: what begins as the polite consultation of authority ends in the total rejection of it: "For in writing what I have set about, I shall confine myself neither to his rules, nor to any man's rules that ever lived" (1.4).

Sterne's text is full of comments that shift perspective or mood, as in the altered expectations in "I know there are readers in the world, as well as many other good people in it, who are no readers at all," in which both expectation and emphasis shift radically from the first to the third unit. This technique, like the array of types of discourse in the first four chapters, exemplifies Sterne's interest in the texture of his work, its discontinuities and disruptions. Clearly, one of his chief structural devices is the interrupted narrative (about which I shall say more later). But quite beyond a natural (or perhaps unnatural) interest in interruption, Sterne also creates intertextuality within a single text, through his fondness for disjunctiveness creating an apparently spontaneous flow marked by

Sterne: *Tristram Shandy*

highlights and emphasis.[24] There are insertions evident in the physical features of the text—differences in typeface, blank and black pages, etc.—but more persistently in the narrative itself: "The article in my mother's marriage settlement, which I told the reader I was at the pains to search for, and which, now that I have found it, I think proper to lay before him,—" (1.15). Sterne is plainly interested in the inserted tale (a technique he shares with Fielding and other writers of the period), even in the inserted curse.[25] Tristram includes the opinion, in French, of the doctors of the Sorbonne on the validity of baptism of infants in utero (1.20); Yorick's sermon on conscience (2.17); Ernulf's curse (3.11) in a dual language version; not to mention Slawkenbergius's tale, the tale of Amandus and Amanda, Tristram's travel narratives, the story of the Abbess of Andouillets, of Maria and her goats, and the story of Le Fever. Indeed, the more one enumerates, the more one realizes that nearly the entire text consists of such insertions, to the extent that the supposed subject of the novel, the life (and opinions) of Tristram Shandy, comes to be an insertion within this welter of material. Sterne's disparate materials acquire definition by being set off against one another so that we are made aware of them as particular kinds and genres of texts. This procedure raises the question of genre once again, not just with regard to the whole—is this a novel or is it something else?—but with regard to individual texts, jostling for our attention, making *Tristram Shandy* a book of books. Sterne's ostensibly spontaneous text calls attention to its own disjunctiveness, highlighting and emphasizing its departures, becoming in effect a metatext on spontaneity.

The strong tendency to digressiveness in Burton and Sterne is related not only to the associative process by which their prose, with apparent arbitrariness, moves but also to their love of language and linguistic play. In his initial digression Burton speaks of "many hard words [that] will often occurre," with the implication that his purpose is to avoid confusion; the choice of a phrase like "hard words" (the sort of thing to be avoided in speaking to a lady, for example) suggests a deliberate, courteous, pedagogical preference for simplicity. But Burton then immediately favors us with some of the hardest and least polite words he might choose—"*Myrache, Hypocondries, Hemrods,*" before going on to others, perhaps equally hard, but more elevated: "*Imagination, Reason, Humours, Spirits, Vitall, Naturall, Animall, Nerves, Veines, Arteries,*" "which of the vulgar will not so easily bee perceaved" (1.139).

Sterne, like Burton, also delights in *copia,* in *congeries,* in the heaping up of examples, the making of lists. For example, Tristram gives us a list of things that will undoubtedly fall in the writer's way to divert him from the straight line that the reader might desire:

> He will have views and prospects to himself perpetually soliciting his eye, which he can no more help standing still to look at than he can fly; he will moreover have various
> > Accounts to reconcile:
> > Anecdotes to pick up:
> > Inscriptions to make out:
> > Stories to weave in:
> > Traditions to sift:
> > Personages to call upon:
> > Panegyricks to paste up at this door:
> > Pasquinades at that:——— (1.14)

He lists the kinds of behavior Mr. Shandy will not tolerate in his son's governor: he "shall neither lisp, or squint, or wink, or talk loud, or look fierce, or foolish;———or bite his lips, or grind his teeth, or speak through his nose, or pick it, or blow it with his fingers . . ." ad infinitum (6.5). He lists the articles of ancient dress (6.19). And more.

We have already noted how, in Burton, such lists or examples acquire a life of their own, leading writer and reader in unexpected directions. The element of surprise is there in Sterne as well, but the surprises are more obviously orchestrated. For example, Sterne emphasizes the shifting character of his discourse by arranging the list of digressions vertically on the page; he emphasizes the absurdity of Mr. Shandy's qualifications for a governor by making these a parody of Pellegrini and by making Uncle Toby comment (as is his wont, discreetly to himself), "Now this is all nonsense again."[26] While the method, the tendency, and even the root cause—love of language—remains the same, the effect in Sterne is yet more dramatic than in Burton. The instability of tone that results from Burton's lists becomes in Sterne a deliberate reversal of expectations and variation of tone, a text elaborately ludic.[27]

For Sterne as for Burton, the writing of the chief text for which he is known was literally his life's work. Although Sterne wrote and published four volumes of sermons (under the title *The Sermons of Mr. Yorick*) as well as *A Sentimental Journey* and although Burton wrote a play in his early years and explicitly refrained from publishing his sermons, *Tristram Shandy* and *The Anatomy of Melancholy* are their authors' dominant and defining texts.[28] Sterne promised early on "to go on leisurely, writing and publishing two volumes of my life every year;----which, if I am suffered to go on quietly, and can make a tolerable bargain with my bookseller, I shall continue to do as long as I live" (1.14); he did in fact publish volumes of *Tristram Shandy,* if not quite at the rate promised, until a year before his death.[29] Sterne's remarkably various work was published sequentially during the last nine years of his life; Burton's *Anatomy,* already substantial at its first publication in 1621, continued to grow (increasing by half its volume) in four further editions issued over seventeen years. In both cases the book served as a kind of record of the author's changing attitudes and opinions as well as of the continuity of his interest.[30] For example, in the section on clerical preferment, Burton revised his text from "Preferment as I could not get" to "Greater preferment as I could not get" upon his obtaining the promise of the living of Seagrave;[31] moreover, references to additional authorities on subjects already treated in earlier editions of the *Anatomy* provide evidence of Burton's continuing reading and interest in his subject. Readers of Sterne have found a kind of record of the author's developing attitudes in the increasing tendency toward sentimentality (and the cultivation of it) in *Tristram Shandy,* culminating logically in the writing of *A Sentimental Journey* as the last work of his life.

These works were also uniquely identified with their authors, partly through the creation of personae with strong resemblances to their creators. Democritus Junior both is and is not Burton: despite Burton's disclaimer, "'tis not I, but *Democritus, Democritus dixit*" (1.110), Burton was buried under his name in Christ Church Cathedral, Oxford. In Sterne's case both Yorick and Tristram have close affinities with Sterne: Tristram, like Sterne, endures the unfavorable remarks of his critics, is tall and thin, suffers from "a vile cough" that makes him flee England and undertake a continental journey that parallels Sterne's own; Tristram refers to one "dear, dear Jenny," who resembles Catherine Fourmantel, the singer in whom Sterne was romantically interested early in his career.[32] Sterne goes further, not only in creating resemblances but in calling attention to them, playing with our sense of the degree to which the frame separating novel from life is permeable. He obviously encouraged the association of Yorick with himself, mounting a kind of self-defense with the suggestion that Yorick was the author of many a charitable action for which he was not duly credited, but also opening himself to criticism, since readers took offense at the notion of a clergyman as fascinated by bawdry as Sterne, or as delighted with performance as Yorick, whose name Sterne used in publishing his own sermons. Just as Burton acknowledged that for him the writing of the text was therapeutic — "I write of Melancholy, by being busie to avoid Melancholy" (1.6) — so for Sterne, writing is a contest against a deadly and persistent foe: "There is no *living,* Eugenius, . . . at this rate;" Tristram confesses, "for as this *son of a whore* [Death] has found out my lodgings———" (7.1).

For Sterne, then, as for Burton, the text is in some sense life itself, and that text is dialogic, antiphonal, and digressive. I have already argued that in a quite particular sense Burton maintained a dialogue with his own text, adding to it, altering it, responding to it over a series of editions as he might to another text or to a human interlocutor. Sterne's narrator likewise conveys a strong sense of conversation with the reader (or the imaginary hearer). He even makes the case as a point of principle: "Writing, when properly managed, (as you may be sure I think mine is) is but a different name for conversation: As no one, who knows what he is about in good company, would venture to talk all; — so no author, who understands the just boundaries of decorum and good breeding, would presume to think all: The truest respect which you can pay to the reader's understanding, is to halve this matter amicably, and leave him something to imagine, in his turn, as well as yourself" (2.11). Sterne maintains dialogue with those readers whom he rebukes for missing clues, for paying inadequate attention; he likewise challenges the reader who expects some sort of straightforward narration, who dares to care about plot (the sort rebuked for a "vile pruriency for fresh adventures" and "a vicious taste . . . of reading straight forwards . . . in quest of . . . adventures"[1.20]), or who looks for some proportion between the duration of the event and the duration of the narration.[33]

Yet Sterne, though maintaining the appearance of a dialogue with his reader, is, like Burton, perhaps in a more profound sense in dialogue with his own text.[34] In his explanation (4.13) of the difficulties of moving forward with his narrative, he provides a marvelous image of the writer who is completely involved with, implicated in, wound up in, inseparable from his text:

> I will not finish that sentence till I have made an observation upon the strange state of affairs between the reader and myself. . . .
> I am this month one whole year older than I was this time twelve-month; and having got, as you perceive, almost into the middle of my fourth volume — and no farther than to my first day's

life—'tis demonstrative that I have three hundred and sixty-four days more life to write just now, than when I first set out; so that instead of advancing, as a common writer, in my work with what I have been doing at it—on the contrary, I am just thrown so many volumes back—was every day of my life to be as busy a day as this—And why not?—and the transactions and opinions of it to take up as much description—And for what reason should they be cut short? as at this rate I should just live 364 times faster than I should write—It must follow, an' please your worships, that the more I write, the more I shall have to write—and consequently, the more your worships read, the more your worships will have to read. (4.13)

Analogous to the diagrams in volume 6 of the line of the narrative, Sterne's verbal account here shows a never-ending sequence of digressions and complications, with the parentheses within this long, loose period mimicking the eruption of fresh matter into an already overfilled agenda. Although the narrator speaks of the "strange state of affairs between the reader and myself," the focus of the passage is on the narrator's infinitely tangled relationship with his own text.[35] The comic conclusion, "Will this be good for your worships eyes?," clearly undercuts what is in danger of becoming a philosophical discussion about the divergence of art and life, fictional time and life time; but it also creates a discontinuity between the readers, mocked as "your worships," and the author, who plainly writes not to instruct the reader but to delight himself and whose particular delight is in the construction of an impossible problem with which to amuse and perplex.

Tristram Shandy, I need hardly remark, is filled with images of interruption, impotence, and failure, from the unseasonable question with which Mrs. Shandy interrupts her husband, to the digressions that make up the text, to the failure of the family bull with which the novel concludes. Sterne never seems to fail to find such tales and images amusing, dwelling as he does on the near mis-conception of Tristram, his mis-naming, the unwitting substitution of a name of grief for a name of power, Tristram's near-castration, the mutilation of his pointedly symbolic nose, the failure of Walter Shandy to make any impression on his wife, the significant and highly suspicious injury of Toby Shandy, the broken bridges, dangerous crevices and passages, Uncle Toby's peril at the hands of the predatory, venereal Widow Wadman—all these amount to a concentration of interest that several critics have found less indicative of a sense of humor than of a personal concern. Not only do the main and subordinate events of the narrative focus on such matters: they are also borne out by seemingly minor and irrelevant asides, as for example in Yorick's consideration that he might as well support a midwife for the village as continue to lend his horse, because "it confined all his charity into one particular channel, and where, as he fancied, it was the least wanted, namely, to the child-bearing and child-getting part of his parish; reserving nothing for the impotent,---nothing for the aged,---nothing for the many comfortless scenes he was hourly called forth to visit" (1.10). *Tristram Shandy* is a novel in which there is a particular interest, charitable and otherwise, in the impotent.

Certainly one might argue for a connection between the frequent images of sexual failure and interruption or inadequacy and the instances of narrative interruption: the one becomes a metaphor for the other. But it is also true that the one may become a compensation for the other. For it is a curious fact that Tristram, whose biographical facts suggest practically unmitigated disaster, who might seem, like the other male members of his family, doomed to impotence and frustration, is nevertheless a powerful storyteller.[36] Like his father the rhetorician, who fails so badly to achieve the desired effect with either his wife or his brother, Tristram too has a way with words; the son of a father embarrassed about the means by which he might engender a child and of a mother more concerned with the clock and the calendar than with sexual relations, offspring of a nearly universal blank and a less than overpowering passion, Tristram is a captivating weaver of tales, one who at first invites us to consider him inept and out of control and then triumphantly, if ironically, points out the success and appropriateness of what he's done. In fact, it is precisely through his mastery of digressions that Tristram controls the text and the reader, emerging as a potent narrative voice, a persona who, while endlessly flirting with chaos, dominates otherwise uncontrollable experience through language.

There is undoubtedly a strong relation between words and power in *Tristram Shandy* as well as a relation between words and sexuality. Sterne establishes, indeed cultivates, the relation between language and sexuality by suggesting possibilities that are then denied, by accusing the reader of imagining things that the author never intended: so persistently does Sterne make these denials that even the most unsuspecting reader must be convinced that he protests too much. Several other instances suggest the unusual potency of words in this novel. Witness, for example, Tristram's assertion that "'twas not by ideas,———by heaven! [Uncle Toby's] life was put in jeopardy by words!" (2.2). The ambiguity about just where Uncle Toby received his wound—in the groin or at the siege of Namur—is sexually charged, not to say full of pitfalls. And we see the connection between sexuality and words, between sexual innuendo and power, in the story of the chestnut.

When Yorick picks up the chestnut that has burned *Phutatorius* (the name means lecher) in his most vulnerable spot and rolled onto the floor, his action may be seen as emblematic of Sterne's professed attitude toward words, that is, that a good word is unharmed—and may even be enhanced—by its connotations: "He did it, for no reason, but that he thought the chesnut not a jot worse for the adventure—and that he held a good chesnut worth stooping for" (4.27). Yorick has been described as a sentimentalized version of the author,[37] an amiable satirist and moralist, kindly and charitable, but unhappily for his own fortunes, too quick to offend the great of the world by attention only to the merits of a case rather than to the politics. But Yorick is also the jester who establishes the relationship between apparently innocent words and bawdry, for although he did not initially aim the chestnut, he did, musingly, pick it up. While Sterne's presentation of Yorick amounts to a self-defense of the innocent, unworldly-wise wit and jester, the actions that Tristram recounts allow of another interpretation: "But this incident, trifling as it was, wrought differently in *Phutatorius*'s head: He considered this act of *Yorick*'s, in getting off his chair, and picking up the chesnut, as a plain acknowledgment in him, that the chesnut was originally his,—and in course, that it must have been the owner of the chesnut, and no one else, who could have plaid him such a prank with it" (4.27). Tristram implies here, as he has earlier insisted about Slawkenbergius's tale, that the fault is in the mind of the perceiver, that Yorick's supposed guilt resides only in Phutatorius's mind, just as anyone who assumes that nose may mean anything other than nose is imposing his own corrupt or salacious reading onto the text. Yorick's action, according to the narrator, suggests that a chestnut that has had a risqué adventure is no less worthy than one that has not, just as words, Tristram would insist, are not the worse just because certain people cannot keep from thinking that something else is meant by them.

But of course Sterne goes out of his way to supply us with other meanings for the words he uses by the very act of insisting that they can have but one meaning, and that meaning strictly innocent. Just as words, in Sterne, acquire a life of their own, so the chestnut is earlier described as "of more life and rotundity than the rest" (4.27), having a kind of vigor appropriate to a sexually tinged adventure. Its physical action is analogous to the effect of words on the imagination: "The genial warmth which the chesnut imparted, was not undelectable for the first twenty or five and twenty seconds, — and did no more than gently solicit *Phutatorius*'s attention towards the part." Ultimately more than the attention is engaged: his faculties — "imagination, judgment, resolution, deliberation, ratiocination, memory, fancy" — are wholly devoted to attempting to determine the cause. Phutatorius's conjectures range from the neutral (even that state being sexually tinged in the telling) — "his imagination continued neuter" — to comically figured images of castration: "a thought instantly darted into his mind, that tho' the anguish had the sensation of glowing heat — it might, notwithstanding that, be a bite as well as a burn; and if so, that possibly a *Newt* or an *Asker*, or some such detested reptile, had crept up, and was fastening his teeth — ." And though Sterne / Tristram seems to mock and reject Phutatorius's corrupt imagination, he also encourages the lively action of words, which, like the chestnut, happily careen through a series of decent and indecent meanings.

Sterne, while ostensibly rejecting salacious material through Yorick's expressed opposition to Phutatorius's treatise, entitled *de Concubinis retinendis*, of course constantly flirts with such possibilities. Writing, which might be a balm for genital inflammations or wounds, cannot so function here: the pages of Phutatorius's treatise, cool off the press, are rejected for the purpose because its "doctrines . . . had inflamed many an honest man in the same place" (4.27). Yet Yorick, like Sterne, also opposes affected gravity, in telling a bawdy story for his reader's enjoyment, in declaring "Heaven forbid the stock of chastity should be lessen'd by the life and opinions of Tristram Shandy."[38] Much of the humor of this tale consists in the discrepancy between the simple incident of low comedy and the elevated style in which it is described; thus the pleasure is dual: a rather simple, backroom story, provoking guffaws, is recounted with elegant diction and rhetorical flourishes, so that the pleasures of the text are bawdy, narrative, and linguistic.

It is perhaps not entirely irrelevant that Sterne and Burton, the one a bachelor and the other a not altogether successfully married man, express in their writing a very particular degree of interest in sexuality. The bulk of the third partition of the *Anatomy* is given over to the symptoms, causes, and cures of Love Melancholy; Burton is nowhere more eloquent than in his account of the madness of love, his detailing of the deformities that can disfigure a woman without rendering her unattractive to the opposite sex (3.164). Burton documents with enthusiasm instances of love among the palm trees, love between species, instances of unnatural lust (given in Latin), and the inflammatory effects of "heroical love." He describes love out of control: "They cannot, I say, containe themselves, they will be still not only joyning hands, kissing, but embracing, treading on their toes, &c. diving into their bosomes, and that *libenter, & cum delectatione,* as *Philostratus* confesseth to his mistris; and *Lamprias* in *Lucian, mammillas premens, per sinum clam dextrâ, &c.* feeling their paps, and that scarce honestly sometimes" (3.145). And then he realizes that his own enthusiasm has carried him away: "But I rove, I confesse" (3.277); "But I am too lavish peradventure in this subject" (3.257), he says, only to plunge once more into an infinity of examples. Burton confesses, about midway through his treatment of the subject, "I confesse I am but a novice, a Contemplator only, *Nescio quid sit amor nec amo,* . . . yet *homo sum, &c.* not altogether inexpert in this subject" (3.195–96). For a novice, a contemplator only, Burton shows a good deal of interest, and displays a good deal of expertise, even if acquired second-hand.[39]

For all that *The Anatomy of Melancholy* and *Tristram Shandy* may appear at first to be generically diverse, they resemble each other in their subject matter, their attitudes, their representation of spontaneity, and their manipulation of the reader. Both works are characterized by a considerable misogyny, conventional to be sure, yet noteworthy.[40] Burton reports with enthusiasm a good many of the commonly held opinions of the faults and weaknesses of women, and then, several times, rather lamely draws back: "Let *Simonides, Mantuan, Platina, Pet. Aretine,* and such women haters bare the blame, if ought bee said amisse, I have not writ a tenth of that which might bee urged out of them and others. . . . And that which I have said (to speake truth) no more concernes them then men, though women be more frequently named in this tract" (3.229). Sterne's presentation of women is also predominantly negative, ranging from the rather Popean dictum that "the females [of the Shandy family] had no character at all" (1.21), to the utter blankness of Mrs. Shandy, to the predatory Widow Wadman. But whereas Burton's misogyny is conventional, overt, and based in centuries of patristic and other authority, Sterne's is more suggestive and insidious, based in the innuendoes directed against Madam, of whose reading Sterne particularly complains, as she misses clues he has placed for her, and, according to his insinuations, reads matters into his text which he never intended.[41]

But the female inquisitiveness and lack of insight found in *Tristram Shandy* are balanced by elaborate representations of masculine incompleteness and inadequacy, and once again, Burton's text provides provocative models for Sterne. Not only does *Tristram Shandy* resemble *The Anatomy of Melancholy* in its view of women and its reliance on digression and interruption; both texts contain gaps and omissions that do not merely remain blank but become spaces for the reader's directed imagination. While citing an overwhelming multiplicity of examples, Burton often ends by suggesting that there are more: a list of ten or twenty examples is likely to conclude with an "etc." or with suggestions for further reading. For example, regarding the remedies of love, Burton writes: "Plura qui volet de remediis amoris, legat *Jasonem Pratensem, Arnoldum, Montaltum, Savanarolum, Langium, Valescum, Crimisonum, Alexandrum Benedictum, Laurentium, Valleriolam;* è Poetis *Nasonem,* è nostratibus *Chaucerum, &c.* with whom I conclude" (3.272). In the midst of a discussion of the most alluring part of a woman ("some peculiar part or other which pleaseth most, and inflames him above the rest"), Burton first records the possibilities — "some said the forhead, some the teeth, some the eyes, cheekes, lips, necke, chinne, &c." — and then cites Lais of Corinth, a famous courtesan and favorite Burtonian example: "But shee smiling, said, they were a company of fooles; for suppose they had her where they wished, what would they first seeke?" (3.84). Burton is so eager to pass over the suggestion made by Lais's question that he nearly stumbles over his own prose in moving on to another part, that which proves to be Widow Wadman's best weapon against Uncle Toby: "Yet this notwithstanding I doe easily grant, *neque quis vestrum negaverit, opinor,* All parts are attractive, but especially the eyes, . . . which are Loves Fowlers, . . . *the hookes of Love*" (3.84).[42] Although the gaps in Burton are less obviously crafted, less elaborately constructed than those in *Tristram Shandy,* the techniques are analogous: the blank sheet on which we may draw a picture of the beautiful Widow Wadman may have its origin, not in a physical space, but an imaginative space in Burton.

Indeed, what may have been a mild tendency in Burton becomes one of Sterne's favorite devices, richly present in a text full of gaps and spaces for the imagination, gaps in the story, the language, and the time sequence. Sterne leads us to imagine Uncle Toby's wooing of the Widow

Wadman, then leaves a gap in which it takes place, then enters the narrative in the middle, then urges his reader, "Now give me all the help you can" (9.20); only after the intervention of an invocation and the story of Maria the goatherd does he finally return to the original narrative line. Not only are digressions the very substance of *Tristram Shandy;* so also are gaps, crevices, covered ways, omissions, dashes, misunderstandings, implications, etc., which have their antecedent in the numerous *et ceteras* and indeterminacies of Burton, seen in those instances in which he invites us to make up our own minds or to treat the text as text rather than as truth: "Whether this bee a true story, or a tale, I will not much contend, it serves to illustrate this which I have said" (3.122). Of many that might be cited, one anecdote from Burton may suggest how much he and Sterne share in method and subject matter. Recounting the stringent confinement of a Turkish seraglio, Burton speaks of wives "so penned up they may not conferre with any living man, or converse with younger women, have a Coucumber or Carret sent in to them for their diet but sliced, for feare, &c."; he concludes, "and so live and are left alone to their unchast thoughts all the dayes of their lives" (3.301).

The unchaste thoughts that now and again emerge in Burton's text, sometimes camouflaged in Latin, become, like Burton's fondness for digressions, the life and soul of *Tristram Shandy*. In Sterne, of course, the narrative persona and the narrative structure are much more fully developed, and bawdiness is much more conscious and explicit.[43] But not only Burton's matter and his sources find their way into *Tristram Shandy;* so does his manner. Sterne lifted a good deal from many texts besides *The Anatomy of Melancholy;* his strong resemblance to Burton consists in the handling of that material, in his flamboyant following of associations, and his use of persona. Both Burton and Sterne take a pronounced interest in matters, not so much of the heart, as of the body and the psyche; in both there is a fascination with words, a delight in them for their own sake, a sense of their power; in both the stream of ideas and instances goes where it will; both demonstrate the power of the incomplete narrative; and both manipulate the reader and the text.

One of the consequences of Sterne's emphasis on interruption and digressiveness is, as we have seen, to divert attention from the content of a narrative to its method, to problems and techniques of narrative itself. As with several of the techniques they share, this too is developed more strongly by Sterne than by Burton. Most dramatically, by erecting a series of frames around an incident or a narrative sequence, Sterne progressively recontextualizes a given event or passage, presenting it first from one and then from another point of view as it is reseen in a subsequent remark or chapter: "In the beginning of the last chapter, I inform'd you exactly *when* I was born; — but I did not inform you, *how*" (1.6); "To my uncle Mr. *Toby Shandy* do I stand indebted for the preceding anecdote, to whom my father, who was an excellent natural philosopher, and much given to close reasoning upon the smallest matters, had oft, and heavily, complain'd of the injury" (1.3). Such interruptions may serve to tantalize the reader, but they also resolutely draw our attention to the narrative process itself, even as they make evident to the reader the degree to which his reactions to the text are being manipulated.

A prime example is the account of the death of Le Fever (6.6–10), an inserted and extended narrative in which the unambiguously kindhearted and generous Uncle Toby stars and in the course of which Sterne cultivates the vein of sentimentality. But just as we get to the end of the story, and in the chapter that follows, Sterne makes it apparent that he is playing with the reader. It has been suggested that Sterne himself realized he had gone too far in the sentimental mode and so drew back,[44] but it is precisely when the story is at its most sentimental that Sterne draws our attention to the process of cultivating emotional response, by turning it on and off again: "the pulse fluttered————stopp'd———— went on————throb'd————stopp'd again————moved———— stopp'd————shall I go on?————No" (6.10).

In this sequence the question "shall I go on?" may be seen first as a response to the reader's sympathy, which Sterne insinuates must be wellnigh intolerable, but it is quickly reseen as a question about whether the narrator should continue to play with our emotions. Sterne speedily finishes the narrative at the beginning of the next chapter but then sets it off with additional information and comments that in effect provide an ever-expanding series of frames for the simple story. First we hear that the governor of Dendermond paid Le Fever military honors, then that Yorick paid him ecclesiastic honors, and next that Yorick preached a funeral sermon; but the series is here disrupted and framed, for mention of this sermon leads to an account of Yorick's habit of commenting on the rhetorical merits of his work and his use of musical terminology to do so. In the further frames provided for this story, in an extended sequential description of the manuscript, Sterne, step by step, elaborates the description of the insignificance of the comment that puts the whole prior performance, the narrative of Le Fever's death, in doubt. He tells

Sterne: *Tristram Shandy*

us in a series of ever more definitive phrases — that the comment "Bravo!" had been written "at two inches, at least, and a half's distance from, and below the concluding line of the sermon, at the very extremity of the page, and in that right hand corner of it, which, you know, is generally covered with your thumb; and, to do it justice, it is wrote besides with a crow's quill so faintly in a small *Italian* hand, as scarce to sollicit the eye" (6.11). The result of this carefully punctuated string of minute designations is to place the original experience at such a remove that we can no longer regard it seriously. Comment upon comment and comment upon context frame and distance narrative, in a process that is elaborate, extended, teasing, and playful.[45]

Advancing, retreating, retracting at great length and with many complexities what has been rather startlingly advanced, Sterne repeatedly modifies our vision and perception of this narrative, focusing our attention first on the tale and then on the framework, then on the many possible refinements in our understanding of it. Thackeray's remark, that Sterne is always standing at our side, to see how we react to his art, is appropriate here, but this passage is less a leering authorial intrusion into a pure emotionalism than vintage Sterne, who is part sentimentalist, part anatomist of his own art, and who cultivates the first in the service of the second. Tristram's comment, that Yorick "has left us the two sermons marked *Moderato,* and the half dozen of *So, so,* tied fast together in one bundle by themselves" (6.11), implies that what we have for a moment been led to regard as fact within fiction, as a narrative in its own right, is now to be regarded as performance, and that it is by the author himself so regarded.

These suspicions are borne out by the revelation that Yorick has marked this very sermon, which "seems to have been his favourite composition———It is upon mortality," with the applause of "Bravo!" Sermons on mortality, like sermons on any other subject, are judged in this novel as rhetorical performances. Sterne draws attention to Yorick's self-congratulation, partly to shock, partly to amuse; but the thought of mortality, like the related thought of sexuality, brings out the rhetorical streak in Sterne, whose writing of this novel was a race against death (7.1–2). Although he speaks of "that particular sermon which has unaccountably led me into this digression" (6.11), the linking of death and performance is as characteristic of Sterne as it was of his seventeenth-century predecessors.

Laurence Sterne, who took more than one leaf from Burton's book, creates a text that is apparently spontaneous yet artfully constructed, that calls attention both to its construction and to its deconstruction, a text of which he said: "My work is digressive, and it is progressive too,—and at the same time" (1.22). Like Burton's *Anatomy of Melancholy, Tristram Shandy* is shamelessly dependent on its predecessors and yet idiosyncratic, indeed unique. In both works the persona thrusts himself upon the reader, drawing us into the text as collaborators and co-conspirators. This interactive quality of the text, in which Burton and Sterne invite, even demand, response from readers, to whom they issue both invitations and challenges, is one of the most basic features of the two works. Moreover, Burton and Sterne interact with what they have written: they modify and revise, whether over a period of years or on the instant, responding and adding to what they have written. These are texts that call attention to the process of generation, texts that leave the scaffolding up so that we may admire the intricacy and skill of the construction. Thus, although Sterne has written a novel or private history and Burton a systematic medical treatise, there is a similarity in the process by which these texts are generated and in the nature of the result, a similarity of attitude and method as determinative of their essential qualities as questions of fiction and nonfiction, novel or scientific treatise.

Although the direct influence of one author on another is not the primary concern of this study, the way in which Sterne drew on Burton for the materials as well as for the methodology of his text underscores my contention that genre is not only, as Fowler argues, a matter of familial resemblances rather than a set of minimum requirements but something that develops with time. Sterne's novel is not only profoundly reliant on Burton's text for source material but also profoundly analogous in approach; indeed, it represents a further elaboration of Burton's rhetorical technique. Burton's *Anatomy of Melancholy,* like Donne's *Devotions* and Browne's *Religio Medici,* is not only a text powerful in itself but one whose generative pattern operates again, I would submit, in its lively progeny.

VIII

QUESTIONS OF HISTORY

Damn Sir T. Browne, a writer I never got much kick from: I suppose it is a reminiscence, though I was thinking of the Ballet.

–T. S. Eliot, writing to John Hayward

ELIOT IN EXASPERATION puts his finger on one of the questions that may be raised by this book: what is reminiscence, what is new invention; what is influence, what analogy; what, exactly, is the relation between the pairs of writers considered here? In the case in point, Eliot's line in *Little Gidding* on the raising of the ghosts of the past — "Nor is it an incantation / To summon the spectre of a Rose" — is part of an assertion that the past cannot be recaptured:

> We cannot revive old factions
> We cannot restore old policies
> Or follow an antique drum.

But of course Eliot makes the statement in the context of a linking of past, present, and future, following hard upon images that join the death of Charles I with that of Christ, preceding the linking of apostolic and martial flame, of dove and rocket. He finds himself caught in the act of using even what he does not remember, an unintentional effect in the midst of his extraordinarily deliberate craft. Eliot, who drew so heavily on seventeenth-century writers, would here reject, if he could, this particular borrowing.

The texts that I have considered are, as I noted at the outset, also marked by reminiscences, borrowings, memories, allusions, parodies, and distortions, many of which have been noted by other readers and critics. But more important than the issue of whether Eliot or the other post-Renaissance writers considered or made use of Browne, Donne, or Burton is the question of whether they adopted the same rhetorical strategies, the same mode, the same method; it is the similarity of conception — of the nature of the persona or voice, the nature of the quest, the nature of the inquiry — and of the structure that emerges to which I have tried to turn attention. The paired works considered seem to fall into three categories: meditative texts, those that discover the self within the context of time and eternity, whether pursued within the context of Donne's sickness or Eliot's thoughtful return to significant places; autobiographical and celebratory texts, texts that present the self and its experiences to others in an exuberant and revelatory way; and deconstructive texts, those that dramatize and exploit a discrepancy between our expectations and the work that we find, that lay out an elaborate structure only to undermine it. All of the seventeenth-century works are nonfiction prose, only one of the subsequent ones is. But I have argued that genre, conceived of as the function of an attitude, the expression of a conception, is useful in understanding these and other works, that the designations of meditation, autobiographical celebration, and deconstructive self-presentation are not only useful in describing the original texts but also meaningful for what I have called their progeny. These early texts are generative as well as generic; their techniques of cyclical meditation, of linguistic exploration and explosion, and of associative construction are potent and determinative forces in the three subsequent texts. In the works in question, and, I believe, in other texts as well, what I have called the generative impulse is as significant a shaping and interpretive factor as such formal considerations as verse or prose, fiction or nonfiction.

But as I remarked in the case of Donne and Eliot, the more one notes similarities, the more also one must acknowledge differences, differences that are perhaps not so much generic as generational, or perhaps historical. Eliot adopts a meditational method similar to Donne's, a method that has structural, even syntactic consequences, a tendency to turn over, to modify a phrase until it more nearly suits his latest apprehension of the truth. That method resembles Donne's pushing a statement until it yields both its truth and its limitations or his examining it to the point of annihilation. But despite a common approach and a common concern with time and eternity, there are distinctions in the content of these meditations. One finds in Eliot a movement from the secular toward the sacred, from an apprehension in which the numinous is dimly sensed toward one in which it has a quite dominant position. By contrast, Donne's position is from the beginning schematic, involving certain notions of the relation between the divine and the human, the cosmic and the mundane, that he elaborates with unusual brilliance but that he shares with earlier writers. Nevertheless, his prose is far from the tired rehearsal of truths universally acknowledged; it is rather the highly charged expression of a soul trying to ward off terror with conviction, rhetoric, and logic. The fatigue, and the eclecticism, are rather to be found in Eliot.

Both Browne and Thoreau also see in nature more than the merely physical; both owe much to the medieval notion of the Book of Creatures. But whereas Browne, like Donne, is explicitly grounded in a Christian reading of that book, Thoreau is less explicit, more Romantic in his sense of the divine as immanent within nature. Never naming God as such, Thoreau finds within nature some sense of its Author, of the original settler, and the like, using designations that seem to grow progressively more explicit as the work proceeds. Besides the fundamental presentation of themselves in relation to larger theological and social structures, strategies by which their apparently modest descriptions of their own preferences become normative, Browne and Thoreau resemble each other also in their determination to cast things in a new light, to use rhetorical and syntactical means to push a word beyond its original meaning. They open up a phrase or a concept to a blazing new understanding, not simply by assertion but by a careful rhetorical and syntactical process — in Thoreau's frequent use of puns, in Browne's use of open-ended analogies. But once again one must mark differences between the paired works, differences that point toward an increasing secularization and an eclecticism in Thoreau's choice of texts, a tendency that might be seen as the extension of Browne's frequent declarations of tolerance.

Finally, let us admit that, for all the prominence of a persona in Burton's *Anatomy*, Sterne does after all develop his characters more fully and that the structure he creates is novelistic rather than analytical. In fact, precisely the sense of the power of the author first conveyed by Burton in the *Anatomy* is, I have suggested, what emboldens Sterne to play so outrageously with his readers in *Tristram Shandy*. But if, as one might assert, there is something resolutely sophomoric about Sterne's text, a sense that structure exists primarily to be flouted, to be contested and controverted, the ambiguity between the author and the persona, which becomes a site of deliberate play, is a quality shared by these two texts; and the instability of Burton's text is the mode that makes *Tristram Shandy* possible.

Much recent critical attention, appropriately, has been given to the circumstances of composition, to texts as participating in a broad political and cultural context, not simply as reflecting it. My interest in finding connections across centuries and across genres, conventionally defined, might seem to weaken those concerns, for the emphasis of this book is more on the rhetorical, the formal, and the personal. But the very similarities, the analogies and approaches I have considered, also point up historical differences.

Sir Thomas Browne writes as if outside of time, pointing to an eternal, universal structure, yet his treatise has marked political implications; recent critics have found in it a carefully calculated royalism, a precisely articulated position within the highly charged religious disputes of his day. Thoreau, engaging in a meditation on nature and on the metaphysical within it, may be seen as responding to Browne, yet *Walden* is surely prompted also by the threat of industrialization and urbanization.[1] Donne, treating human sickness and sinfulness per se, also writes out of his own illness, one case in a particular London epidemic. Eliot, finding his true intellectual home in the seventeenth century, also marks distinctly the mood of the Second World War and its physical and intellectual terrors. Burton, sometimes described as the academic cut off from the world, yet continually adding new books to his stock, provides a picture not only of his own reading but of the intellectual life of his century. Sterne, like Burton, innovative yet kleptomaniacal, is himself a player with genres, deliberately cutting across the boundary between comic and serious, mingling texts of all periods to create his effects.

In examining these three pairs of texts I have argued that genre is not fixed but always in flux, that impulse, occasion, and response are as crucial as external form in determining genre. Rather than finding a single way in which a later work resembles an earlier one I have argued that analogous approaches create analogous rhetorical and syntactic structures even as they operate in a variety of literary forms. The pairing of these texts also enables us to note certain general tendencies within time. The later works often manifest a greater eclecticism: whereas Browne and Donne are firmly grounded in biblical and patristic language and theology, Thoreau and Eliot range much more widely across Eastern and Western culture in the construction of their meditations and the representations of their selves. That the tendency does not hold with Sterne is perhaps no counterargument, for nothing could be more eclectic than Burton's *Anatomy*. But the Burton/Sterne pairing does suggest another shared tendency: the later work develops more fully an approach established in the first: the persona of Democritus Junior, shifting, unreliable, often irascible, becomes the more fully developed, equally undependable

Questions of History

Tristram Shandy. Sometimes this elaboration of a technique yields, as in Sterne, greater freedom to apply an approach even more boldly than his generic predecessor. Sometimes, as with Thoreau, the later writer must express more carefully an idea easily assumed in the earlier work: there may be a need to articulate, even to preach, what had been a given. The loss of the clear theological context so central to Donne may mean, if not more fear, at least more work for the individual, who, like Eliot, must construct the very context of his meditations. Sometimes in Thoreau and Eliot the effect of such construction is subtle, allusive, probing; at other times, artificial, ornate, or strained.

A full account of such differences would be another project, amounting to something like a cultural history, a demonstration of how the same impulse in a new context yields a new form. But such differences emerge especially clearly in the context of generic identity, of differing manifestations of generating impulses. As Eliot put it, "Time the destroyer is time the preserver"; yet the more things stay the same, the more they change. Eliot, who considered all this at length, describes the paradoxical quality of the interaction between past and present, life and life:

> I have said before
> That the past experience revived in the meaning
> Is not the experience of one life only
> But of many generations —
>
> (*The Dry Salvages* 2)

Such generations, and such generative processes, I have hoped to show, are not only those of men and women but also of texts.

APPENDIX

NOTES

SELECT BIBLIOGRAPHY

INDEX

APPENDIX
Burton's Revisions

AN EXAMINATION of the following section will indicate how Burton built up a passage, step by step, phrase by phrase, even as he continued to apologize for its roughness and unpolished quality. The 1621 text is taken from the STC Microfilm version of the first edition (STC 4159); the subsequent versions, those of 1624, 1628, and 1632 (STC 4160, 4161, 4162), have also been checked against the Oxford edition, 1.16–17.

New material added in 1624 [   ]
Additions 1624 taken from Conclusion to the Reader (1621) [[   ]]
Additions 1628 {   }
Additions 1632 <   >

In 1621 the passage that appeared in Democritus Junior to the Reader was relatively brief:

> One or two things yet I would have amended if I could, That is, first to have revised the copie, and amended the stile which now floues *ex tempore*, as it was first written: but my leasure would not permit, *Feci nec quod potui nec quod volui*. For the rest it went against my *Genius*, to prostitute my Muse in English, my intent was to have it exposed this more contract in *Latin*, but I could not get it printed. Any scurrile pamphlet is welcome to our mercenary Printers in *English*, but in *Latin* they will not meddle with it, which is one of the reasons that *Nicholas Carre* in his Oration of the paucity of *English* writers gives, that so many flourishing wits are smothered in oblivion, lye dead and buried in this our nation.

In 1624 and thereafter the passage is a composite of insertions from the Conclusion and later additions:

> One or two things yet I would {I was desirous to} have amended if I could, [concerning the manner of handling this my subject, for which I must Apologize, *deprecari*,] {& upon better advice} give the friendly reader notice. [It was not mine intent] to prostitute my Muse in *English*, [or to divulge *secretae Minervae*, but to have] exposed this more contract in *Latin*, {If I could have got} it printed. Any scurrile Pamphlet is welcome to our mercenary Stationers in *English*, {they print all,
>   ———*cuduntque libellos*
>   *In quorum foliis vix simia nuda cacaret;*}
> But in *Latin* they will not [deal];[1] which is one of the reasons *Nicholas Car* in his Oration of the paucity of *English* Writers, gives; that so many flourishing wittes are smothered in oblivion, ly dead and buried in this our Na-

tion. [Another maine fault is, that I have not revised the Copie, and amended the stile, which now flowes remissely, as it was first conceived, but my leisure would not permit, *Feci nec quod potui, nec quod volui.* I confesse it is neither as I would, or as it should be.]

[[*Cum relego scripsisse pudet, quia plurima cerno,*
Me quoque quae fuerant judice digna lini:[2]
When I peruse this Tract which I have writ,
I am abash'd, and much I hold unfit.]]

{*Et quod gravissimum,* in the matter it selfe, many things I disallow at this present, which then I writ, *Non eadem est aetas non mens,* I would willingly retract much, &c. but 'tis too late, I can only crave pardon now for what is amisse.}

[[I should {might} indeed (had I wisely done) observed that Precept of the Poet,

———— *nonumque prematur in annum,* and have taken more care: Or as *Alexander* the Physitian would have done by *Lapis Lazuli,* fifty times washed before it be used, I should have [revised (1621 perused)], corrected, and amended this Tract; but I had not [(as I say)][3] that happy leisure, no *Amanuenses* {or} assistants.]] {*Pancrates* in *Lucian,* wanting a Servant as he went from *Memphis* to *Coptus* in *Aegypt,* tooke a doore barre, and after some superstitious words pronounced (*Eucrates* the relator was then present) made it stand up like a Serving-man, fetch him water, turne the spit, serve in supper, and what worke he would besides; and when he had done that service he desired, turned his man to a stick againe. I have no such skill to make new men at my pleasure, or meanes to hire them; no whistle to call like the Master of a Ship, and bid them runne, &c. I have no such authority,} <no such Benefactors as that noble *Ambrosius* was to *Origen,* allowing him sixe or seven *Amanuenses* to write out his dictats,> I {must for that cause, doe my busines my selfe,} [[and was [therefore] enforced, as a Beare doth her whelpes, to bring forth this confused lumpe, and had not time[4] to licke it into forme, as she doth her yong ones, but even so to publish it, as it was first written, *quicquid in buccam venit,* in an extemporanean stile, as I doe commonly all other exercises, *effudi quicquid dictavit Genius meus,* out of a confused company of notes, and writ with as small deliberation as I doe ordinarily speake,]][5] [without all affectation of big words, fustian phrases, jingling termes, {tropes,} strong lines, <that like *Acesta's* arrowes cought fire as they flew;> [straines of] wit, {brave heats,} elogies, {hyperbolicall} exornations, {elegancies}, &c. which many so much affect. I am *aquae potor,* {drinke no wine at all, which so much improves our moderne wits,} a loose, plaine, rude writer, *ficum voco ficum, & ligonem ligonem,* and as free, as loose, *idem calamo quod in mente,* I call a spade a spade, *animis haec scribo, non auribus,* I respect matter, not words; remembering that of *Cardan, verba propter res, non res propter verba:* and seeking with *Seneca, quid scribam non quemadmodum,* rather what, then how to write. For as *Philo* thinks, *He that is conversant about matter, neglects wordes, and those that excell in this art of speaking, have no profound learning,*]

{*Verba nitent phaleris, at nullas verba medullas*
Intus habent————}

Notes

Notes

1. 1621: meddle with it
2. 1621: qui scripsi Judice
3. 1628 and thereafter: as I said
4. 1621: space
5. The section "as it was first written . . . doe ordinarily speake" contains slight variations in wording and word order. The 1621 version is quoted in chap. 6.

NOTES

Chapter I: Questions of Genre

1. In the view of some, earlier, although this notion has been challenged by Anne Whaling, "Studies in Thoreau's Reading," cited by Harding and Meyer, *The New Thoreau Handbook*, 99.
2. Frye, *Anatomy of Criticism*, 332; Imbrie, "Defining Nonfiction Genres," 61; Cohen, "Innovation and Variation," 9.
3. I here quote Imbrie, "Defining Nonfiction Genres," 60; her argument, like my own, owes a good deal to Colie, *Resources of Kind*.
4. Olney, *Metaphors of Self*, 261.
5. Browne, *Religio Medici* 1.11, *Religio Medici and Other Works*, ed. Martin.
6. Thoreau, *Walden*, ed. Shanley, 320.
7. Burton died in 1639, but the 1651 edition includes approximately 2,268 words that Burton added to a copy of the 1638 edition (Burton, *The Anatomy of Melancholy*, ed. Faulkner, Kiessling, and Blair, 1.xliii).
8. Colie, *Resources of Kind*, 1.
9. Jameson, *The Political Unconscious*, 105.
10. Fowler, *Kinds of Literature*, 25. In a related essay, "The Life and Death of Literary Forms," Fowler elaborates the point: "Some regard all genres as obsolete. They imagine them as sets of old rules, irrelevant to post-Romantic literature. But all literature may in fact be genre-bound, without this being consciously realized" (203).
11. Lewalski, *Renaissance Genres*, 1.
12. Dubrow, *Genre*, chap. 1. As Dubrow points out, we respond very differently, for example, if we take a story to be a murder mystery or a history. The point is also made by Bruss in *Autobiographical Acts*: "The genre does not tell us the style or construction of a text as much as how we should expect to 'take' that style or mode of construction—what force it should have for us. And this force is derived from the kind of action that text is taken to be" (4).
13. Hirsch, *Validity in Interpretation*, 76, 98.
14. Guillén, *Literature as System*, 114; Robertson, "Some Observations on Method," 73.
15. See the discussion by Imbrie, "Defining Nonfiction Genres," 45–69.
16. Miner, "Some Issues," 37–39.
17. Imbrie, in "Defining Nonfiction Genres," notes that "nonfiction prose, almost by definition nonliterary, seems outside—or beneath—the view of generic criticism" (45; see also 55).
18. Graham Hough, *An Essay on Criticism* (London, 1966); cited by Imbrie, "Defining Nonfiction Genres," 63.

167

Notes to pages 9 to 14

19. Fowler, *Kinds of Literature*, 41, traces the notion to Wittgenstein, *Philosophical Investigations* (Oxford, 1953), sections 65–77.

20. Cohen concurs, stating in "History and Genre": "Members of a genre need not have a single trait in common since to do so would presuppose that the trait has the same function for each of the member texts. Rather the members of a generic classification have multiple relational possibilities with each other, relationships that are discovered only in the process of adding members to a class" (210).

21. Radcliffe, *Forms of Reflection*, 29.

22. See Miner's comments on this point in "Some Issues," 24–26.

23. Ibid., 25–27; Cohen, "History and Genre," 204.

24. Colie states: "Rhetorical education, always a model-following enterprise, increasingly stressed *structures* as well as styles to be imitated in the humane letters—epistles, orations, discourses, dialogues, histories, poems—always discoverable to the enthusiastic new man of letters by kind" (*Resources of Kind*, 4).

25. Fowler, *Kinds of Literature*, 26.

26. Culler, *Structuralist Poetics*, 116.

27. Colie, *Resources of Kind*, 23–24; Imbrie, "Defining Nonfiction Genres," 56–62. Although it has been frequently asserted that the seventeenth century was much more flexible in its generic notions than the eighteenth, Cohen disagrees, arguing in "On the Interrelations of Eighteenth-Century Literary Forms" that mixed forms were as important to the eighteenth century as to the Renaissance, but that the hierarchical relation of forms had shifted, away from lyric to didactic, leading to a different understanding of what was appropriate in terms of the effect on the reader.

28. Miner notes, "Western medieval matter well illustrates that prose and verse are alternatives to each other rather than matters classifiable as genres. There are romances in verse and romances in prose. . . . It is very strange that so little study has been made, for example, of resemblances and differences between narrative in verse and narrative in prose" ("Some Issues," 37).

29. Dubrow, *Genre*, 86, quotes Paul Van Tieghem, "La question des genres litteraires," *Helicon* 1 (1938).

Chapter II: Donne

1. St. François de Sales, *A Treatise of the Love of God*, [trans. Thomas Carre, i.e., Miles Pinkney] (Douay, 1630); cited by Martz, *The Poetry of Meditation*, 14, 15.

2. Martz, *The Poetry of Meditation*, 4. Martz cites the influence of Jesuit meditative patterns on the poetry of Hopkins and refers to the meditative poetry of Yeats, Eliot, and others. He develops this insight in his later study, *The Poem of the Mind*, which treats Donne, Edward Taylor, Whitman, Dickinson, Eliot, Williams, Roethke, and Stevens.

3. Clearly both were important, and since they are not mutually exclusive, I am less concerned with determining primacy of influence than in making use of these analyses to understand Donne; I concur here with Raspa's Introduction to the Oxford edition of the *Devotions,* vii-viii (the text cited throughout). The work of Martz and Lewalski has been elaborated by further studies; those who have paid particular attention to the meditative structure of the *Devotions* are Janel M. Mueller, "The Exegesis of Experience"; Van Laan, "John Donne's *Devotions*"; and Andreasen, "Donne's *Devotions.*" See also Webber, *Contrary Music* and *The Eloquent "I"*; Novarr, *The Disinterred Muse;* and Quinn, "Donne's Christian Eloquence."

4. Hall, *The Arte of Divine Meditation* (London, 1606); quoted by Andreasen, "Donne's *Devotions,*" 208.

5. Lewalski is here characterizing the explicitly Christian and, in her view, Protestant, meditation of the seventeenth century, but the description of the meditative method of appropriation of paradigms has a much broader application.

6. Martz, *The Poetry of Meditation,* 330.

7. Goldberg, "The Understanding of Sickness in Donne's *Devotions,*" expounds the traditional connection between sin and sickness.

8. See the studies cited in note 3 above. Andreasen, "Donne's *Devotions,*" raises the issue of dual structure explicitly but briefly. Andreasen and Webber note the repeating action of the *Devotions,* but as Novarr points out in a review article, "The Two Hands of John Donne," 152, Webber "does not inquire into the cumulative effect of using the same technique twenty-three times in the same work; she does not talk of the *Devotions* as a developed whole."

9. Janel M. Mueller, "The Exegesis of Experience," calls attention to Donne's use of biblical texts not as a simple authoritative source but in a questioning, problematic way (3); she finds in the *Devotions* "a singular blend of soul-searching and exegetical inquiry" (9) and emphasizes the congruence of the devotional and the homiletic.

10. Guibbory, *The Map of Time,* 90, speaks of the importance of memory for Donne: "Donne tries to understand his sickness by recalling biblical history, by discerning parallels between himself and those whom, despite their suffering, God blessed."

11. See the account by Raspa in his Introduction to the *Devotions,* xiii-xvii.

12. Donne, *The Divine Poems,* ed. Gardner.

13. Although Carey does not explicitly apply this notion to the *Devotions,* his views on the nature and origin of Donne's anxieties are relevant to its conclusion. His comment on the "Holy Sonnets" in *John Donne,* 57–58, is characteristic: "The love poems display, in their obsession with woman's inconstancy, a profound anxiety about his own ability to attract or merit stable affection. [Donne's] fear of damnation and of exclusion from God's love in the 'Holy Sonnets' reflects the same anxiety, transposed to the religious sphere." See also Fish's argument in *Self-Consuming Artifacts.*

14. One might compare George Herbert's description of man as "a wonder tortured in the space, / Betwixt this world and that of grace," "Affliction" (IV), 5–6.

15. Janel M. Mueller, "The Exegesis of Experience," 14, notes Donne's reliance on the Fathers, particularly Basil, Bernard, and Augustine, for his figurative exegesis of biblical texts. I would agree with Mueller, who stresses the traditional, exegetical elements of Donne's approach, and take issue with Carey's view of Donne as perversely obsessed with self, terrified by what he believes and cannot believe. Yet Donne's articulation of these ideas is so brilliant as to make purely scholarly accounts of his work seem inadequate. His tendency to read variously surely has its roots in medieval practices of biblical exegesis, but his practice is both narrowly focused and dramatic; these opposing readings work as a structural principle of the *Devotions*.

16. See for example Mulder, *The Temple of the Mind*, chap. 1.

17. Webber, *Contrary Music*, 4–5.

18. One finds oneself here in the midst of the classic definition of the baroque.

19. The pattern of the first clause is basically anapestic; that of the second shifts awkwardly from iambic to trochaic.

20. I here follow the edition of Sparrow in reading "*sound* that word, *present*," which seems to make more sense in context, over Raspa's text, which reads "found that word."

21. The centrality of the idea of decay to Donne's work is comprehensively demonstrated by Guibbory, *The Map of Time*, chap. 3.

22. The figure at the opening of the *Devotions* is epanalepsis, the repetition at the end of the sentence of the word or phrase with which it begins; the occurrence of the phrase "this minute" at the end and the beginning of the *Devotions* might itself be seen as epanalepsis on a very large scale.

23. Olney, *Metaphors of Self*, 313–14.

Chapter III: Eliot

1. Eliot, "Lancelot Andrewes" (1926), in *Selected Essays, 1917–1932*, 293–94; Eliot here quotes at length from F. E. Brightman's introduction to a translation of Andrewes's *Preces Privatae*. Kenner, *The Invisible Poet*, 244–45, notes Eliot's interest in Andrewes as a factor in the shaping of Eliot's verse.

2. Traversi, *T. S. Eliot*, 89.

3. Quotations throughout are taken from T. S. Eliot, *The Complete Poems and Plays, 1909–1950*.

4. Gardner, for example (*Art*, chap. 2), outlines the structure:
   1. a first section of statement and counter-statement which articulates the contradictions the poem will attempt to reconcile and delineates the landscape or setting from which each poem takes its name.

2. a second section in which a single subject is handled in two boldly contrasting ways, first a lyric passage and then a colloquial passage.
3. a third section which forms the core of the poem, its attempt at reconciliation.
4. a brief lyrical section.
5. recapitulation, a resumption and resolution of the themes of the poem.
Other versions are offered by Stead, "The Imposed Structure of the *Four Quartets*"; Matthiessen, "The *Quartets*"; and Traversi, *T. S. Eliot*.

5. This passage of descent occurs in the second rather than the third section of *Little Gidding*.

6. Once again, Eliot's correspondence with Hayward shows his deliberate choice of the term. Eliot wrote: "How great is the resistance to 'quartets'? I am aware of general objections to these musical analogies: there was a period when people were writing long poems and calling them, with no excuse, 'symphonies'. . . . But I should like to indicate that these poems are all in a particular set form which I have elaborated, and the word 'quartet' does seem to me to start people on the right tack for understanding them ('sonata' in any case is *too* musical). It suggests to me the notion of making a poem by weaving in together three or four superficially unrelated themes: the 'poem' being the degree of success in making a new whole out of them" (Letter to Hayward, 3 Sept. 1941, quoted by Gardner, *Composition*, 26).

7. Eliot made the comparison explicit when he wrote to Stephen Spender on 28 Mar. 1931: "I have the A minor Quartet [of Beethoven] on the gramophone, and I find it quite inexhaustible to study. There is a sort of heavenly or at least more than human gaiety about some of his later things which one imagines might come to oneself as the fruit of reconciliation and relief after immense suffering; I should like to get something of that into verse before I die" (quoted by Gordon, *Eliot's New Life*, 143). Matthiessen also notes the similarity (and differences) between the structure of *The Waste Land* and *Four Quartets*, "The Quartets," 188, as does Gardner, *Art*, 42–44.

8. Eliot makes the point in a letter to William Matchett, quoted by Gardner, *Composition*, 18, n. 8; see also *New York Times Book Review* 29 Nov. 1953, reprinted in Bergonzi, ed., *T. S. Eliot*, 23. Martz, in "Origins of Form in *Four Quartets*," describes his initial experience of *Burnt Norton* as the end of Eliot's collected poems rather than as the beginning of a new sequence.

9. From an interview with Donald Hall in *Writers and their Work: The Paris Review Interviews*, 2d ser. (New York, 1965), quoted by Gardner, *Composition*, 14–15.

10. One of the reasons that Eliot took longer with the composition of *Little Gidding* than the other three poems was that it was "the culminating poem of the series," as he wrote to John Hayward in July and August 1941 (quoted by Gardner, *Composition*, 22–23).

11. Lobb, "Limitation and Transcendence in *East Coker*," points to a reader's experience of the *Quartets* both as a sequence and as a single unit: "In the ideal

reader's mind the diachronic experience of reading the *Quartets* becomes finally a synchronic or spatial vision of the whole consort" (*Words in Time,* 33–34).

12. Gordon, *Eliot's New Life,* 45–47; Gardner, *Composition,* 34–35.

13. Donne addresses that God who has "cald me up, by casting me further downe, and clothd me with thy selfe, by stripping me of my selfe, and by dulling my bodily senses, to the meats, and eases of this world, hast whet, and sharpned my spirituall senses, to the apprehension of thee" (Prayer 2).

14. The opening lines of *Burnt Norton,* for example, sound like a philosophic disquisition:

> "Time present and time past
> Are both perhaps present in time future,
> And time future contained in time past."

But in going on to use the word *unredeemable,* Eliot evokes inescapably theological meanings.

15. Levenson, in a challenging essay, "The End of Tradition and the Beginning of History," finds an essential contradiction in Eliot's work between his view of the past as present to us, spatial, and of the past as receding, becoming ever more distant; accordingly, he finds no such satisfactory conclusion in *Little Gidding.*

16. Olney, *Metaphors of Self,* 314.

17. There are unseen eyebeams, and unheard music; beside the ghosts of Keats and Donne and Milton that arise in Eliot's fragmentary quotations from them, Eliot and his readers have also noted echoes of Elizabeth Barrett Browning, Kipling, Lewis Carroll, and D. H. Lawrence in this section. It is beyond the scope of my discussion, and would in any case be a needless duplication of previous criticism, to document all the allusions of *Four Quartets.* I shall note only those essential to my argument and refer the reader especially to Gardner, *Composition,* and to the many predecessors listed in the bibliography, from whose detailed and painstaking work I have profited greatly.

18. The principle of "as above, so below"; for an elaboration see Tayler, *Nature and Art,* especially chap. 1.

19. Martz, "The Wheel and the Point," argues that "the still point of the turning world" that gives order to the whole is the governing concept for Eliot's later poetry.

20. Eliot's method here is also the negative way of mysticism. Many critics have noted his borrowings from St. John of the Cross, both *The Ascent of Mount Carmel* and *The Dark Night of the Soul.* Hugh Kenner also cites Aristotle (*De Anima* III:10), who treats the still point not as a vacuum but as the energizing point (*The Invisible Poet,* 298).

21. D. W. Harding aptly describes the use of abstract and concrete in *Burnt Norton* as representing a new method for Eliot and a means of discovery: "In this poem the new meaning is approached by two methods. The first is the presentation of concrete images and definite events, each of which is checked and passes over into another before it has developed far enough to stand mean-

ingfully by itself.... And the complementary method is to make pseudo-statements in highly abstract language, for the purpose, essentially, of putting forward and immediately rejecting ready-made concepts that might have seemed to approximate to the concept he is creating" ("A Note on *Burnt Norton*," *Scrutiny* [1936]; reprinted in Bergonzi, ed., *T. S. Eliot*, 30).

22. Traditionally the Logos, the Word, is the creative power, as defined in John 1:1–3: "In the beginning was the Word, and the Word was with God, and the Word was God. The same was in the beginning with God. All things were made by him; and without him was not any thing made that was made." In verse 14 the Word is identified with Christ: "the Word was made flesh and dwelt among us." But for Eliot the Word also seems to have some of the qualities of the Unmoved Mover, usually associated with the First Person of the Trinity.

23. For Milton's use of the word *prevent* (Lat. *praevenire*) see the *Nativity Ode:* "O run, prevent them with thy humble ode" (24). Eliot's use of Browne, though effective, may be unconscious: in a letter to Hayward regarding another passage, Eliot wrote: "Damn Sir T. Browne, a writer I never got much kick from: I suppose it is a reminiscence, though I was thinking of the Ballet [the reference is to *Le Spectre de la Rose*]"; cited by Gardner, *Composition*, 202.

24. The famous statement reads: "What happens when a new work of art is created is something that happens simultaneously to all the works of art which preceded it. The existing monuments form an ideal order among themselves, which is modified by the introduction of the new (the really new) work of art among them. The existing order is complete before the new work arrives; for order to persist after the supervention of novelty, the *whole* existing order must be, if ever so slightly, altered; and so the relations, proportions, values of each work of art toward the whole are readjusted; and this is conformity between the old and the new. Whoever has approved this idea of order, of the form of European, of English literature will not find it preposterous that the past should be altered by the present as much as the present is directed by the past" (*Selected Essays, 1917–1932*, 5).

For a provocative discussion of the contradictions embodied in Eliot's view of tradition, see Levenson, "The End of Tradition and the Beginning of History."

25. As Donne puts it in Prayer 18, "Thou presentest mee *death* as the *cure* of my *disease*, not as the *exaltation* of it."

26. This is the view of Davie, who in "T. S. Eliot: The End of an Era," says that *The Dry Salvages* "sticks out among the rest like a sore thumb.... it is quite simply *rather a bad poem*" (153). But Gardner retorts (*Composition*, 4, n.4) that "Eliot's twice expressed view that *The Dry Salvages* improves on its predecessors explodes Donald Davie's extraordinary suggestion that the 'badness' of the poem was deliberate." Kenner takes an intermediate position: "Not that he has deliberately written a second-rate poem.... [Rather] the poem leads us *out of* 'poetry'—the river and the sea—down into small dry air in which to consider in an orderly fashion what 'most of us' are capable of" (*The Invisible Poet*, 314–15).

27. Indeed, in its repeated patterns (isocolon, parison, anaphora, and epistrophe), the first line of section 1b approaches iambic meter; the third line with its internal rhyme gives an almost mirror image of trochaic followed by iambic rhythms, before moving from iambic to anapestic rhythms in the fourth line.

28. In October 1940 Eliot moved out of London to Shamley Green, near Guildford, Surrey, making weekly trips into London; *The Dry Salvages* and *Little Gidding* were both composed during his residence there (Gordon, *Eliot's New Life*, 122–33).

29. See Hartwig's explanation of the nature of parody in *Shakespeare's Analogical Scene*, 3.

30. Psalm 107:23–24 reads: "They that go down to the sea in ships, that do business in great waters; / These see the works of the Lord, and his wonders in the deep." As Kenner points out, Eliot's manner was itself parodied by Henry Reed: "Oh, listeners, / And you especially who have switched off the wireless" (*Chard Whitlow*, quoted in *The Invisible Poet*, 314).

31. These are the terms that Eliot chose to define himself in the Preface to *For Lancelot Andrewes* in 1928: "Classicist in literature, royalist in politics, and anglo-catholic in religion."

32. Although Brooker ("From *The Waste Land* to *Four Quartets*") argues that *Little Gidding* runs the risk of closing the sequence, providing the final abstraction, I find it a brilliant articulation, not of abstract statement, but of paradox.

33. George Herbert's "The Flower" and Vaughan's "The Morning-Watch," for example, use a blossom to show the human spirit's vulnerability and its susceptibility to divine influence.

34. Eliot, "Tradition and the Individual Talent," *Selected Essays, 1917–1932*, 4.

35. "The Altar," *The Works of George Herbert*, ed. Hutchinson.

36. Dante, *The Divine Comedy*.

37. Eliot, writing to Hayward on 27 August 1941, makes the connection; having altered "Where you must / learn your measure, / like a dancer" to "Where you must move in measure, like a dancer," he wrote, "I . . . rather like the suggestion of the new line which carries some reminder of a line, I think it is about Mark Antony" (quoted in Gardner, *Composition*, 196). Interestingly, Eliot alters the context in his partial remembering: in *Antony and Cleopatra* 3.11.36 Antony scornfully refers to the prudent Caesar, who "at Philippi kept / His sword e'en like a dancer," while Antony himself boldly struck Cassius and Brutus. The line as transformed by Eliot retains Shakespeare's phrasing, but renders the line more fluid to depict Antony's grace rather than Caesar's lack of daring. Such modification of texts in allusion and quotation is altogether characteristic of Eliot. Eliot's phrase "the intolerable shirt of flame" (*Little Gidding* 4) may owe something to Antony's reference, one act later, to "the shirt of Nessus" (4.12.43).

38. The three may be Thomas Wentworth, earl of Strafford, Archbishop William Laud, and Charles himself, although they did not, of course, die on the scaffold together.

39. The joining of destruction and creation is like that of the refiner's fire

of Malachi 3:2, associated with the Messiah, powerful and frightening, yet redemptive.

40. The sentence that concludes Prayer 23 is stretched between the fears and dangers of the opening and those of the conclusion, the hope but not the certainty that his petitions will be heard. The mercy of which Donne speaks in the central independent clause—"then thy *long-livd,* thy *everlasting Mercy*"—is actually astonishingly brief in comparison to the rest of the sentence. The moment of security in this final sentence, though physically central, is fleeting, beset by fears before and after; the syntax expresses the radical dependency of Donne's faith: "though *that,* which I most earnestly pray against, should fall upon mee, a *relapse* into those *sinnes* which I have *truely repented,* and thou hast *fully pardoned.*" See discussion above, chap. 2.

41. Eliot himself validated this approach when he wrote, "But I believe that the critical writings of poets, of which in the past there have been some very distinguished examples, owe a great deal of their interest to the fact that the poet, at the back of his mind, if not as his ostensible purpose, is always trying to defend the kind of poetry he is writing, or to formulate the kind that he wants to write.... What he writes about poetry, in short, must be assessed in relation to the poetry he writes" ("The Music of Poetry" [1942], in *On Poetry and Poets,* 26).

42. Gish writes of *Four Quartets* that "the primary experience they articulate is the experience of thought.... Their merit lies not only in evocative power but in integrity of thought and precision of statement. Most importantly, it lies in the accuracy with which the poems convey a movement of the mind, the form of mental exploration" (*Time in the Poetry of T. S. Eliot,* 92).

Chapter IV: Browne

1. See Bottrall, *Every Man a Phoenix,* 33–34, on the presentation of a self that is "necessarily unique, yet not singular or unrelated to larger human issues."

2. *Religio Medici,* in Browne, *Religio Medici and Other Works,* ed. Martin, 1.34. Unless otherwise noted, all references to *Religio Medici* are to this edition, with part and section number indicated in the text.

3. Thoreau, *Walden,* ed. Shanley, 5, 10. All further references to *Walden* are to this edition.

4. Harding and Meyer, *A New Thoreau Handbook,* 98–103; Whaling, "Studies in Thoreau's Reading"; Van Doren, *Henry David Thoreau,* 81; Matthiessen, *American Renaissance,* 110–30; Krutch, "Thoreau and Sir Thomas Browne." The copying into the commonplace book is noted by Matthiessen, *American Renaissance,* 100.

5. Poirier, *A World Elsewhere,* 84.

6. *Walden* was published in 1854, when Thoreau was thirty-seven, though his stay at Walden Pond was earlier, between 1845–47, when he was twenty-eight to thirty. The authorized version of *Religio Medici* was published in 1643, when

Browne was thirty-eight, though according to his preface he wrote it "about seven yeares past." Thoreau says he is responding to the "very particular inquiries . . . made by my townsmen" (1), though the *Journal* entries out of which *Walden* is shaped, if not antedating such inquiries, are at least as powerful an impulse to composition. And Browne, though he claims to have written *Religio Medici* "for my private exercise and satisfaction . . . at leisurable houres" needed little time and relatively minor changes to transform that "most depraved copy" (the pirated version published in 1642) into a "full and intended copy" which he saw fit to publish.

7. Sir Kenelm Digby read *Religio Medici* on the advice of his friend Edward Sackville, fourth earl of Dorset, and sat up all night to write a detailed response, which was then printed as *Observations upon Religio Medici* (London, 1643); reprinted in *The Works of Sir Thomas Browne*, ed. Wilkin. Digby asks, "What should I say Of his making so particular a narration of personal things, and private thoughts of his own?—the knowledge whereof cannot much conduce to any man's betterment; which I make account is the chief end of his writing this discourse" (2:469). See the account in Huntley, *Sir Thomas Browne*, chap. 9; and Wise, *Sir Thomas Browne's Religio Medici*.

8. Most outspoken among these is Fish, "The Bad Physician: The Case of Sir Thomas Browne," in *Self-Consuming Artifacts,* 353–73. These questions are also considered by Webber, *The Eloquent "I"*; Hall, *Ceremony and Civility,* 171–90; and Ziegler, *In Divided and Distinguished Worlds*. I have elsewhere considered the peculiar intensity of response to Browne's rhetoric, the assumption by a number of modern critics that there is something not merely aesthetically but morally suspect about his approach, in "Sir Thomas Browne and Stanley Fish: A Case of Malpractice."

9. *Religio Medici* was published first in an unauthorized edition in 1642, and then, in one somewhat amended, in 1643. Although the individual changes are relatively slight, as a whole they seem intended to respond to the criticisms offered by Sir Kenelm Digby in his *Observations,* and to make Browne's position less contentious, more conciliatory in expression. For an authoritative discussion of the revisions, see Post, "Browne's Revisions of *Religio Medici*"; and for a view of their political significance, Wilding, *Dragons Teeth,* 87–113.

10. Although twentieth-century readers, until rather recently, tended to think Browne was outside religious controversy, *Religio Medici* was in fact vigorously responded to by contemporaries who disagreed with it. According to Waddington, "Browne's contemporary critics Digby and Ross were wrong in most particulars but right in their general assumption that Browne was engaging in religious controversy" ("The Two Tables in *Religio Medici*," 98).

11. Hall, "Epistle," notes Browne's negotiation between the private and the public modes.

12. Waddington asserts that "the Two Tables . . . supply a structure of topics and themes that ought to be recognizable to any reader sufficiently beguiled by Browne's title to open the book" ("The Two Tables in *Religio Medici*," 98).

Waddington elaborates the point made by Huntley, *Sir Thomas Browne,* 107–17. The biblical reference is to Matthew 22:36–40.

13. See Hall on the informality of the epistolary mode in "Epistle."

14. Fish, *Self-Consuming Artifacts,* chap. 7; Webber, *The Eloquent "I,"* 181. Roston, on the other hand, sees a deliberate rhetorical device: "The *Religio Medici* ... is not a tortuous search for certitude ... but rather the celebration of an achieved equilibrium of spirit" ("The 'Doubting' Thomas," 74).

15. Samuel Johnson's Life of Sir Thomas Browne (1756), originally prefixed to an edition of Browne's *Christian Morals,* reprinted in *The Major Works,* ed. Patrides, 488. Thoreau understood rather better than Johnson, commenting in *A Week on the Concord and Merrimack Rivers,* "The wonder is, rather, that all men do not assert as much" (noted by Matthiessen, *American Renaissance,* 111).

16. In addition to Hall, "Epistle," see also the extended discussion by Nathanson, *The Strategy of Truth,* 111–41.

17. See Wilding, *Dragons Teeth,* 89–113; and Guibbory, "'A rationall of old Rites,'" 229–41. The phrase "warfaring Christian," from Milton's *Areopagitica,* is itself something of a textual crux (see *Complete Prose Works,* 2.515, for a statement of the reasons for preferring this reading to "wayfaring"). In the case of Browne also, "warfaring," suggesting the rigor of the campaign, is preferable to "wayfaring," suggesting the faithfulness of a pilgrimage.

18. Post, "The Politics of Laughter," chap. 5 of *Sir Thomas Browne.*

19. Hall connects this point with the negotiation between public and private modes of discourse. Of the opening, she says: "Despite the startling immediacy of the first sentence, the opening lines still contain a good deal of polite deference. These 'protestation[s], parenthesis ... and digressions' ... though borrowed from an earlier tradition of the letter, are directed here not to Browne's confidant but to 'the world,' whose menacing hostility the speaker is quite aware of. In explaining himself to an intimate associate, Browne also politely defers to the better judgment of a faceless public ('the generall scandall of my profession')" ("Epistle," 235).

20. In Genesis the spirit of God moved upon the face of the waters. But the birdlike image of the divine spirit hatching the world, which had its source in Hermetic texts, appears of course not only in Browne but also in *Paradise Lost,* in which the Spirit "with mighty wings outspread / Dove-like satst brooding on the vast Abyss / And mad'st it pregnant" (1.20–22).

21. Roston, "The 'Doubting' Thomas," 74.

22. Martin, ed., *Religio Medici,* 291, supplies the genealogy of Browne's series of definitions, noting Ficino's *De lumine* and Ralegh's *History of the World* as likely sources, the former, of the idea and the latter, of something very close to the phrase.

23. If one needed evidence for Browne's text as construct, the representation of discovery rather than the thing itself, one could note that some of the most dramatic of Browne's effects were added to the 1643 text, in particular, the climactic ending of 1.59: "and thus was I dead before I was alive ... and *Eve*

miscarried of mee before she conceiv'd of *Cain*"; as well as the heart of 2.11: "The earth is a point not onely in respect of the heavens above us . . . . to begin the Alphabet of man."

24. See for instance Webber, *The Eloquent "I,"* 154.

25. I speak here of modern readers, who may well have on this and other subjects doubts not shared by Browne's contemporaries.

26. Hall, "Epistle," notes how Browne characteristically shifts style and rhythm in the course of a section, as he moves from earthly to heavenly considerations: "In the *Religio*, it is the meditation that generates the incantatory lilt in the rhythm, the roll of the cursus, and the ritualized utterances of Hebraic symphony, all of which frequently move Browne's style from middle to elevated" (236).

27. Browne here canvasses a well-known philosophical principle, but the function of his prose is to make the ordinary reader experience the insufficiency of sense perception. On fideism and skepticism in Browne, see Nathanson, *The Strategy of Truth*, 143–76.

Chapter V: Thoreau

1. Thoreau, *Walden*, ed. Shanley, 84, 49; all further references to *Walden* are to this edition. Galligan, "The Comedian at Walden Pond," connects the matter of universality with the tone of *Walden*, making a point that applies also to *Religio Medici*. Galligan argues that *Walden* must be a comedy to solve its inherent technical problems: "to manage a first-person narrative celebrating the goodness of life and the divinity of the individual in such a way that it would not become cloying or pompous, bland or arrogant, blind or smug" (31). Yet not everyone has been persuaded of the celebratory quality of *Walden;* most notably, see Bridgman, *Dark Thoreau.*

2. Cavell raises these darker possibilities in *The Senses of Walden*, 65. On the word play of the opening, see Lane, "Thoreau's *Walden*," 35; Lane finds sixteen examples in the first three paragraphs.

3. One might argue that this is the result of *Walden*'s not having a preface, so that the apologetic matter is mixed with the text proper. But such explicitness is typical of Thoreau. Indeed, this tendency to extend, to make the qualities of the seventeenth-century text more explicit, is one of the characteristics of generic extension in the works I'm considering.

4. Cavell speaks of "the fiction . . . that some unknown people have asked him these prompting questions" (45–46). On the generic backgrounds of *Walden*, see Buell, *Literary Transcendentalism;* Buell cites the sermon and the essay as bases for *Walden,* and (103) the lyceum lecture.

5. Thoreau gives us a sample of these questions: "Some have asked what I got to eat; if I did not feel lonesome; if I was not afraid; and the like. Others have been curious to learn what portion of my income I devoted to charitable

purposes; and some, who have large families, how many poor children I maintained" (3).

6. See the account by Mazzeo, "A Seventeenth-Century Theory of Metaphysical Poetry" and "Metaphysical Poetry and the Poetic of Correspondence," 29–59.

7. *Religio Medici* 1.16. For an account of the tradition, see Wallerstein, *Studies in Seventeenth-Century Poetic*, 181–277.

8. Cudworth, *The True Intellectual System of the Universe*, 1678. Matthiessen noted early "the intimate kinship to the seventeenth-century metaphysical strain that was felt by Emerson, Thoreau, and Melville" (*American Renaissance*, xiii). Thoreau's position within transcendentalism is a vast subject in itself. See for example the discussions of Lawrence Buell, *Literary Transcendentalism*; McIntosh, *Thoreau as Romantic Naturalist*; and Frederick Garber, *Thoreau's Redemptive Imagination*. Emerson, as Matthiessen notes, articulates the principle of meaning in nature: "Particular natural facts are symbols of particular spiritual facts. Nature is the symbol of spirit" (Emerson, "Language," cited by Matthiessen, *American Renaissance*, 40). Buell associates Emerson with the "tradition of Christian typology in western thought, leavened by pantheistic influences. He imbibed these traditions from a variety of sources, including the neoplatonic tradition from Plotinus to Cudworth; more recent German, French, and English Unitarian pantheism as digested and transmitted by Coleridge; Swedenborgianism; seventeenth-century metaphysical poetry; and Goethe's idea of the metamorphosis of plants." Buell concludes, "But rather than insist on specific sources, it is fairer to say that the idea of correspondence was generally in the air" (*Literary Transcendentalism*, 149–50).

9. Cavell describes these passages as "parodies of America's methods of evaluation" (*The Senses of Walden*, 30).

10. See Woodson, "The Two Beginnings of *Walden*."

11. Seybold describes Thoreau as "a youthful mystic" who later "lost the ability to enter the ecstatic state" (*Thoreau*, 73). Thorp also held that "his delight in Nature correspondingly dried" (quoted by Wagenknecht, *Henry David Thoreau*, 30, who provides a list of others who hold this view). In moving toward a greater concern with facts and documentation later in life, Thoreau resembles Browne, who in *Religio Medici* emphasized the wondrous quality of the natural world and in *Pseudodoxia Epidemica* (popularly known as *Vulgar Errors*) sought to discredit superstition, turning to more precise observation of natural phenomena.

12. As an example of too specific determinations, I would cite Paul's introduction to the Riverside Edition, *Walden and Civil Disobedience*. By contrast, the indeterminacy of *Walden* may be seen in Cavell's elucidation of *The Senses of Walden*.

13. Like Walden Pond itself, the beans are an expression of something in the earth: "making the yellow soil express its summer thought in bean leaves

and blossoms rather than in wormwood and piper and millet grass, making the earth say beans instead of grass" (157).

14. Thoreau's tendency to use separate sentences reflects in part the movement toward shorter syntactic units in the two hundred years that separate Thoreau from Browne. Given that historical shift, the effect is not significantly different, although it does make Thoreau's representation of the process of discovery perhaps more tentative and less celebratory than Browne's.

15. This whole scene may remind the reader of the interchanging of meadow and sea, the world of water and land, in Andrew Marvell's "Upon Appleton House."

16. Matthew 6:19–20.

17. Matthiessen, *American Renaissance*, 65 et passim.

18. See the accounts of Shanley, *The Making of Walden*, and Cameron, *Writing Nature*.

19. Broderick describes the movement of Thoreau's prose from observation to speculation and back again in "The Movement of Thoreau's Prose," 133–42.

20. "I did not read books the first summer; I hoed beans. Nay, I often did better than this" (111).

21. The circumstantial quality of this description reminds one of the ongoing attempts by Jewish and Christian scholars to fix the precise moment of creation in time. The most popular date was 4000 B.C., the time of the year, spring; see the discussion by Nicolson, *The Breaking of the Circle*, 108–12. In *Pseudodoxia Epidemica* (6.1), Sir Thomas Browne examines the question at some length, finding not only the date but the season of the year indeterminate.

22. Garber, *Thoreau's Redemptive Imagination*, notes the association of the West with Eden (216–17).

23. See the account by Wallerstein, *Studies in Seventeenth-Century Poetic*, 44–55.

24. Arbitrary though Thoreau's finding of words and letters in the thawing bank may seem, his literalism here is related to the language theories of Charles Kraitsir, *Significance of the Alphabet* (1846), and *Glossology: Being a Treatise on the Nature of Language and the Language of Nature* (1852), described by Gura, *The Wisdom of Words: Language, Theology, and Literature in the New England Renaissance*, chap. 4; and West, "Charles Kraitsir's Influence on Thoreau's Theory of Language."

25. The statement might well be an oblique reference to Browne himself, whose testimony in 1665 at a Norfolk witch trial has occasioned much comment. See the accounts of Finch, *Sir Thomas Browne*, 214–18; Bennett, *Sir Thomas Browne*, 11–16; and Post, *Sir Thomas Browne*, 16–18.

Chapter VI: Burton

1. Noted by Dewey, "Burton's Melancholy," 292–93. Since *anatomy* was a frequently used designation in the Renaissance, denoting a systematic treatment

of a subject (see Hodges, *Renaissance Fictions of Anatomy*), the designation by subject would have been the more definitive in Burton's day.

2. On the systematic nature of the *Anatomy*, see Bensly, "Some Alterations and Errors," and Hodges, *Renaissance Fictions of Anatomy*. For Osler, the *Anatomy* is a "great medical treatise, orderly in arrangement" ("Burton's Anatomy of Melancholy," 252); Frye terms it "the greatest Menippean satire in English before Swift" (*Anatomy of Criticism*, 311). Lyons, *The Voices of Melancholy*, and Lawrence Babb, *Sanity in Bedlam*, point to the strong contemporary interest in the subject.

3. Vicari, in *The View from Minerva's Tower*, does refer to the *Anatomy* as a "manual of hygiene" (5, 58–67, 144, et passim), but she stresses the idea of Burton as a healer of souls.

4. Bamborough, Introduction to *The Anatomy of Melancholy*, ed. Faulkner, Kiessling, and Blair, 1.xx-xxvi, argues that Burton is trying for encyclopedic mastery at a time when it was no longer possible; Fox, *The Tangled Chain*, sees an attempt to bring all things together, arguing that structure is the most important thing a reader sees in the *Anatomy*, that Burton attempts to impose order on a disorderly subject. Babb has described the *Anatomy* as a work that combines a diversity of kinds of writing; King, *Studies in Six Seventeenth-Century Writers*, 83–84, sees an author overwhelmed by his material, facing it with obviously inadequate equipment, a writer comically unable to handle the basic writing of a book. Other critics, such as Lyons, have seen Burton's work as primarily satiric (this is especially true of the preface, but it's hard to make this description fit the whole). Colie, in *Paradoxica Epidemica* and "Some Notes on Burton's Erasmus," has stressed the *Anatomy*'s place within the tradition of learned paradox, of learned self-reflexivity, seeing a particular connection between Burton and Erasmus: like the voice of folly praising folly, Burton is the melancholy scholar who writes about melancholy to avoid melancholy. Fish, *Self-Consuming Artifacts*, characteristically sees Burton as the supremely manipulative author, and Vicari, one of the most recent critics of Burton, sees him as the quintessential Christian humanist.

5. In *Renaissance Fictions of Anatomy*, one of the most helpful of recent treatments, Hodges notes the *Anatomy*'s connection both with encyclopedic approaches and with analytical ones; but, as she points out, the anatomist's method of revealing order also turns its subject into fragments (108).

6. Fox, *The Tangled Chain*, 40, uses the analogy to make a rather different point.

7. See ibid., 36–40, 211–31, et passim.

8. The connection here with Ramist methodology has been noted by several scholars, especially Renaker, "Robert Burton and the Ramist Method," and most recently by Höltgen, "Literary Art and Scientific Method," 24. See also Ong, *Ramus, Method and the Decay of Dialogue*.

9. Burton, *The Anatomy of Melancholy*, ed. Faulkner, Kiessling, and Blair, 1. 1. All references are to this edition; volume and page numbers will be cited in the

text; occasional translations of Burton's Latin quotations are from Jackson's edition.

10. Fish, *Self-Consuming Artifacts,* chap. 6.

11. Bamborough, putting this method in the context of Burton's scholarly training, takes a rather different view of its effect (*The Anatomy of Melancholy,* 1.xxvi).

12. See MacDonald, *Mystical Bedlam,* and Porter, *Mind-Forg'd Manacles.*

13. The warning (1.387) was inserted in 1628 and expanded in 1632.

14. Richard Lanham, in a lecture at Smith College, Spring 1982, on the kinds of language appropriate to certain occasions and situations, produced as an example a brief section of the California highway code that attempts to specify exactly which shrubs (or plants) (or trees), etc. one may not cut — or remove — or injure, etc. from the side of the highway. In legal language as in *The Anatomy of Melancholy,* the attempt at inclusiveness leads inevitably to the possibility of omission. I am grateful to Marian Macdonald for helping me recall the date of this presentation.

15. For example Fish, *Self-Consuming Artifacts,* chap. 6. Baker, in *The Wars of Truth,* also suggests this as the effect, if not the intention, of Burton's treatise.

16. Frye, *Anatomy of Criticism,* notes that Burton's "'digressions,' . . . when examined turn out to be scholarly distillations of Menippean forms" (311); Vicari, *The View from Minerva's Tower,* 131, associates them with the oral tradition.

17. See, for example, Renaker, "Robert Burton and the Ramist Method," 210–20.

18. Lyons, *Voices of Melancholy,* 121–41.

19. For Milton's use of tradition and his indebtedness to Burton, see Grace, "Notes on Robert Burton and John Milton."

20. The vast literature on the subject includes the essays by Croll, "Attic Prose" and "The Baroque Style in Prose"; the work of Williamson, *The Senecan Amble;* as well as of their more recent successors.

21. Burton's copy is Bodleian 4to G8 Art, which includes thirteen other texts bound together with Dekker.

22. Burton's annotations in the back flyleaf of *The Anatomy of Melancholy* (1624) record how the book has grown over its first edition (Bodl. NN 17 Th. Rous). He lists the number of leaves for each partition or section of the book and concludes: "added ——— 20 sheetes and a leafe in the third Edition" (see Höltgen, "Literary Art and Scientific Method," 30 and 35 n. 42); he also makes notes about the misprints and misreadings of his manuscript. Burton's concern with the physical text, his literal counting of pages, is one more link with Sterne, who tells us not that he will continue the story of Tristram but that he will publish two volumes a year.

23. Bacon, "Of Truth," *The Essayes,* 7.

24. O'Connell, *Robert Burton,* chap. 4, "Words against Melancholy," comments on Burton's playing off English against Latin and further suggests that Burton uses Latin in a talismanic way (63).

25. See the Appendix for a complete version of the original text and Burton's revisions.

26. Hallwachs, "Additions and Revisions."

27. In 1624 Burton added "I care, I feare" to the sentence beginning "No, I recant" and in 1628 added "(Reader)" after "I owe thee nothing."

28. That the technique still thrives as artistic strategy is to be seen in its (relatively) recent appearance in a Monty Python skit in which John Cleese alternately insults and speaks civilly to a job applicant.

29. Sterne, *The Life and Opinions of Tristram Shandy, Gentleman*, ed. Melvyn New and Joan New, 1.22.

30. This sense is borne out by the fact that the majority of the additions to subsequent editions of the *Anatomy* are to the non-medical sections of the work (noted by Vicari, *The View from Minerva's Tower*, 5). As O'Connell puts it, "The real energy of the *Anatomy*, in fact, goes into the great non-medical sections of the book." "The therapeutic medium . . . is language" (*Robert Burton*, 58, 62).

31. Lord Byron said that by reading Burton one could gain a reputation for being learned with the least effort; noted by Jackson, Introduction to *The Anatomy of Melancholy*, 1.xvi.

32. See Nardo, "Robert Burton's Play Therapy," *The Ludic Self*, 139–57.

Chapter VII: Sterne

1. Ferriar, *Illustrations of Sterne*, 4. Ferriar noted that Sterne drew a good deal of his erudition from "the ludicrous writers," a line beginning with Rabelais, Beroald, D'Aubigné, and Bruscambille (mentioned in *Tristram Shandy* 3.35), and continuing through Swift. Ferriar's investigations actually began with an address to the Literary and Philosophical Society of Manchester in 1791 (published in the Society's *Memoirs* [1793] 4:45–86; noted by New, ed., *Tristram Shandy*, 3.13, n. 21). Ferriar's insights are pursued in much greater detail by Booth in "*Tristram Shandy* and its Precursors"; see also Jackson, "Sterne, Burton, and Ferriar."

2. There's a comic twist in the plagiarism: Burton, *Anatomy of Melancholy*, 2.3.5.1, notes how Cicero triumphed over grief by philosophical consolation: "Then he began to triumph over fortune and griefe, and for her reception into heaven to be much more joyed, then before he was troubled for her losse" (2.181); Sterne goes further, mocking the fact that the orator's delight in the speech he is about to compose overcomes his grief for the loss of his daughter: "But as soon as he began to look into the stores of philosophy, and consider how many excellent things might be said upon the occasion—no body upon earth can conceive, says the great orator, how happy, how joyful, it made me" (5.3).

3. Especially in the notes to the editions of Work and of Melvyn and Joan New.

4. On learned wit, see Jefferson, "Sterne and the Tradition of Learned Wit";

Traugott, *Tristram Shandy's World*; and New, *Laurence Sterne as Satirist*. With regard to interrupted narratives, see Booth's discussion in *The Rhetoric of Fiction*, chap. 8, and in "The Self-Conscious Narrator in Comic Fiction before *Tristram Shandy*"; Hunter, "Response as Reformation"; and Harries, *The Unfinished Manner*, especially chap. 2.

5. Lanham, *Tristram Shandy*, chap. 1; Lanham provides a summary of previous criticism, giving particular prominence to Traugott, *Tristram Shandy's World*; see also Day, "*Tristram Shandy*."

6. See the summary by Hartley, "Yorick Redivivus"; Hartley, *Laurence Sterne in the Twentieth Century*, 21–23; and New, *Telling New Lies*, chaps. 3 and 4.

7. Booth, "*Tristram Shandy* and Its Precursors," 65.

8. Lanham, *Tristram Shandy*, 6–18, describes the Victorian reaction; see also Howes, *Yorick and the Critics*.

9. Stephen, "Sterne," 3:151; Woolf, "Sterne," *Collected Essays*, 3:90. Woolf does acknowledge that when in certain passages "it becomes obvious that he has now time to think of himself our attention strays also, and we ask irrelevant questions—whether, for instance, Sterne was a good man" (92). But for Woolf such questions arise only when the art falters; for Sir Leslie they seem to be a persistent concern.

10. The phrase, of course, is Matthew Arnold's, from "The Study of Poetry."

11. On the subject of the transition from predominantly oral to predominantly visual texts and on textual space as a representation of silence, see Ong, *Orality and Literacy*, chap. 5. Ong cites *Tristram Shandy* but not *The Anatomy of Melancholy* on the use of typographic space (128).

12. For a full account of the frontispiece, see William R. Mueller, "Robert Burton's Frontispiece." Bamborough, in his Introduction to the *Anatomy*, 1.xxxi, gives an account of the appearance and disappearance of Burton's name from the text, a sequence that seems to reflect the vagaries of publishing rather than any attempt at authorial concealment.

13. The extent of Burton's revisions and additions is startling. When *The Anatomy of Melancholy* was first published in 1621, it was already a hefty volume of some 300,000 words of text and another 50,000 of marginalia. The next edition, of 1624, added another 60,000 words; the edition of 1628, nearly 50,000 words; the 1632 edition, a mere 28,000 words, and the 1638 edition, only 3,000 words of text; so that the final edition, of 1651, published posthumously, was almost half again as long as the first edition. See Faulkner, Kiessling, and Blair, Textual Introduction, 1.xxxvii-xxxix.

14. The text cited throughout is *The Life and Opinions of Tristram Shandy, Gentleman*, ed. Melvyn New and Joan New; volume and chapter numbers are cited in the text.

15. Lamb, *Sterne's Fiction*, 48, points out how Sterne can establish authenticity only by demonstrating inauthenticity.

16. As noted above, Ferriar finds the origin of the first four chapters of

Tristram Shandy in Burton. A further point of similarity: not only does Tristram, for comic narrative purposes, calculate the day and hour of his conception, but also Burton, who notes in the *Anatomy,* "Saturn was lord of my geniture," and calculates the date of his conception with great care. Burton also cast numerous other horoscopes; these calculations are preserved in a notebook of Burton's bound together with Claudius Ptolemaeus, *Quadripartium judicorum opus,* 1519, Bodleian 4to R9 Art. For a detailed account of this text, see Bamborough, "Robert Burton's Astrological Notebook."

17. As Price says in *To the Palace of Wisdom,* "Readers of fiction are generally eager to surrender themselves to belief; so long as a novel is conducted with sufficient skill, its conventions are rapidly accepted. Sterne insists upon making us conscious of all we have commonly taken for granted. By pretending incompetence or indecision, by teasing us with false leads or cheating our logical expectations, he exposes the forms at every point" (326).

18. And as Bamborough notes in his Introduction to the *Anatomy,* 1.xxvii, digressions were seen as generically appropriate to long works.

19. Yet a concern with encyclopedic knowledge has also been seen in Sterne. New cites Sterne's extensive use of Chambers's *Cyclopaedia* and of Ozell's notes to Rabelais as evidence of a Bloomian anxiety of influence; his account recalls Bamborough's view of Burton: "Sterne was the century's last great seeker for 'heterogeneous matter,'" someone who fought against the "ever-increasing fragmentation of knowledge and experience" (*Telling New Lies,* 102–3).

20. Babb's description of the digressions as "separable compositions" (*Sanity in Bedlam,* 6–10) gives some notion of the nature of the text; Fox, *The Tangled Chain,* 45–52, argues for the pertinence and necessity of the digressions; Lyons, *Voices of Melancholy,* describes the digressions as better integrated into the structure than has been thought, but also as a "manifestation of the melancholy character" (127). On Sterne's digressiveness see Hunter, "Response as Reformation"; Jefferson, "Sterne and the Tradition of Learned Wit"; and Booth, "*Tristram Shandy* and Its Predecessors."

21. With regard to the question of whether Sterne lived to complete *Tristram Shandy,* Booth, "Did Sterne Complete *Tristram Shandy?,*" has argued persuasively that in the last volume Sterne accomplished all that he wanted to accomplish in the last volume of his novel. This is different from saying that if Sterne had lived longer he might not have written more before arriving at that last volume, or from my point that Sterne was involved in the writing of *Tristram Shandy* as long as he had breath and energy to be so, just as Burton continued to add to the *Anatomy* throughout his life.

22. Of course the commonplace book has grown to the proportions of an encyclopedia — hence again the difficulty of identifying genre in conventional terms.

23. It has been well argued by Traugott, *Tristram Shandy's World,* chaps. 1, 2, that what Sterne gives us in *Tristram Shandy* is not Locke's association of ideas but an instance of the mad application of this notion, not so much a parody of

Locke as a reinterpretation of him. For Locke, such a way of thinking meant the breakdown of all rational discourse; in *Tristram Shandy* it is the norm—though clearly, from Sterne's view, Shandean or Shandaiacal. See also Nuttall, *A Common Sky*, chap. 2; and Lamb, *Sterne's Fiction*.

24. See the discussion of Harries, *The Unfinished Manner*, chap. 2.

25. On the tradition of maledictions on which Sterne draws, see Little, *Benedictine Maledictions*.

26. Sterne's note calls attention to his lifting of the list from another source, although not, as New points out (*Tristram Shandy* 3.404), the source he cites. Sterne refers to Pellegrini, whose categories enable a gentleman to write "many pages concerning any the meanest subject proposed to him"; but there is a possible further parody in that his list is actually based on Obadiah Walker, *Of Education*; see New 3.397, 405. A similar situation seems to obtain in 6.19; see ibid., 3.417–22.

27. The point is brilliantly developed by Lanham, *Tristram Shandy*.

28. Sterne of course also wrote *A Journal to Eliza*, which did not appear in print until 1904. Burton's *Philosophaster*, a Latin play about university life, dates from 1606; Burton makes the point about his sermons in Democritus Junior to the Reader, 1.20–21.

29. Sterne published volumes 1–2 in 1759; 3 and 4 in January 1761; 5 and 6 in December 1761; 7 and 8 in January 1765; and 9 in January 1767; on March 18, 1768, a month after the publication of *A Sentimental Journey*, he died.

30. In *The Library of Robert Burton*, Kiessling gives a detailed account of the contents of Burton's library, showing the nature of Burton's interest, including his continuing interest in new materials in many fields, and the nature of his annotations, which "reveal a bibliophile who read with a purpose. He was always ready to underscore, mark with a check in the margin, or highlight an interesting passage with a word or two in the margin. Many of these marked passages found their way into various editions of the *Anatomy*, even into the sixth, published in 1651, more than a decade after his death" (xxxiv).

31. In 1621 Burton dedicated *The Anatomy of Melancholy* to George, Lord Berkeley; on September 3, 1624, Lord Berkeley granted Burton the advowson, or right of presentation, of the living of Seagrave; in June of 1632, when the then rector died, Robert Burton was finally inducted into it. See O'Connell, *Robert Burton*, 21–22; and Höltgen, "Robert Burton and the Rectory of Seagrave."

32. The degree of identification was such that a letter addressed to "Tristram Shandy, Europe," was successfully delivered to Sterne at his home in Coxwold; noted by Cross, *The Life and Times of Laurence Sterne*, 225.

33. Hartley, *Laurence Sterne in the Twentieth Century*, 65–74, gives an account of the rapidly shifting identities attributed to Sterne's readers; Harries, "The Sorrows and Confessions of a Cross-Eyed 'Female-Reader' of Sterne," 113–14, notes the particular abuse heaped on "Madam." On matters of time in *Tristram*

Shandy, see Baird, "The Time-Scheme in *Tristram Shandy* and a Source"; and Lehman, "Of Time, Personality, and the Author."

34. There certainly were revisions of the text of *Tristram Shandy*, although the News' edition shows that these almost entirely predated the publication of individual volumes (*Tristram Shandy*, 2.814–62).

35. According to Lamb, "Sterne's illusion that he was inhabiting his own text, or that his life had become a quotation or a continuation of it to the point where he could read himself in what he had already written, shows him exploiting (perhaps beyond reasonable bounds) two related associationist positions" (*Sterne's Fiction*, 83).

36. See Booth, *Rhetoric of Fiction*, chap. 8, on the power of the narrator as a unifying force in *Tristram Shandy*.

37. See for example Booth, "The Self-Conscious Narrator"; this aspect of Yorick comes through most strongly in the introductory chapters (1.10–12).

38. Yorick "had an invincible dislike and opposition in his nature to gravity;----not to gravity as such;----for where gravity was wanted, he would be the most grave or serious of mortal men for days and weeks together;---but he was an enemy to the affectation of it, and declared open war against it, only as it appeared a cloak for ignorance, or for folly" (1.11). Sterne's statement is from a letter dated Jan. 30, 1760, perhaps to Dr. Noah Thomas, a Scarborough physician (Sterne, *Letters*, 90).

39. Burton continues, "and what I say, is meerely reading, *ex aliorum forsan ineptiis*, by mine owne observation, and others relation" (3.196).

40. Although Sterne addresses his readers, male and female, in diverse ways, treating them more like a competitive school than a community, chiding some for what they have missed, representing others as forward and eager, his female readers, as Harries has noted, fare particularly badly; that view is shared by Benedict, "'Dear Madam.'" But for a quite different view of women, as taking central and sympathetic roles in *Tristram Shandy*, see New, "Job's Wife and Sterne's Other Women," 55–74; and Telotte, "'Fire, Water, Women, Wind,'" 118–22.

41. See the discussion by Harries, "The Sorrows and Confessions of a Cross-Eyed 'Female-Reader' of Sterne," 113–14, on the consequences for female readers of Sterne's depiction of women in *Tristram Shandy*.

42. Tristram (8.24) compares the Widow Wadman's beautiful eyes to those of Rhodopis of Thrace, and Sterne supplies a Latin footnote cribbed from Burton (8.24); Work, *Tristram Shandy*, 577, makes the connection to Burton, *Anatomy of Melancholy* (3.92).

43. Indeed, Burton is not in this instance bawdy; it's just that his *etc.* leaves room for thought. In "A Note on Annotating *Tristram Shandy*," 18–19, New notes one of the definitions of "et cetera" (*OED* 2.b): "as substitute for a suppressed substantive, generally a coarse or indelicate one."

44. Sterne's intention of course remains indeterminable; my concern, in any case, is with what he does next.

45. That Yorick's own comment, "BRAVO," is later crossed out is but the culminating instance of this characteristic process. The gesture, Elizabeth Harries informs me, was characterized by Martin Price in a note to her as "Sterne's styptic pencil."

VIII: Questions of History

1. On this point see Buell, *The Environmental Imagination,* who notes that "Thoreau largely edited out the pipe smoke and wagon traffic on the Wayland road (now Route 126)" (71).

SELECT BIBLIOGRAPHY

I have listed below primarily sources referred to or cited in the text and notes, but I include as well a number of sources that were important in shaping my views of genre and the texts I write about.

Primary Texts

Dante Alighieri. *The Divine Comedy*. Trans. John D. Sinclair. New York: Oxford Univ. Press, 1961.
Bacon, Sir Francis. *The Essayes or Counsels, Civill and Morall*. Ed. Michael Kiernan. Cambridge: Harvard Univ. Press, 1985.
Browne, Sir Thomas. *Pseudodoxia Epidemica*. Ed. Robin Robbins. Oxford: Clarendon Press, 1981.
———. *Religio Medici and Other Works*. Ed. L. C. Martin. Oxford: Clarendon Press, 1964.
———. *The Major Works*. Ed. C. A. Patrides. Harmondsworth, Middlesex: Penguin, 1977.
———. *The Works of Sir Thomas Browne*. Ed. Geoffrey Keynes. Chicago: Univ. of Chicago Press, 1964.
———. *The Works of Sir Thomas Browne*. Ed. Simon Wilkin. London: Bohn, 1852.
Burton, Robert. *The Anatomy of Melancholy*. Ed. Thomas C. Faulkner, Nicolas K. Kiessling, and Rhonda L. Blair; with an introduction by J. B. Bamborough. Oxford: Clarendon Press, 1989–94.
———. *The Anatomy of Melancholy*. Ed. Holbrook Jackson. London: J. M. Dent & Sons, 1932.
Donne, John. *Devotions upon Emergent Occasions*. Ed. Anthony Raspa. New York: Oxford Univ. Press, 1987.
———. *Devotions upon Emergent Occasions*. Ed. John Sparrow. Cambridge: Cambridge Univ. Press, 1923.
———. *The Divine Poems*. Ed. Helen Gardner. Oxford: Clarendon Press, 1952.
Eliot, T. S. *The Complete Poems and Plays, 1909–1950*. New York: Harcourt Brace, 1958.
———. *For Lancelot Andrewes*. Garden City, N.Y.: Doubleday, Doran, 1929.
———. *On Poetry and Poets*. London: Faber and Faber, 1957.
———. *Selected Essays, 1917–1932*. New York: Harcourt Brace, 1932.
Herbert, George. *The Works of George Herbert*. Ed. F. E. Hutchinson. Oxford: Clarendon Press, 1941.
Milton, John. *Complete Prose Works of John Milton*. Ed. Don M. Wolfe. New Haven: Yale Univ. Press, 1953–1982.

Select Bibliography

Sterne, Laurence. *Letters.* Ed. Lewis Perry Curtis. Oxford: Clarendon Press, 1935.
———. *The Life and Opinions of Tristram Shandy, Gentleman.* Ed. Melvyn New and Joan New. Gainesville: Univ. Presses of Florida, 1978–84.
———. *The Life and Opinions of Tristram Shandy, Gentleman.* Ed. James A. Work. New York: Odyssey Press, 1940.
Thoreau, Henry David. *Walden.* Ed. J. Lyndon Shanley. Princeton: Princeton Univ. Press, 1971.
———. *Walden and Civil Disobedience.* Ed. Sherman Paul. Cambridge: Houghton Mifflin, 1960.

Secondary Texts

Anderson, Howard. "Tristram Shandy and the Reader's Imagination." *PMLA* 86 (1971): 966–73.
Andreasen, N. J. C. "Donne's *Devotions* and the Psychology of Assent." *Modern Philology* 63 (1965): 207–16.
Babb, Lawrence. *Sanity in Bedlam: A Study of Robert Burton's Anatomy of Melancholy.* East Lansing: Michigan State Univ. Press, 1959.
Baird, Theodore. "The Time-Scheme in *Tristram Shandy* and a Source." *PMLA* 51 (1936): 803–20.
Baker, Herschel. *The Wars of Truth.* Cambridge: Harvard Univ. Press, 1952.
Bakhtin, Mikhail. *Rabelais and His World.* Trans. Hélène Iswolsky. Bloomington: Indiana Univ. Press, 1984.
Bamborough, J. B. "Burton and Cardan." In *English Renaissance Studies Presented to Dame Helen Gardner,* ed. John Carey. Oxford: Oxford Univ. Press, 1980, 180–93.
———. *The Little World of Man.* London: Longmans, Green, 1951.
———. "Robert Burton's Astrological Notebook." *Review of English Studies,* n. s. 32 (1981): 267–85.
Benedict, Barbara M. "'Dear Madam': Rhetoric, Cultural Politics and the Female Reader in Sterne's *Tristram Shandy.*" *Studies in Philology* 89 (1992): 485–98.
Bennett, Joan. *Sir Thomas Browne.* Cambridge: Cambridge Univ. Press, 1962.
Bensly, Edward. "Some Alterations and Errors in Successive Editions of the *Anatomy of Melancholy.*" *Proceedings and Papers of the Oxford Bibliographical Society* 1 (1922–26): 198–218.
Bergonzi, Bernard, ed. *T. S. Eliot: Four Quartets.* London: Macmillan, 1969.
Booth, Wayne. "Did Sterne Complete *Tristram Shandy?*" *Modern Philology* 48 (1951): 171–83.
———. *The Rhetoric of Fiction.* Chicago: Univ. of Chicago Press, 1961.
———. "The Self-Conscious Narrator in Comic Fiction before *Tristram Shandy.*" *PMLA* 67 (1952): 163–85.
———. "*Tristram Shandy* and Its Precursors: The Self-Conscious Narrator." Ph.D. diss., University of Chicago, 1950.

Select Bibliography

Bottrall, Margaret. *Every Man a Phoenix*. London: John Murray, 1958.
Bridgman, Richard. *Dark Thoreau*. Lincoln: Univ. of Nebraska Press, 1982.
Broderick, John. "The Movement of Thoreau's Prose." *American Literature* 33 (1961): 133–42.
Brooker, Jewel Spears. "From *The Waste Land* to *Four Quartets:* Evolution of a Method." In *Words in Time,* ed. Lobb, 84–106.
Bruss, Elizabeth. *Autobiographical Acts*. Baltimore: Johns Hopkins Univ. Press, 1976.
Buell, Lawrence. *The Environmental Imagination: Thoreau, Nature Writing, and the Formation of American Culture*. Cambridge: Belknap Press of Harvard Univ. Press, 1995.
———. *Literary Transcendentalism: Style and Vision in the American Renaissance*. Ithaca and London: Cornell Univ. Press, 1973.
Burckhardt, Sigurd. "*Tristram Shandy*'s Law of Gravity." *ELH* 28 (1961): 70–88.
Cameron, Sharon. *Writing Nature: Henry Thoreau's Journal*. New York: Oxford Univ. Press, 1985.
Carey, John. *John Donne: Life, Mind, and Art*. London: Oxford Univ. Press, 1981.
———, ed. *English Renaissance Studies Presented to Dame Helen Gardner*. Oxford: Oxford Univ. Press, 1980.
Cavell, Stanley. *The Senses of Walden*. New York: Viking Press, 1972.
Claridge, Laura, and Elizabeth Langland, eds. *Out of Bounds: Male Writers and Gender(ed) Criticism*. Amherst: Univ. of Massachusetts Press, 1990.
Cohen, Ralph. "History and Genre." *New Literary History* 17 (1986): 203–18.
———. "Innovation and Variation: Literary Change and Georgic Poetry." In *Literature and History,* a Clark Library Seminar. Los Angeles: University of California, William Andrews Clark Memorial Library, 1974.
———, ed. *New Directions in Literary History*. Baltimore: Johns Hopkins Univ. Press, 1974.
Colie, Rosalie L. *Paradoxica Epidemica*. Princeton: Princeton Univ. Press, 1966.
———. *The Resources of Kind: Genre-Theory in the Renaissance,* ed. Barbara K. Lewalski. Berkeley: Univ. of California Press, 1973.
———. "Some Notes on Burton's Erasmus." *Renaissance Quarterly* 20 (1967): 335–41.
Croll, Morris. "Attic Prose: Lipsius, Montaigne, Bacon." In *Schelling Anniversary Papers*. New York: Century, 1923, 117–50.
———. "The Baroque Style in Prose." In *Studies in English Philology in Honor of Frederick Klaeber,* ed. Kemp Malone and Martin B. Ruud. Minneapolis: Univ. of Minnesota Press, 1929; rpt. in *Seventeenth-Century Prose,* ed. Stanley Fish. New York: Oxford Univ. Press, 1971, 26–52.
Cross, Wilbur. *The Life and Times of Laurence Sterne*. New Haven: Yale Univ. Press, 1929.
Culler, Jonathan. *Structuralist Poetics*. Ithaca: Cornell Univ. Press, 1975.
Davie, Donald. "T. S. Eliot: The End of an Era." *Twentieth Century* (Apr. 1956); rpt. in Bergonzi, ed., *T. S. Eliot: Four Quartets,* 153–67.

Select Bibliography

Day, W. G. "*Tristram Shandy:* Locke May Not Be the Key." In Myer, ed., *Laurence Sterne: Riddles and Mysteries,* 75–83.

Dewey, Nicholas. "Burton's Melancholy: A Paradox Disinterred." *Modern Philology* 68 (1971): 292–93.

Dubrow, Heather. *Genre.* New York: Methuen, 1982.

Ferriar, John. *Illustrations of Sterne: with Other Essays and Verses.* London, 1798. Published in facsimile from a copy in the Beinecke Library, Yale University. New York: Garland, 1971.

Finch, Jeremiah S. *Sir Thomas Browne.* New York: Henry Schuman, 1950.

Fish, Stanley E. *Self-Consuming Artifacts.* Berkeley and Los Angeles: Univ. of California Press, 1972.

Fowler, Alastair. *Kinds of Literature: An Introduction to the Theory of Genres and Modes.* Cambridge: Harvard Univ. Press, 1982.

———. "The Life and Death of Literary Forms." *New Literary History* 2 (1971): 199–216.

Fox, Ruth A. *The Tangled Chain: The Structure of Disorder in the Anatomy of Melancholy.* Berkeley and Los Angeles: Univ. of California Press, 1976.

Frye, Northrop. *Anatomy of Criticism: Four Essays.* Princeton: Princeton Univ. Press, 1957.

Galligan, Edward L. "The Comedian at Walden Pond." *South Atlantic Quarterly* 69 (1970): 20–37.

Garber, Frederick. *Thoreau's Fable of Inscribing.* Princeton: Princeton Univ. Press, 1991.

———. *Thoreau's Redemptive Imagination.* New York: New York Univ. Press, 1977.

Gardner, Helen. *The Art of T. S. Eliot.* London: Faber and Faber, 1949; rpt. 1969.

———. *The Composition of Four Quartets.* New York: Oxford Univ. Press, 1978.

Gish, Nancy. *Time in the Poetry of T. S. Eliot.* Totowa, N. J.: Barnes and Noble, 1981.

Glick, Wendell, ed. *The Recognition of Henry David Thoreau.* Ann Arbor: Univ. of Michigan Press, 1969.

Goldberg, Jonathan. "The Understanding of Sickness in Donne's *Devotions.*" *Renaissance Quarterly* 24 (1971): 507–17.

Gordon, Lyndall. "The American Eliot and 'The Dry Salvages.'" In *Words in Time,* ed. Lobb, 38–51.

———. *Eliot's Early Years.* New York: Oxford Univ. Press, 1977.

———. *Eliot's New Life.* New York: Farrar, Straus and Giroux, 1988.

Grace, William J. "Notes on Robert Burton and John Milton." *Studies in Philology* 52 (1955): 578–91.

Greene, Thomas M. *The Light in Troy: Imitation and Discovery in Renaissance Poetry.* New Haven: Yale Univ. Press, 1982.

Guibbory, Achsah. *The Map of Time: Seventeenth-Century English Literature and Ideas of Pattern in History.* Urbana and Chicago: Univ. of Illinois Press, 1986.

Select Bibliography

———. "'A rationall of old Rites': Sir Thomas Browne's *Urn Buriall* and the Conflict over Ceremony." *Yearbook of English Studies* 21 (1991): 229–41.

Guillén, Claudio. *Literature as System: Essays toward the Theory of Literary History*. Princeton: Princeton Univ. Press, 1971.

Gura, Philip F. *The Wisdom of Words: Language, Theology, and Literature in the New England Renaissance*. Middletown, Conn.: Wesleyan Univ. Press, 1981.

Hall, Anne Drury. *Ceremony and Civility in English Renaissance Prose*. University Park: Pennsylvania State Univ. Press, 1991.

———. "Epistle, Meditation, and Sir Thomas Browne's *Religio Medici*." *PMLA* 94 (1979): 234–46.

Hallwachs, Robert G. "Additions and Revisions in the Second Edition of Burton's *Anatomy of Melancholy*." Ph.D. diss., Princeton University, 1942.

Harding, Walter, and Michael Meyer. *The New Thoreau Handbook*. New York: New York Univ. Press, 1980.

Harries, Elizabeth W. "The Sorrows and Confessions of a Cross-Eyed 'Female-Reader' of Sterne." In *Approaches to Teaching Sterne's Tristram Shandy*, ed. New, 111–17.

———. *The Unfinished Manner: Essays on the Fragment in the Later Eighteenth Century*. Charlottesville: Univ. Press of Virginia, 1994.

Hartley, Lodwick. *Laurence Sterne in the Twentieth Century: An Essay and a Bibliography of Sternean Studies 1900–1965*. Chapel Hill: Univ. of North Carolina Press, 1966.

———. "Yorick Redivivus: A Bicentenary Review of Studies on Laurence Sterne." *Studies in the Novel* 1 (1969): 81–87.

Hartwig, Joan. *Shakespeare's Analogical Scene: Parody as Structural Syntax*. Lincoln: Univ. of Nebraska Press, 1983.

Hernadi, Paul. *Beyond Genre: New Directions in Literary Classification*. Ithaca: Cornell Univ. Press, 1972.

Hirsch, E. D. *Validity in Interpretation*. New Haven: Yale Univ. Press, 1967.

Hodges, Devon L. *Renaissance Fictions of Anatomy*. Amherst: Univ. of Massachusetts Press, 1985.

Höltgen, Karl Joseph. "Literary Art and Scientific Method in Robert Burton's *Anatomy of Melancholy*." *Explorations in Renaissance Culture* 16 (1990): 1–35.

———. "Robert Burton and the Rectory of Seagrave." *Review of English Studies* 27 (1976): 129–36.

Howes, Alan B. *Yorick and the Critics: Sterne's Reputation in England, 1760–1868*. New Haven: Yale Univ. Press, 1958.

Hunter, J. Paul. "Response as Reformation: *Tristram Shandy* and the Art of Interruption." *Novel* 4 (1971): 132–46.

Huntley, F. L. *Sir Thomas Browne: A Biographical and Critical Study*. Ann Arbor: Univ. of Michigan Press, 1962.

Hyman, Stanley Edgar. "Henry Thoreau in Our Time." *Atlantic Monthly* 178 (Nov. 1946): 137–46.

Select Bibliography

Imbrie, Ann E. "Defining Nonfiction Genres." In *Renaissance Genres: Essays on Theory, History, and Interpretation,* ed. Lewalski. Cambridge: Harvard Univ. Press, 1986, 45–69.

Iser, Wolfgang. *Laurence Sterne: Tristram Shandy.* Trans. David Henry Wilson. Cambridge: Cambridge Univ. Press, 1988.

Jackson, H. J. "Sterne, Burton, and Ferriar: Allusions to the *Anatomy of Melancholy* in Volumes Five to Nine of *Tristram Shandy.*" *Philological Quarterly* 54 (1975): 457–70.

Jameson, Fredric. *The Political Unconscious.* Ithaca: Cornell Univ. Press, 1981.

Jauss, Hans Robert. "Literary History as a Challenge to Literary Theory." In *New Directions in Literary History,* ed. Cohen, 11–41.

Jefferson, D. W. "Sterne and the Tradition of Learned Wit." *Essays in Criticism* 1 (1951): 225–48.

Kenner, Hugh. *The Invisible Poet: T. S. Eliot.* New York: Harcourt Brace, 1932.

Kiessling, Nicolas K. *The Legacy of Democritus Junior: Robert Burton.* Exhibition Catalogue. Oxford: Bodleian Library, 1990.

———. *The Library of Robert Burton.* The Oxford Bibliographical Society, n. s. 22 (1988).

———. "Two Notes on Robert Burton's Annotations." *Review of English Studies* n. s. 36 (1985): 375–79.

King, James Roy. *Studies in Six 17th-Century Prose Writers.* Athens: Ohio Univ. Press, 1966.

Krutch, Joseph Wood. "Thoreau and Sir Thomas Browne." *Thoreau Society Bulletin* 29 (1949): n.p.

Lamb, Jonathan. *Sterne's Fiction and the Double Principle.* Cambridge: Cambridge Univ. Press, 1989.

Lanham, Richard. *Tristram Shandy: The Games of Pleasure.* Berkeley and Los Angeles: Univ. of California Press, 1973.

Lane, Lauriat, Jr. "Thoreau's *Walden,* I, Paragraphs 1–3." *Explicator* 29 (1971): 35.

Lebeaux, Richard. *Thoreau's Seasons.* Amherst: Univ. of Massachusetts Press, 1984.

Lehman, B. H. "Of Time, Personality, and the Author. A Study of *Tristram Shandy:* Comedy." In *Studies in the Comic.* University of California Studies in English, vol. 3, no. 2 (1941), 233–50.

Levenson, Michael. "The End of Tradition and the Beginning of History." In *Words in Time,* ed. Lobb, 158–78.

Lewalski, Barbara Kiefer. *Protestant Poetics and the Seventeenth-Century Religious Lyric.* Princeton: Princeton Univ. Press, 1979.

———, ed. *Renaissance Genres: Essays on Theory, History, and Interpretation.* Cambridge: Harvard Univ. Press, 1986.

Little, Lester K. *Benedictine Maledictions: Liturgical Cursing in Romanesque France.* Ithaca: Cornell Univ. Press, 1993.

Lobb, Edward. "Limitation and Transcendence in 'East Coker.'" In *Words in Time,* ed. Lobb, 20–37.

Select Bibliography

———, ed. *Words in Time: New Essays on Eliot's Four Quartets*. Ann Arbor: Univ. of Michigan Press, 1993.
Loveridge, Mark. *Laurence Sterne and the Argument about Design*. Totowa, N.J.: Barnes and Noble, 1982.
Lyons, Bridget Gellert. *Voices of Melancholy: Studies in Literary Treatments of Melancholy in Renaissance England*. London: Routledge, 1971.
MacDonald, Michael. *Mystical Bedlam: Madness, Anxiety, and Healing in Seventeenth-Century England*. New York: Cambridge Univ. Press, 1981.
McCanles, Michael. "The Authentic Discourse of the Renaissance." *Diacritics* 10 (1980): 77–87.
McIntosh, James. *Thoreau as Romantic Naturalist: His Shifting Stance toward Nature*. Ithaca and London: Cornell Univ. Press, 1974.
Martz, Louis L. "Origins of Form in *Four Quartets*." In *Words in Time*, ed. Lobb, 189–204.
———. *The Poem of the Mind: Essays on Poetry English and American*. New York: Oxford Univ. Press, 1966.
———. *The Poetry of Meditation: A Study of English Religious Literature of the Seventeenth Century*. New Haven: Yale Univ. Press, rev. ed., 1962.
———. "The Wheel and the Point: Aspects of Imagery and Theme in Eliot's Later Poetry." *Sewanee Review* 55 (1947): 126–47.
Matthiessen, F. O. *American Renaissance*. New York: Oxford Univ. Press, 1941.
———. "The *Quartets*." In *The Achievement of T. S. Eliot*, 3d ed. (New York: Oxford Univ. Press, 1958); rpt. in Bergonzi, ed., *T. S. Eliot: Four Quartets*, 88–104.
Mazzeo, Joseph A. "A Seventeenth-Century Theory of Metaphysical Poetry" and "Metaphysical Poetry and the Poetic of Correspondence." In *Renaissance and Seventeenth-Century Studies*. New York: Columbia University Press, 1964, 29–59.
Miner, Earl. "Some Issues of Literary 'Species, or Distinct Kind.'" In *Renaissance Genres: Essays on Theory, History, and Interpretation*, ed. Lewalski, 15–44.
Moldenhauer, Joseph J. "*Walden*: The Strategy of Paradox." In *The Thoreau Centennial*, ed. Walter Harding. Albany: State Univ. of New York Press, 1964, 16–30.
Mueller, Janel M. "The Exegesis of Experience: Dean Donne's *Devotions*." *JEGP* 67 (1968): 1–19.
Mueller, William R. "Robert Burton's Frontispiece." *PMLA* 64 (1949): 1074–88.
Mulder, John R. *The Temple of the Mind: Education and Literary Taste in Seventeenth-Century England*. New York: Pegasus, 1969.
Murray, Paul. *T. S. Eliot and Mysticism: The Secret History of Four Quartets*. New York: St. Martin's Press, 1991.
Myer, Valerie Grosvenor, ed. *Laurence Sterne: Riddles and Mysteries*. London and Totowa, N.J.: Vision and Barnes and Noble, 1984.
Nardo, Anna K. *The Ludic Self in Seventeenth-Century English Literature*. Albany: State Univ. of New York Press, 1991.

Select Bibliography

Nathanson, Leonard. *The Strategy of Truth: A Study of Sir Thomas Browne*. Chicago: Univ. of Chicago Press, 1967.

New, Melvyn. "'At the backside of the door of purgatory': A Note on Annotating *Tristram Shandy*." In *Laurence Sterne: Riddles and Mysteries,* ed. Myer, 15–23.

———. "Job's Wife and Sterne's Other Women." In *Out of Bounds,* ed. Claridge and Langland, 55–74.

———. *Laurence Sterne as Satirist*. Gainesville: Univ. of Florida Press, 1969.

———. *Telling New Lies: Seven Essays in Fiction, Past and Present*. Gainesville: Univ. Press of Florida, 1992.

———, ed. *Approaches to Teaching Sterne's Tristram Shandy*. New York: Modern Language Association of America, 1989.

Nicolson, Marjorie Hope. *The Breaking of the Circle*. New York: Columbia Univ. Press, 1962.

Nochimson, Richard Leonard. "Robert Burton: A Study of the Man, His Work, and His Critics." Ph.D. diss. Columbia University, 1967.

Novarr, David. *The Disinterred Muse: Donne's Texts and Contexts*. Ithaca: Cornell Univ. Press, 1980.

———. "The Two Hands of John Donne." *Modern Philology* 62 (1964): 142–54.

Nuttall, A. D. *A Common Sky: Philosophy and the Literary Imagination*. Berkeley: Univ. of California Press, 1974.

O'Connell, Michael. *Robert Burton*. Boston: [Twayne Publishers] G. K. Hall, 1986.

Olney, James. *Metaphors of Self*. Princeton: Princeton Univ. Press, 1972.

Ong, Walter J. *Orality and Literacy: The Technologizing of the Word*. London: Routledge, 1982.

———. *Ramus, Method and the Decay of Dialogue*. Cambridge: Harvard Univ. Press, 1958.

Osler, William. "Burton's *Anatomy of Melancholy*." *Yale Review*, n. s. 3 (1914): 251–71.

Patrides, C. A., ed. *Approaches to Sir Thomas Browne: The Ann Arbor Tercentenary Lectures and Essays*. Columbia: Univ. of Missouri Press, 1982.

Piper, William Bowman. *Laurence Sterne*. New York: Twayne, 1966.

Poirier, Richard. *A World Elsewhere: The Place of Style in American Literature*. New York: Oxford Univ. Press, 1966.

Porter, Roy. *Mind-Forg'd Manacles: A History of Madness in England from the Restoration to the Regency*. London: Athlone Press, 1987.

Post, Jonathan F. S. "Browne's Revisions of *Religio Medici*." *Studies in English Literature* 25 (1985): 145–63.

———. *Sir Thomas Browne*. Boston: G. K. Hall, 1987.

Price, Martin. *To the Palace of Wisdom: Studies in Order and Energy from Dryden to Blake*. Garden City, N.Y.: Doubleday, 1964.

Quinn, Dennis. "Donne's Christian Eloquence." *ELH* 27 (1960): 276–97.

Select Bibliography

Radcliffe, David. *Forms of Reflection*. Baltimore: Johns Hopkins Univ. Press, 1993.

Renaker, David. "Robert Burton and the Ramist Method." *Renaissance Quarterly* 24 (1971): 210–20.

Robertson, D. W., Jr. "Some Observations on Method in Literary Studies." In *New Directions in Literary History*, ed. Cohen, 63–75.

Roston, Murray. "The 'Doubting' Thomas." In *Approaches to Sir Thomas Browne*, ed. Patrides, 69–80.

Schneider, Richard J. *Henry David Thoreau*. Boston: G. K. Hall, 1987.

Seelig, Sharon Cadman. "Sir Thomas Browne and Stanley Fish: A Case of Malpractice." *Prose Studies* 11 (1988): 72–84.

Seybold, Edith. *Thoreau: The Quest and the Classics*. New Haven: Yale Univ. Press, 1951.

Shanley, J. Lyndon. *The Making of Walden*. Chicago: Univ. of Chicago Press, 1957.

Siskin, Clifford. *The Historicity of Romantic Discourse*. New York: Oxford Univ. Press, 1988.

Stapleton, Laurence. *The Elected Circle: Studies in the Art of Prose*. Princeton: Princeton Univ. Press, 1973.

Stead, C. K. "The Imposed Structure of the *Four Quartets*." In Bergonzi, ed., *T. S. Eliot: Four Quartets*, 197–211.

Stedmond, John M. *The Comic Art of Laurence Sterne*. Toronto: Univ. of Toronto Press, 1967.

Stephen, Leslie. "Sterne." In *Hours in a Library*. 3 vols. New York: G. P. Putnam's Sons, 1894, 139–74.

Tayler, Edward W. *Nature and Art in Renaissance Literature*. New York: Columbia Univ. Press, 1964.

Telotte, Leigh Ehlers. "'Fire, Water, Women, Wind': *Tristram Shandy* in the Classroom." In *Approaches to Teaching Sterne's Tristram Shandy*, ed. New, 118–22.

Traister, Barbara H. "New Evidence about Burton's Melancholy." *Renaissance Quarterly* 29 (1976): 66–70.

Traugott, John. *Tristram Shandy's World: Sterne's Philosophical Rhetoric*. Berkeley and Los Angeles: Univ. of California Press, 1954.

Traversi, D. A. *T. S. Eliot: The Longer Poems*. London: Bodley Head, 1976.

Van Doren, Mark. *Henry David Thoreau: A Critical Study*. New York: Houghton Mifflin, 1916.

Van Laan, Thomas F. "John Donne's *Devotions* and the Jesuit *Spiritual Exercises*." *Studies in Philology* 60 (1963): 191–202.

Waddington, Raymond. "The Two Tables in *Religio Medici*." In *Approaches to Sir Thomas Browne*, ed. Patrides, 81–99.

Wagenknecht, Edward. *Henry David Thoreau*. Amherst: Univ. of Massachusetts Press, 1981.

Select Bibliography

Wallerstein, Ruth. *Studies in Seventeenth-Century Poetic.* Madison: Univ. of Wisconsin Press, 1950.

Webber, Joan. *Contrary Music: The Prose Style of John Donne.* Madison: Univ. of Wisconsin Press, 1963.

———. *The Eloquent "I": Style and Self in Seventeenth-Century Prose.* Madison: Univ. of Wisconsin Press, 1968.

West, Michael. "Charles Kraitsir's Influence on Thoreau's Theory of Language." *Emerson Society Quarterly* 19 (1973): 262–74.

Whaling, Anne. "Studies in Thoreau's Reading of English Poetry and Prose, 1340–1660." Ph.D. diss., Yale University, 1946.

Wilding, Michael. *Dragons Teeth: Literature in the English Revolution.* Oxford: Clarendon Press, 1987.

Williamson, George. *The Senecan Amble.* Chicago: Univ. of Chicago Press, 1951.

Wise, James N. *Sir Thomas Browne's Religio Medici and Two Seventeenth-Century Critics.* Columbia: Univ. of Missouri Press, 1973.

Woodson, Thomas. "The Two Beginnings of *Walden*: A Distinction of Styles." *ELH* 35 (1968): 440–73.

Woolf, Virginia. *Collected Essays.* 3 vols. New York: Harcourt, Brace, and World, 1967.

Ziegler, Dewey Kiper. *In Divided and Distinguished Worlds: Religion and Rhetoric in the Writings of Sir Thomas Browne.* Cambridge: Harvard Univ. Printing Office, 1943.

INDEX

Anatomy, 8, 105, 106, 137, 180 n. 1
Andrewes, Lancelot, 37
Aristotle, 2, 139
Attitude: in relation to genre, 1–6, 11–13, 154, 156; toward reader, 105, 108, 122–23, 135, 144–45, 146, 149
Augustine, St., 17
Authority, use of, 5, 6, 105, 108, 110–20, 125, 131–32, 139–40
Autobiography, forms of, 2, 3, 5, 8, 12, 13, 156; *see also* Normative autobiography

Babb, Lawrence, 108, 181 n. 4
Bacon, Francis, 118, 128
Bamborough, J. B., 109, 181 n. 4, 184 n. 12, 185 nn. 16 and 18
Book of Creatures, 157; *see also* Book of Nature
Book of Nature, 87, 98, 99–100, 103
Booth, Wayne, 130, 185 n. 21
Browne, Sir Thomas, 1–5, 62–82, 155; as Anglican, 65, 67, 70–72; and Burton and Donne, 154, 157–58; and Donne, 62, 65, 67, 71–72; and Eliot, 70; and Thoreau, 63, 75, 83–87, 89, 93, 96, 98–104, 157; *Garden of Cyrus*, 100
—*Religio Medici:* biblical references in, 73, 79, 80–81; facts of publication, 175 n. 6, 176, n. 9; meditation in, 65–66, 70, 76; as normative autobiography, 70–71; persona in 66, 72; political context of, 176 n. 10; prose style of, 68–70, 77–82, 93; revisions of, 177 n. 23; rhetorical patterns in, 67–69, 72, 77–79; rhetorical strategy in, 62–82, 155; structure in, 65
Bruss, Elizabeth, 167 n. 12
Buell, Lawrence, 178 n. 4, 179 n. 8, 188 n. 1
Burton, Robert, 1–3; as reader, 186 n. 30; and Sterne, 112, 122, 126–44, 157; and Thoreau, 86
—*Anatomy of Melancholy*, 1, 2, 5, 10–12, 105–27; 128–36, 140–43, 154; attitude toward material in, 108, 113; Democritus Junior in, 105, 108, 110–11, 116–17, 120–25, 128, 133–35, 138, 143, 158; Digression of the Air, 112–13, 136; editions of, 167; as encyclopedic, 10, 105–6, 109, 112, 130; genre of, 105; lists in, 150; misogyny in, 149; persona in, 106, 108, 110, 117, 122–28, 132–35, 138–43, 154, 157–58; prose style of, 115–20; revisions of, 120–22, 126, 143, 182 n. 22, 183 n. 30, 184 n. 13, 186 n. 31; rhetorical strategy in, 110, 117–27; structure in, 65, 110–13, 116, 126, 137; structure as Ramist, 113, 116; synopsis of, 105, 107, 113, 131, 134, 135, 140; use of sources in, 132, 183 n.2, *see also* Digression; Persona

Cardan, (Jerome), 114, 117
Carey, John, 169 n. 13, 170 n. 15
Cavell, Stanley, 178 nn. 2 and 4, 179 nn. 9 and 12
Charles I, 40, 54, 56, 155, 174 n. 38
Christian Platonism, 87
Church fathers, 115, 170 n. 15
Cohen, Ralph, 2, 10, 13, 168 nn. 20 and 27
Colie, Rosalie, 6, 7, 10, 11, 106, 168 n. 24, 181 n. 4
Croll, Morris, 116
Cudworth, Ralph, 87
Culler, Jonathan, 10

Dante, 10, 43, 55, 56, 59, 60
Davie, Donald, 173 n. 26
Dekker, Thomas, 118
Democritus, 109, 112, 123, 124; *see also* Burton, *Anatomy of Melancholy,* Democritus Junior
Digby, Sir Kenelm, 64, 176 nn. 7 and 9
Digression, 6, 112, 113, 126, 137, 140–42, 145, 150–51, 185 n. 20; in *Anatomy of Melancholy*, 111–13, 126–27, 135–36,

Index

Digression (*cont.*)
140–41, 151, 154; Digression of the Air, 112–13, 136; *see also* Sterne, *Tristram Shandy,* digression in
Discovery, process of, 3; in Browne, 66–68, 70, 76; in Burton, 111, 116, 125; in Donne and Eliot, 15–16; in Thoreau, 93–98, 102
Donne, John, 1–4, 155; and Browne 62, 154; and Eliot, 15–16, 36–42, 44–45, 47–49, 51, 55–61, 156; and Thoreau, 71, 104; *First Anniversarie,* 31
— *Devotions upon Emergent Occasions,* 1–2, 4, 11–12, 13–35, 38–40; attitude to death in, 21–25; biblical references in, 17–18, 20–21; formal structure of, 16–21, 26, 33–35, 37–38, 57–58; meditation in, 15–21, 25–35; rhetorical approach in, 21–35, 175 n. 40; rhetorical figures in, 25–26, 27–34, 43, 51
Dubrow, Heather, 7, 11, 167 n. 12

Eliot, T. S., 1–3, 26, 36–62; and Browne 70; and Donne, 14–16, 35, 36–37, 38, 39, 40, 42, 44, 49, 55–61; *Murder in the Cathedral,* 38; "The Music of Poetry," 175 n. 41; "Tradition and the Individual Talent," 48, 54, 173 n.24
— *Four Quartets,* 1–2, 4, 12–13, 15; formal structure in, 38–40, 43; meditation in, 35–37, 39–40, 42–43, 60; persona in, 47, 54; rhetorical figures in, 43, 50, 54; rhetorical strategy in, 37–60, 174 n. 27; use of biblical sources in, 46–47, 51; use of literary sources in, 41, 43, 47–48, 49, 51, 55–57, 155, 172 nn. 17 and 20, 173 nn. 22 and 23, 174 nn. 30, 37, and 39; — *Burnt Norton,* 38, 39, 40–45, 46, 47, 48, 49, 55; — *East Coker,* 38, 39, 43, 45–49, 55, 57–58; — *The Dry Salvages,* 39, 42, 43, 49–52, 54, 55, 58; — *Little Gidding,* 37, 38, 39, 40, 42, 43, 46, 52–61, 155
Emerson, Ralph Waldo, 87, 89, 96
Erasmus, 122

Ferrar, Nicholas, 39
Ferriar, John, 128, 129, 184 n. 16

Fish, Stanley, 66, 79, 108, 114, 181 n. 4
Fowler, Alastair, 6, 7, 9, 10, 154, 167 n. 10
Fox, Ruth A., 181 n. 4
François, de Sales, St., 13
Frye, Northrop, 2, 7, 8, 9, 182 n. 16

Galligan, Edward L., 178 n. 1
Gardner, Helen, 38, 170–71 n. 4, 173 n. 26
Generation of texts, 1, 12, 154, 159
Genre: and familial resemblances, 9, 11, 154; genre in *The Anatomy of Melancholy,* 105–7, 109–10, 127; genre in *Tristram Shandy* and *The Anatomy of Melancholy* 129–30, 149; meditation as, 13; nature of, 6, 7, 10, 11; questions of, 105, 109, 130, 141, 159; related to attitude, 11–12, 13, 36, 106, 129, 130, 156, 158–59; Renaissance attitudes toward, 6, 10–11; *see also* Play, generic
Goldberg, Jonathan, 169 n. 7
Gracián, Baltasar, 87
Guibbory, Achsah, 67, 169 n. 10
Guillén, Claudio, 7, 8, 9

Hall, Anne Drury, 66, 86, 177 n. 19, 178 n. 26
Hall, Joseph, 14, 128
Harding, D. W., 172 n. 21
Harries, Elizabeth W., 187 nn. 40 and 41, 188 n. 45
Hayward, John, 38, 155, 171 nn. 6 and 10, 174 n. 37
Heraclitus, 51
Herbert, George, 39, 41, 44, 54, 87
Hermetic philosophy, 73–74
Hernadi, Paul, 7
Hirsch, E. D., 7, 9
Hodges, Devon, 106, 181 n. 5
Horace, 139–40
Hough, Graham, 8
Huntley, F. L., 65

Ignatius Loyola, St., 13
Imbrie, Ann, 7, 10, 11, 13, 36, 167 n. 17
Influence, literary, 1, 129, 154, 155

Index

Jameson, Fredric, 6
Johnson, Samuel, 56, 66, 87, 127
Julian of Norwich, 60

Kenner, Hugh, 173 n. 26
Kiessling, Nicolas K., 186 n. 30
King, James Roy, 181 n. 4
Kraitsir, Charles, 180 n. 24

Lanham, Richard, 130, 131, 182 n. 14
Levenson, Michael, 172 n. 15, 173 n. 24
Lewalski, Barbara, 6, 7, 14, 16, 35, 38, 169 n. 5
Linguistic play: in Donne, 19; in Thoreau, 84, 86, 87, 90–93; in Sterne, 134, 141, 147
Literary influence, *see* Influence, literary
Lobb, Edward, 171 n. 11
Locke, John, 140, 185 n. 23
Loyola, Ignatius, *see* Ignatius Loyola, St.
Lyons, Bridget Gellert, 108, 114, 181 n. 4

Macrobius, 125
Mallarmé, 41, 56
Martz, Louis, 13–14, 15, 16, 35, 38, 39, 76, 88, 168 n. 2, 171 n. 8, 172 n. 19
Matthiessen, F. O., 38
Melancholy, 5, 106, 109–15, 118, 124, 130, 135
Meditation, 2, 4, 8, 13, 129, 156, 158–59; in Browne, 65–66, 70, 76; in Donne, 15–21, 25–35; in Eliot, 35–37, 39–40, 42–43, 52–53, 60; forms of, 4, 12, 13–15, 58; and Senecan style, 116, 159; and structure, 15–16, 36, 39; in Thoreau, 88, 97, 100, 102
Metaphysical, the, 57, 83–84, 87, 88, 93, 101, 103–4
Metaphysical poets, 13, 41, 60, 62
Milton, John, 148; *Il Penseroso*, 115; *Paradise Lost*, 127
Miner, Earl, 8, 10, 168 n. 28
Montaigne, Michel de, 8, 128, 129
Mueller, Janel M., 169 n. 9, 170 n. 15

Nardo, Anna K., 127
Narrator: in relation to author, 186 n. 32; in Sterne, 132–34, 137–39, 144–46, 152–53; *see also* Persona
Nicholas of Cusa, 76
Normative autobiography, 62, 64, 70–71, 85, 157

Olney, James, 3, 35, 40
Ong, Walter, 184, n. 11

Persona, 1, 6, 155, 158; in Browne, 66, 72; in Burton, 106, 108, 110, 117, 122–28, 132–35, 138–43, 154, 157–58; in Eliot, 47, 54; in relation to the author, 143, 146–48, 157; in Sterne, 132–33, 146, 151, 154; in Thoreau, 86, 93; *see also* Narrator; Reader
Plato, 73, 74
Play, generic, 127, 130–31, 133, 158; *see also* Genre
Poirier, Richard, 63, 104
Price, Martin, 185 n. 17
Prose, nonfiction, 8, 11, 12, 105, 156; anti-Ciceronian, 118; mimetic, 27, 54, 93–96, 114–17, 125–26; representing process, 132, 138; Senecan, 15, 93, 116
Prose style: in Browne, 68–72, 77–82, 93; in Burton, 115–17; in Donne, 21–23, 24–35; in Sterne, 133–34, 148; in Thoreau, 88–89, 93–96, 102; *see also* Rhetoric; Rhetorical strategy

Rabelais, François, 129
Radcliffe, David, 9
Ramist organization, 113, 116
Reader, manipulation of, 6; in Burton, 108, 114, 122–23; in Sterne, 152–54, 157
Reader, relation to: in Burton, 126; in Sterne, 133–34, 138, 144; in Thoreau, 85–86
Rhetoric: and discovery, 66–68, 76; in relation to worldview, 1–5, 21–34, 70–71, 75–82, 83, 92–95, 158; *see also* Rhetorical strategy
Rhetoric, figures of: in Burton 141; in Burton and Sterne, 150; in Donne, 25–26, 27–34, 43, 51; in Eliot, 43, 51, 54; in

Index

Rhetoric, figures of (*cont.*)
  Thoreau 90–93, 96; in Thoreau and Browne, 83–84, 180 n. 14
Rhetorical strategy: in Browne, 62–82; in Burton, 110, 117–27; in Donne, 21–34, 175 n. 40; in Eliot, 37–60, 174 n. 27; in Thoreau, 83, 84–88, 90–96
Robertson, D. W., 8
Roston, Murray, 74, 177 n. 14

Scaliger, J. C., 10, 11
Self: definition of, 3, 117; discovery of, 66; presentation of, 3, 114, 135, 156–57; representation of in Thoreau, 86, 87; revelation of, 65
Seneca, 117, 125
Shakespeare: analogies to, 118, 123; and Burton, 123; and Eliot, 47; and Thoreau, 96; *Hamlet,* 10, 23–24, 47, 49
Sidney, Sir Philip, 10, 11
Stephen, Sir Leslie, 131, 184 n. 9
Sterne, Laurence, 2, 3; anticipated by Burton, 117; borrowing from Burton, 128–29; compared to Burton, 128–44, 148–51, 153–54, 157; *Journal to Eliza,* 186 n. 28; *A Sentimental Journey,* 142, 143
— *Tristram Shandy,* 1, 2, 5, 12, 128–59; digression in, 126, 135–37, 139–42, 144–46, 150–51, 153–54; genre in, 130, 134, 141; interruptions in, 129, 133, 134, 140–42, 145–46, 150; linguistic play in, 147–48; lists in, 141–42; manipulation of reader in, 138, 144, 145, 146, 149, 151–52; misogyny in, 149; and modern novel, 129, 131; narrator in, 132–34, 137–39, 144–46, 152–53; publication of, 143, 186 n. 29; spontaneity in, 138, 141; structure in, 134–35, 140; text as object, 131–32; use of sources in, 128–29, 132, 139, 154, 186 n. 26; and Yorick, 132, 142–44, 147–48, 153, 187 n. 38

Stuart, Mary, 49, 58
Swift, Jonathan, 129
Synopsis, 65; in Burton, 105, 107, 113, 131, 134–35, 140

Tertullian, 65
Tesauro, Emanuele, 87
Text: author and, 122, 129, 144, 154; reader and, 125, 154; reality as, 22, 24–25; text as object, 131–32; *see also* Generation of texts
Thoreau, Henry David, 1–4, 83–104; and Browne, 83–87, 89, 93, 96, 98–104, 147; comment on Browne, 177 n. 15; and Burton, 112; and Donne and Eliot, 87
— *Walden,* 1, 2, 4, 5, 12, 63–64, 83–104; allusions and religious references in, 96–99, 102; generic backgrounds of, 178 n. 4; meditation in, 88, 95, 96, 97, 100, 102; persona in, 86, 93; prose style of, 88–89, 93, 95, 96; publication of, 175 n. 6; rhetorical figures in, 90–93, 96, 170 n. 22; rhetorical strategy in, 83–88, 90–96; structure of, 96–98; tone of, 178 n. 1; word play in, 86–87, 90–93, 99
Traversi, D. A., 37, 38

Vaughan, Henry, 87
Vicari, Patricia, 130, 181 n. 4

Waddington, Raymond, 65, 176 nn. 10 and 12
Walton, Izaak, 89
Webber, Joan, 27, 66
Wilding, Michael, 67
Williamson, George, 116
Woolf, Virginia, 129, 131, 184 n. 9